D1598235

Afro-Catholic Festivals in the Americas

AFRICANA RELIGIONS

Edited by

Sylvester A. Johnson, *Virginia Tech*

Edward E. Curtis IV, *Indiana University–Purdue University, Indianapolis*

ADVISORY BOARD:

Afe Adogame, *Princeton Theological Seminary*

Sylviane Diouf, *Historian of the African Diaspora*

Paul C. Johnson, *University of Michigan*

Elizabeth Pérez, *University of California, Santa Barbara*

Elisha P. Renne, *University of Michigan*

Judith Weisenfeld, *Princeton University*

Adopting a global vision for the study of Black religions, the Africana Religions book series explores the rich diversity of religious history and life among African and African-descended people. It publishes research on African-derived religions of Orisha devotion, Christianity, Islam, and other religious traditions that are part of the Africana world. The series emphasizes the translocal nature of Africana religions across national, regional, and hemispheric boundaries.

Afro-Catholic Festivals in the Americas

Performance, Representation, and the Making of Black Atlantic Tradition

EDITED BY CÉCILE FROMONT

The Pennsylvania State University Press
University Park, Pennsylvania

Library of Congress Cataloging-in-Publication Data

Names: Fromont, Cécile, editor.
Title: Afro-Catholic festivals in the Americas : performance,
    representation, and the making of Black Atlantic tradition /
    edited by Cécile Fromont.
Other titles: Africana religions.
Description: University Park, Pennsylvania : The Pennsylvania
    State University Press, [2019] | Series: Africana religions |
    Includes bibliographical references and index.
Summary: "Explores how, in the Americas, people of African
    birth or descent found spiritual and social empowerment in
    the orbit of the Church. Draws connections between Afro-
    Catholic festivals and their precedents in the early modern
    Christian kingdom of Kongo"—Provided by publisher.
Identifiers: LCCN 2019001030 | ISBN 9780271083292 (cloth :
    alk. paper)
Subjects: LCSH: Africans—America—Religion. | Blacks—
    America—Religion. | Fasts and feasts—America—Catholic
    Church. | African diaspora.
Classification: LCC E29.N3 A555 2019 | DDC 304.8096—dc23
LC record available at https://lccn.loc.gov/2019001030

The Pennsylvania State University Press is a member of the
Association of University Presses.

It is the policy of The Pennsylvania State University Press to
use acid-free paper. Publications on uncoated stock satisfy
the minimum requirements of American National Standard
for Information Sciences—Permanence of Paper for Printed
Library Material, ANSI Z39.48–1992.

TO MY AUNT GIRIANE WHO TOOK ME TO
THE ARCHIVES AS A CHILD, TO LEARN TO TALK
WITH THE ANCESTORS.

C.F.

Contents

Illustrations

Acknowledgments

This book project began at a conference at Yale's Institute for Sacred Music in February 2015. I am grateful for the institute; its director, Martin Jean; and its phenomenal staff, including Kristen Forman, Melissa Maier, and Jacqueline Campoli, as well as the coordinator for ISM Fellows, Glen Segger, for making this event possible. In addition to the authors of this book (with the exception of Michael Iyanaga, who joined the project at a later point), conference speakers included Linda Heywood, Glaura Lucas, Suzel Ana Reily, Tim Barringer, Monique Ingalls, and Stuart Schwartz. Their generous participation in the proceedings and the many insights they shared have greatly contributed to the formulation of this book.

The authors of this volume are indebted to Sylvester A. Johnson and Edward E. Curtis IV, the editors of the Africana Religion series at Penn State University Press, for welcoming the book project into their list, as well as to Penn State University Press director, Patrick Alexander, and editorial assistant Alex Vose for ushering the project from proposal to publication. Their comments and suggestions, as well as those of the anonymous readers of the manuscript, greatly improved the arguments made in the book.

Our thanks also go to the repositories who have kindly allowed us to reproduce images of artworks in their collections: the Bibliothèque Nationale de France, the Biblioteca Nacional de España, the Berardo Collection, the Oliveira Lima Library at the Catholic University of America, the Biblioteca Nacional do Rio de Janeiro, the James Ford Bell Library at the University of Minnesota, and the Rio de Janeiro branch of Brazil's Instituto do Patrimônio Histórico e Artístico Nacional.

This book could not have been published without the financial support of the University of Chicago's Department of Art History and Division of the Humanities. Kenya Senecharles provided me with key administrative and editing support. Yale University's Department of the History of Art and MacMillan Center contributed financially to the publication project in its final phase. I also thank the American Academy in Rome for the time and space to finish this manuscript.

On a personal note, my full-hearted thanks go to Grant, Louis, and Héloïse for their support and enthusiasm.

Introduction

Kongo Christianity, Festive Performances, and the Making of Black Atlantic Tradition

CÉCILE FROMONT AND MICHAEL IYANAGA

Lifting a veil on the secret origins of New Orleans's Mardi Gras Indians, seeing Brazilian Catholic songs anew as an expression of Afro-diasporic devotion, uncovering the deep Afro-Catholic roots of Caribbean Orisa religion and rituals, and analyzing the significance of black kings and queens feted in the Americas and their various forms of representations, the chapters gathered in this volume explore the role that Christianity and its festive traditions have played in the making of black Atlantic cultures since the era of the slave trade. Their arguments move beyond analyses of African diasporic religious traditions that consider their Christian dimensions as inherently exogenous, imposed elements that enslaved or disenfranchised populations of African origins or descent either resignedly accepted or else eventually transformed into syncretic objects of stealthy resistance and identity formation. Instead, authors in this volume draw transatlantic connections between festive traditions from North to South America and the Caribbean and precedents chiefly in the early modern Catholic kingdom of Kongo, an influential polity of west-central Africa and one of the main regions of origin of men and women enslaved in the Americas. This background, they argue, reveals how enslaved and free Africans, and later their descendants, often used Christianity and Christian-derived celebrations as physical and mental spaces for autonomous cultural expression, social organization, and political empowerment.

Scholars have written at length about identifiable aspects of central African and Kongo spiritual practices in African American religions such as Haitian

Vodou.[1] Yet these studies have maintained a strong focus on non-Christian traits of central African religions and often used as a point of departure ethnographies conducted after the end of the slave trade, in the late nineteenth and twentieth centuries. These important works have played a key role in advancing knowledge of the African diaspora but have been ill equipped because of their methods and sources to identify and analyze historically how the worldly, ostentatiously Catholic culture of the Kingdom of Kongo shaped the religious, social, and political experience of the enslaved and free in the Americas. Drawing from scholarship of the early 2000s and reinterpreting older sources on central Africa and the early modern Atlantic world, the chapters in this volume bridge that gap. They identify and study the often elusive marks that early-modern central African Christianity has left on the festive events enslaved or free Africans and their descendants have staged in the Americas in the direct or indirect orbit of the church from the era of slavery to contemporary times. These chapters derive from a conversation begun among most of the authors in 2015 at Yale's Institute for Sacred Music on the occasion of the symposium titled "Afro-Christian Festivals in the Americas: Bridging Methodologies and Crossing Frontiers."

SLAVE TRADE AND CHRISTIANITY BETWEEN TWO SHORES

Between the sixteenth and the nineteenth centuries, the Atlantic commerce in slaves forcibly uprooted close to twelve million men, women, and children from the African continent. The largest number of captives originated from populations in and around Kongo and Angola in west-central Africa, and in Gbe- and Yoruba-speaking areas along the Bight of Benin, although many other parts of the continent, including Senegambia and even the Indian Ocean coast also saw their people caught in the trade. A small number of those embarked reached European shores; the overwhelming majority landed in the Americas, and close to half in Brazil.[2]

This massive, centuries-long movement in population across the Atlantic is one of the two crucial background phenomena that underlie the practices and events analyzed in this book. The other formative element is the path Christianity followed along the routes created by the new political, diplomatic, and commercial networks that emerged across the Atlantic in the early modern period, including, but not exclusive to, those created by the traffic in slaves. Within months of the entrance of what would later be called the Americas into European history, upon the return of Christopher Columbus to

Europe, the pope recognized, with the 1494 Treaty of Tordesillas, Spain's and Portugal's secular claim over extra-European lands and, in exchange, mandated the evangelization of world populations as a task for the two seafaring, expansionist realms to implement and finance. From that moment Catholicism and conquistadors would advance hand in hand in the American, African, and Asian territories Spain and Portugal effectively or nominally controlled. Soon, as Europe tore itself along the Reformation schism, Protestant refugees and proselytizers from northern Europe reached the Americas, where they competed with Catholic Iberian ambitions. The ill-fated Calvinist colony of France Antarctique had settled, then failed, near Rio de Janeiro by the middle of the 1500s. Pilgrims to North America met with more success early in the next century. As their Catholic counterparts, European followers of the Reform made a central mandate the conversion of the people they deported across the waters or who lived enslaved or free under their rule.[3]

Meanwhile, Roman and Reformed Christianity reached the African continent, in sporadic missionary attempts as well as in the Euro-African societies that grew around trading fort enclaves. Most significant, however, in terms of scope and impact on Atlantic cultures, was the independent conversion to Catholicism circa 1500 of the Kingdom of Kongo, an event that started a deep and long lasting engagement among the inhabitants of the region with the religion and with European visual and material culture. The independent conversion of the kingdom, and its enduring appropriation of Catholic rituals, thoughts, and imagery, was a momentous event in the history of the Atlantic world. Not only was the realm influential in its own part of the world among neighboring central African polities who allied with or fought against it, but it also bore much weight on the formation of African-derived cultures in the Americas through the forced migration of massive numbers of its people and neighbors in the Atlantic slave trade.

Starting in the sixteenth century, Catholicism progressively impacted all sectors of Kongo society and reached to various degrees the kingdom's neighboring polities and vassals. But Catholicism did not simply replace Kongo traditions. Rather, a new Kongo Catholicism gradually took shape, built on ritual, aesthetic, and cosmological components drawn from both central African and European traditions. Perhaps one of the most striking examples of the ways in which Catholicism impacted Kongo socioreligious life, mentioned in nearly all the chapters of this volume (Miguel A. Valerio, Kevin Dawson, Jeroen Dewulf, Cécile Fromont, Junia Ferreira Furtado, and Michael Iyanaga), was the danced mock fight ritual known as *sangamento*. The elite of the kingdom performed the sangamento, whose name is a lusitanized version of the Kikongo-language verb *ku-sanga*, on feast days, as part of ceremonies, and prior to important battles.[4] During the ritual the dancers displayed weapons, clothing, and musical instruments of central African origin or European provenance, either in combination or in a clearly delineated binary sequence.[5] Participants in this and other rituals and ceremonies of the Christian Kongo often played a mix of European and central African musical instruments.[6] The enthronization of Kongo kings in particular incorporated such a combination of locally rooted and once foreign symbols, instruments, and pageantry.[7]

Christian cosmology acquired local currency in early modern Kongo in a variety of ways beyond rituals. For example, Kongo Christians recast popular European saints as their patron saints and even as ancestors. The myth of King Afonso I's ascension to the throne with the help of Saint James, an army of divine horsemen, and the cross of Constantine—first written by the Kongo monarch himself in the 1510s—served as an early blueprint of the ways in which Christianity and its holy men and women took on a distinct Kongo significance. These two examples–the adoption of saints and the sangamento (and other rituals)—illustrate how during the early modern period, much of Kongo's Catholicism took on local form and gave once wholly European symbols and imagery distinct central African identities. The chapters in this volume build on the broad notion that this specific, distinctive form of Christianity played a significant role in shaping the worldview of a great many of the millions of central Africans uprooted to the Americas.

Yet if Christianity in the early modern Atlantic world counted a distinct and influential African dimension thanks to the Kongo Church, it was but one of its traits. Many were the entanglements between slavery and Christianity in the Atlantic world, and Africans from many parts of the continent displaced to the Americas experienced the two concurrently. The Church, Catholic or Reformed, was closely linked to European slave owners or merchants, even sometimes a slave owner or trader in its own rights, and was actively involved in the implementation of systems of exploitation. Christianity also became the mandated frame for the spiritual practices of the enslaved and freed, and its precepts ruled over their life, imposing, for instance, its definition of kinship or naming practices. Even so, the history of African American religiosity is one of resilience, resistance, and creativity in spite of the church's relentless cultural and spiritual assaults, but also thanks to the spaces of relative freedom it offered to the disenfranchised, whether enslaved or free. Readings of Christianity as a predominantly external or burdensome influence on African and African

American cultures or else as a thin veneer over deeper, non-Christian allegiances are inaccurate or at least lack nuance.

The chapters in this volume, in contrast, explore how Christianity could be a site for the formation of black Atlantic tradition. They join in this regard earlier scholars who have underlined the role of the church as a locus—albeit, in their views, a temporary one—for the development of African religiosity in the Americas. Anthropologist Roger Bastide, for instance, suggested for Brazil that lay Catholic confraternities often "developed into *candomblés*," framing such sodalities as "incubators" for the later (re)development of a West African–derived religious tradition.[8] Transposing this interpretation to the Cuban context, David Brown and Stephan Palmié have since noted that colonial brotherhoods such as *cabildos de nación* also sequentially, and consequentially, antecede Lucumí houses.[9]

THE ORIGINS AND PATHS OF AFRICAN AMERICAN CULTURES

This volume is in conversation with scholarship on the history of African Christianity in the early modern Atlantic world and contributes to ongoing debates on the origins and trajectory of African American cultures. It comes at a moment when the impact of Atlantic history has pushed studies of the interrelations between Africa and the Americas in new directions. Scholars have become increasingly aware of the depths and reciprocity of the connections between the two continents and of the extent to which the two shores form a single constellation, bound up in a common fate that was largely created by, and intensified through, the commercial, human, and cultural networks of the slave trade. This space of mutual implication, circulation of goods and ideas, and shared transcontinental history, often referred to by scholars today as the "black Atlantic," has not always been imagined as such a fluid, closely interconnected unit.[10] In fact, the field of study that has become African American or African diaspora studies began in large part with an argument about how much of Africa had been transferred and retained in the Americas.

Although the seeds of modern scholarly debates surrounding Africa's link to the then called "New World Negro" are perhaps most accurately found in the late nineteenth- and early twentieth-century work of scholars such as W. E. B. Du Bois, Raymundo Nina Rodrigues, Fernando Ortiz, or Jean Price-Mars, the issue gained lasting traction in the United States only during the 1930s and 1940s.[11] This was in no small part owing to the comprehensive work of anthropologist Melville J. Herskovits and his now famous debate with sociologist E. Franklin Frazier.

The sociologist insisted that the traumatic and devastating nature of slavery all but erased the African past from African American culture, leaving nothing but "scraps of memories" of an African heritage.[12] Despite how odd such an interpretation may seem to our contemporary sensibilities, it was a position that, as Stephan Palmié reminds us, "had [by the early 1940s] clearly come to prevail among liberal North Americans, both white and black."[13] In fact, Herskovits's early writings, such as his 1925 article in *Survey Graphic*, suggest that he, too, saw African American culture as fundamentally American (rather than African).[14] Fieldwork in Suriname, Haiti, West Africa, and Brazil from the end of the 1920s to the 1930s shifted his views, however, and he became the leading oppositional voice to Frazier's position. Indeed, the anthropologist insisted, perhaps most famously in his seminal 1941 book, *Myth of the Negro Past*, that African cultural traits and patterns, "Africanisms," did in fact survive—in some cases even flourishing—in the Americas.[15] Even if the debate did not immediately end, the victor was no doubt Herskovits and his many likeminded colleagues (Fernando Ortiz, Arthur Ramos, Lorenzo Dow Turner, etc.) and students (William Bascom, Richard Waterman, René Ribeiro, Katherine Dunham, etc.).[16]

Landmark publications have since charted ways of approaching this "black Atlantic" that push beyond the models proposed by either Herskovits or Frazier.[17] In 1976, for instance, Sidney W. Mintz and Richard Price circulated *An Anthropological Approach to the Afro-American Past: A Caribbean Perspective*, which was an argument for the need to historicize the Herskovitsian approach while also paying less attention to isolatable traits than to social processes and structures.[18] Although Mintz and Price were careful not to gainsay the African historicity of African American cultures, they turned decidedly away from what Africans (and their descendants) may have "retained" to focus on what was created anew in the Americas. This novel approach to African American religion and culture, however, spurred polemics of its own. Indeed, the decades around the turn of the millennium have seen innumerable debates between those who choose to emphasize a fundamentally American-based creativity as couched in Mintz and Price's work, as in Michel-Rolph Trouillot's idea of the "miracle" of creolization, and those who instead focus on contiguities from one shore to the next, a point of view embraced among others by Gwendolyn Midlo Hall, John Thornton, Linda Heywood, and Pablo A. Gómez—a perspective that historian Paul Lovejoy dubs "Africancentric" or "Afrocentric."[19]

The depth and enduring vitality of the origins debate in its multiple incarnations has brought thinkers to consider its very stakes and players as historical and intellectual artifact worthy of analysis in their own right, yielding a range of metastudies about the trajectory of this fundamental question.[20] Beyond this debate the rise of scholarship favoring an Atlantic-wide perspective has also engendered a deeper interest in the effects on the African continent itself of the transformative "interconnections" the Atlantic world system and the slave trade created between the ocean's two shores.[21] The benefits of such a new emphasis are evidently exponential, as a better grasp of the situation on one shore enlightens approaches to the other.

A FOCUS ON CENTRAL AFRICA

A key moment in the study of African culture and religion in the Americas was the construction and publication of Voyages: The Trans-Atlantic Slave Trade Database in the 1990s, a tool that, despite its limitations, buttressed cultural and historical studies on the slave trade and its effects with the authoritative weight of quantitative data.[22] An effect of the database, for instance, has been a refined attention to the diverse backgrounds of the enslaved as fine demographic data on place of embarkation and disembarkation over time made possible discriminating studies of specific populations in given location and periods.

For instance, using numbers from the online database, we know that between 1551 and 1575, an estimated 61,007 Africans were taken as slaves (81 percent from Upper Guinea, 6 percent from Lower Guinea, and 13 percent from west-central Africa and Saint Helena). However, in the following twenty-five years, when the total number of embarked Africans nearly tripled to an estimated 152,373, the ratio of central Africans became much more significant (29 percent from Upper Guinea, 2 percent from Lower Guinea, and 69 percent from west-central Africa and Saint Helena). Then, from 1601 to 1625 the numbers more than doubled, to an astounding 352,843 people, with captives from west-central Africa and Saint Helena making up more than 91 percent of the total number of enslaved Africans. These numbers suggest that although central Africans were not the first to arrive in the Americas, they were nonetheless the first to arrive on American shores in significant numbers. And the enslavement of central Africans continued well into the nineteenth century. As such, central Africans constituted just under half of all captives (roughly 45 percent or just under six million people), thus making up the largest single origination region of the African continent.[23]

What makes these data—raw numbers and dates—particularly significant is the implication that central Africans may have had an early, strong, and lasting influence on the African American cultures that began to take root in the early years of the slave trade. This is, after all, the general notion Sidney Mintz and Richard Price proposed decades ago. The anthropologists, extrapolating (intuitively, it seems) from their work in Suriname, suggested that the first arrivals had an important role in defining the character of African American culture:

> During the earliest decades of the African presence in Suriname, the core of a new language and a new religion had been developed; subsequent centuries of massive new importations from Africa apparently had little more effect than to lead to secondary elaborations. We would suggest tentatively that similar scenarios may have unfolded in many other parts of Afro-America. . . . The early stages of African-American history . . . stamped these [local slave] cultures with certain general features that strongly influenced their subsequent development and continue to lend to them much of their characteristic shape today.[24]

What is more, as historians have underlined, west-central Africa formed, in the words of Robert Slenes, a "single 'cultural area,'" according to which the peoples from central Africa would share what Jan Vansina called "a common view of the universe and a common political ideology."[25] Consequently, the captives sharing related central African languages and worldviews who were taken in such concentrated numbers may have been foundational in the Americas not only owing to their early arrival but also because they were able to find enough common ground to allow them to rebuild social institutions and practices in ways that other African ethnic groups might have found more challenging.

The power of the quantitative data gathered in the database lies in its ability to outline new questions based on its findings about the enslaved and the cultures they created. It may come as little surprise, therefore, that, in the same years as the database's construction and publication, increased attention on the west-central dimension of the African diaspora started to emerge in scholarship. Yet Linda Heywood still remarked in 2002 how "general interest and knowledge of the history and cultural impact of Central Africans in the Atlantic Diaspora lag far behind that of West Africa."[26] Although the tide has continued to shift since the publication of Heywood's edited volume, studies in the religion and culture of the diaspora have still been to be strongly focused on their connections—however defined—with West Africa and in particular with Gbe-speaking regions and Yorubaland. This historiographic bend partly derived from the increased numbers of enslaved West Africans taken toward the end of the slave trade to Brazil and the Caribbean, two areas of early focus for diasporic studies. In the palimpsestic construction of African American culture over hundreds of years, not only has this later wave left disproportionately visible marks but, as Iyanaga notes in his chapter, specific historiographic reasons, starting in the nineteenth century, inextricably link West Africa to a notion of African "otherness" in both scholarly and more popular ambits. Further, West African traits have been all the more identifiable, as their nineteenth-century counterparts across the waters are well known, thanks to ethnographic work conducted in the Bight of Benin starting only decades after the end of the trade. When ethnographer and photographer Pierre Verger wrote about the fluxes and refluxes between Bahia and Benin, for instance, he talked about trends belonging to some of his informants' living memory.[27] Verger was also the first among a number of later scholars to write from the perspective of a practitioner of West African–derived Afro-Atlantic religion—a *babalawo*, or priest, in his case—explaining the particular emphasis in his observations on elements from his own faith.

While it has been evident that a comparison with central Africa could illuminate many African American practices and objects, the exercise has always been arduous because distance in time multiplies the challenges of spatial disconnect inherent to diasporic studies and complicates possibilities to perform historically grounded rapprochements. The robust scholarship emerging on central Africa before the colonial era contributes little by little to fill this gap.

Indeed, the focus of the chapters in this volume on the central African dimension does not emerge from a vacuum. To varying degrees and in more or less explicit ways, the chapters build on many decades of scholarship that has recognized the central African dimension of the aesthetics and logics of Afro-Christian festivals in the Americas. In fact, in the 1930s Brazilian psychiatrist-turned-anthropologist Arthur Ramos wrote that the Catholic processions, brotherhoods, and feasts of colonial Uruguay, Argentina, Venezuela, Colombia, Cuba, and Peru showed "cultural influences of the Bantu [i.e., central African] Negroes." Importantly, Ramos did not believe that all the Bantu-speaking contributions to religion in the Americas were relegated to the past, observing that "the political organizations of the [central] African monarchies survive in certain popular festivals [of Brazil] . . . such as the *Congos*," which Ramos understood as primarily "folkloric," rather than religious, forms of expression.[28] Why would it be the case, though, that religions of Bantu-speaking Africans fail to "survive" in the way West African–derived religions do or that they might survive only within the structures of West African–derived religious traditions (e.g., *petwo*, the supposedly Kongo-derived "hot" side of Haitian Vodou[29])? It seems not unreasonable to suggest that there has been an ideological shroud over much scholarship, explicated famously in Brazilian journalist-cum-folklorist Edison Carneiro's 1936 assertion that Bantu-speaking peoples had an "extremely poor mythology."[30] The chapters in this book contest these readings, pointing to the religious mark, past and present, of central African Christianity—in all of its own complex integration and redeployment of local and foreign thoughts and symbols—on festivals in the Americas.

One reason central African resonances in the Americas have remained elusive to scholarly attention undoubtedly comes from the large role Christianity played in the formulation of some of its polities' Christian and non-Christian rituals, that already, before the Middle Passage, included cross-culturally resonant forms. The redefinition appeared, for instance, in Kongo Christian crucifixes that mixed and merged local and imported iconography or, more broadly, in the nimble adoption of foreign objects and images, reendowed with local meanings. It seems anything but accidental that so many central African markers—whether sangamento-like practices, crowning ceremonies, musical instruments (e.g., xylophones, bow lutes known as *pluriarcs*, and specific drums types)—are linked to Catholic practices in the Americas.[31] Many aspects of African religious practices that would have been molded in Kongo and Angola, such as the use by different ritual associations of saint statues or crosses, could easily be misinterpreted in the Americas as new, Creole syncretisms.[32] Essentialist conceptions of Christian thoughts, forms, and rituals as strictly European and of African religious practices as necessarily non-Christian fueled these once predominant perceptions.[33]

The emphasis given in this volume to the central African, Christian dimension of the case studies considered contributes to shift the balance. The chapters build on early contributions by, among others, Mary Karasch, Winifred Kellersberger Vass, Robert Farris Thompson and Joseph Cornet, John Thornton, Margaret Washington Creel, and Stuart B. Schwartz.[34] Further interventions emerged in the early 2000s and 2010s, by Robert Slenes, Marina de Mello e Souza, Linda Heywood, Ras MichaelBrown, Jason R. Young, James Sweet, RoquinaldoFerreira, Bárbaro Martínez-Ruiz, and Christina Mobley.[35] The already-mentioned volume Heywood edited in 2002, *Central Africans and Cultural Transformations in the American Diaspora*, was a landmark in English-language scholarship and included many of these older and newer voices.[36] The authors in the present book also mention Fromont's work on Kongo Christian visual and material culture in central Africa and its resonances in Brazil, a line of research inspired and informed by many of the works just mentioned.[37]

Benefiting from the field's maturing bibliography, the authors bring in these pages a new or renewed central African perspective to case studies taken from a range of geographies, from several countries of the Spanish-speaking Americas (Valerio and Iyanaga) to the streets of New Orleans (Dewulf), the waters of northeastern Brazil (Dawson), and the Caribbean island of Trinidad (Stewart), even delving into West Africa (Furtado).[38]

WHY CHRISTIANITY? WHY FESTIVALS?

Religion in general and Christianity in particular have held a place of choice in studies of African and African-derived culture in the Americas because they are key terrains for the construction and expression of identities, power, and social relations. But studies of African diasporic religions have often followed templates dictated by other fields, an approach that has revealed much but also impeded other discoveries. This book is an attempt to bypass this limitation. Analyzing the diasporic experience from the specific perspective of central African Christianity requires crossing historiographic fault lines that have kept scholarship on British, Iberian, or French imperial projects but also on Protestantism or Catholicism too often at odds. A number of studies have explored the African Protestant experience chiefly within the British Atlantic.[39] Others have focused on the relationship between Africans and the Catholic Church, mainly in Latin America.[40] Yet central African Christianity stood as an experiential common ground that brought cohesion and empowerment to forced migrants from the region and their descendants across the Americas and throughout the centuries. Much insight, then, is to be gained in exploring the diasporic experience with a focus on central African-honed religion, a background shared by many in the Americas, across geographies and chronologies, the relevance of which transects scholarly patterns of inquiry defined by different concerns. The chapters in this volume illustrate the new insights that such an approach to diasporic studies, transverse to established fields, can bring. Dianne M. Stewart's chapter, for example, investigates the role of African Catholicism as a background for the formation of Obeah, a black Atlantic phenomenon long seen as the product of both Anglo-Saxon Protestantism and Yoruba religion. Her argument interrogates instead the frictions between Protestantism and Catholicism and between west-central African religion and West African faiths. Dewulf, in another thought-provoking chapter, follows the possibly obfuscated histories of Kongo Catholic ritual in the changing political, religious, and ethnic landscape of contemporary New Orleans.

The chapters in this volume all use, more specifically than religion at large, festive moments unfolding directly or indirectly in the orbit of the church as entry points into their examination of Afro-Christian presence in the Americas and the Atlantic world. Because the authors are historians or scholars of literature, religion, or music, they approach festive occasions as documents rather than objects of study per se. This is a not a book about performance, but it is our hope that it will serve as an invitation to further study the events presented and contextualized here, in particular with a closer and more rigorous attention to the performative mechanics at play in their production and reproduction. If they do not directly grapple with performance theories, the present chapters are nonetheless concerned with historical and contemporary bodies and the ways in which they form and perform social memory. The authors usefully borrow from the field of performance studies its attention to the potential of these performative events, taken in each of their specific contexts, as revealing archives with the potential to fill lacunae in the existing written historical record. The festivals and events considered in the volume all enrich our understanding of past and present by completing and broadening the content and scope of textual archives often constructed specifically to ignore or silence African and African-derived cultural, political, and religious expressions. In some ways, then, the chapters turn us toward what Diana Taylor called the "repertoire," always in a dialogic relationship with the "archive."[41] In the events studied in these pages, those otherwise silenced, overtly or covertly, made themselves heard, "resist[ing]," as Joseph Roach once wrote, "the dominant public transcript by affirming the rites of collective memory."[42] Moreover, the closer look taken here on the central African dimension of the social memory activated in American Christian festivals complicates and enriches understandings of the origins and form of African American religious practice and culture at large with a broadened attention to its multiple, complex, and intermingling forms.

Also emerging from this book's study of bodies in movements within Afro-Christian festivals is a more complex understanding of the multivalent links between African and African-derived pageantry and other dimensions of American cultures. Lisa Voigt's chapter, for instance, reflects on the multiple levels of mimesis in Brazilian baroque festivals, describing multidirectional acts of representation of and by Europeans, Africans, and Afro-Brazilians. Here the festivals, as well as their textual representations, illustrate the limits of official colonial discourses of differentiation and sociopolitical separation. That such textual productions would fail or stop short of performing what is largely understood as the keystone of the colonial system—clear differentiation and insuperable segregation of social actors—is particularly telling. It brings to the fore the porous lines, or rather the deep interpenetration, between elite and African and Native American cultures. Between the lines of the former's self-representation through written histories lay its multivalent entanglements with the latter two, not only in festivals, as highlighted here, but also in other aspects of life. In other words, confronting the written record with embodied social memory, one touches on "the yet unwritten epic of the fabulous cocreation" of history and memory.[43] Such attention to "bodily social memory" is all the more essential, given that it builds spatial and temporal bridges linking the era of slavery to contemporary times.[44]

OUTLINE OF CHAPTERS

In the first part of the book, the authors interpret or reinterpret three different American festivals revolving around ritual mock battles, using precedents from the Christian Kongo as an enlightening background to their staging, either as a direct model or as one of an array of inspirations. In chapter 1 Jeroen Dewulf challenges the idea that the origins of New Orleans's Mardi Gras Indians can be traced solely to Buffalo Bill's touring Wild West shows that wintered in New Orleans in 1884–85. Instead, siding with other historians, he argues that the phenomenon originated in much earlier times, developing out of the "Congo dances" of the city's Congo Square and ultimately linked to the Christian Kongo sangamento ritual dances. As such, Mardi Gras Indians can be approached as one manifestation of the broader, hemispheric phenomenon of Afro-Iberian folk Catholicism. Kevin Dawson turns his attention in chapter 2 to saltwater and freshwater as key sites for the construction, transmission, and staging of African diasporic religion and social memory. Specifically, he probes how enslaved men and women staged a mock naval battle on the island of Itamaracá, in the Brazilian state of Pernambuco, in 1815, in a way that creatively reimaged the Iberian ritual drama of *Moors and Christians*. The transposition, he argues, allowed the enslaved actors to bring freshwater and saltwater west-central African traditions, spiritual and otherwise, to Brazil's social and ecological environment. In a speculative, thought-provoking chapter, Miguel A. Valerio analyzes the first recorded festival staged by black performers in the Americas as part of the 1539 celebration of the truce of Aigues-Mortes in Mexico-Tenochtitlan, seat of the nascent Iberian colonial territory of New Spain. Using demographic data, he argues that the spectacular cavalry of black men and women that staged a mock battle against heathens were *ladinos*, that is, Africans who came to Mexico after having lived in Iberia. These ladinos, moreover, came to Spain and Portugal predominantly from central Africa. They carried not only their African background but also their experience of life in Iberian societies, where free and enslaved Africans already staged festivals and gathered in religious institutions of their own, such as confraternities. Thus, he argues, it would be erroneous to think of the performers in the 1539 cavalcade as powerless actors in a European-designed event. Rather, the mock battle should be seen at least in part as the invention of ladinos.

The second part of the book turns its attention to the figure of black kings and the notion of representation in performance, diplomacy, and the archive. In chapter 4 Lisa Voigt considers the figure of African sovereigns in colonial Brazil not through the repertoire of embodied practices staged in the public sphere but through the archive that governed such performances and represented them narratively. Considering both kings and queens of *congados* festivals and African ambassadors to the Portuguese Crown, she analyzes how Africans found ways to represent themselves and their interests in colonial Brazil in positive and productive ways. Junia Ferreira Furtado, in turn, considers in chapter 5 how the rich Afro-Christian background of two priests born and raised in Brazil shaped their experience of ceremonial life in the African kingdom of Dahomey they were charged with visiting and describing on behalf of the Portuguese Crown in the late eighteenth century. How did these two men of different social and racial backgrounds experience and travel through the black Atlantic? How did their familiarity with the black royalty that the predominantly black populations of their homes in the Brazilian province of Minas Gerais and capital of São Salvador routinely elected and celebrated inform their perception of and interaction with the court of the mighty king of Dahomey?

Part 3 reconsiders well-known primary sources. In chapter 6 art historian Cécile Fromont takes a closer look at a lithograph created in the early nineteenth century after sketches produced by Bavarian artist Johann Moritz Rugendas during his travels in Brazil. The print is one of the earliest and best-known visual representations of the centuries-old celebrations organized by Brazilian socioreligious organizations called congados or congadas, whose very name draws an explicit connection between them and the west-central African region once home to the mighty Kingdom of Kongo. The chapter combines insights gathered from written and visual historical documents, secondary literature, and a careful formal analysis to form a rigorous examination of the image. The chapter interrogates the extent to which the lithograph attempted, and variously succeeded and failed, to make visible the social, religious, and political stakes of the performance. It brings new light to a document that is emblematic but has been seldom critically approached. Dianne M. Stewart reads anew archival records in chapter 7 to propose a new interpretation of Orisa religion in Trinidad. Challenging the predominant interpretation of the genesis of the religious practice as syncretic fusion of Yoruba beliefs and "Euro-Western Christianity," she points to the formative role and lasting impact of preexisting Afro-Catholic communities of the island in its formation in the second half of the nineteenth century. Her chapter brings to the fore the limitations of syncretism as a way of theorizing Afro-diasporic religions.

To close our collection is part 4, which looks at aurality and the making of diasporic tradition. In chapter 8 ethnomusicologist Michael Iyanaga turns our attention more explicitly toward the present, in a comparative, ethnographic examination of domestic patron saint festivals in Venezuela, Brazil, Colombia, and the Dominican Republic. By analyzing music, instruments, dances, and cosmologies together with demographic information about the enslavement and disembarkation of central Africans in the Americas, he suggests that these Catholic celebrations might be contemporary fruits of central African seeds. In so doing, Iyanaga not only asks us to reconsider Catholicism as part of the African legacy in the Americas but also asks us to question the a priori notions at play in identifying the African diaspora in the first place.

NOTES

Thank you to Genevieve Dempsey and Danielle Roper for conversations that enriched this introduction. We also want to point out explicitly that the references cited here focus on the English-language literature because of this volume's intended audience, even if robust, seminal scholarly conversations on similar topics are unfolding outside of Anglo-Saxon academia. Latin American and Caribbean scholarship is paramount to this discussion, and thankfully some U.S.-based university presses have undertaken the crucial task to make these works available to English-language readers.

1. We use the term *African American* in this introduction in a hemispheric sense, to refer to people and phenomena from North and South America and the Caribbean. See, for example,

Robert Farris Thompson, *Flash of the Spirit: African and Afro-American Art and Philosophy* (New York: Random House, 1983); and Donald Cosentino, ed., *Sacred Arts of Haitian Vodou* (Los Angeles: UCLA Fowler Museum of Cultural History, 1995).

2. A full 45 percent of the total of 10,702,654 Africans who disembarked in slaving ports in the period between 1501 and 1875 did so in Brazil. David Eltis, Stephen D. Behrendt, David Richardson, and Herbert S. Klein, eds., Voyages: Trans-Atlantic Slave Trade Database, accessed September 15, 2018, www.slavevoy ages.org/assessment/estimates/.

3. See Katharine Gerbner, *Christian Slavery: Conversion and Race in the Protestant Atlantic*

World (Philadelphia: University of Pennsylvania Press, 2018).

4. Cécile Fromont, *The Art of Conversion: Christian Visual Culture in the Kingdom of Kongo* (Chapel Hill: University of North Carolina Press, 2014), 21; Thomas J. Desch-Obi, "Combat and the Crossing of the Kalunga," in *Central Africans and Cultural Transformations in the American Diaspora*, ed. Linda M. Heywood (Cambridge: Cambridge University Press, 2002), 359.

5. Fromont, *Art of Conversion*, 24.

6. John K. Thornton and Linda M. Heywood, *Central Africans, Atlantic Creoles, and the Foundation of the Americas, 1585–1660* (Cambridge: Cambridge University Press, 2007), 213–14.

7. Fromont, *Art of Conversion*, 40–43.

8. Roger Bastide, *The African Religions of Brazil: Toward a Sociology of the Interpenetration of Civilizations* (1978; repr., Baltimore: Johns Hopkins University Press, 2007), 128; see also Andrew Apter, "Yoruba Ethnogenesis from Within," *Comparative Studies in Society and History* 55, no. 2 (2013): 375–77.

9. David H. Brown, *Santería Enthroned: Art, Ritual, and Innovation in an Afro-Cuban Religion* (Chicago: University of Chicago Press, 2003), 62–67; Stephan Palmié, "Ethnogenetic Processes and Cultural Transfer in Afro-American Slave Populations," in *Slavery in the Americas*, ed. Wolfgang Binder (Würzburg: Königshausen und Neumann, 1993), 341.

10. The term *black Atlantic* has been popularized by Paul Gilroy, *The Black Atlantic: Modernity and Double Consciousness* (Cambridge, Mass.: Harvard University Press, 1993).

11. W. E. B. Du Bois, *Black Folk, Then and Now: An Essay on the History and Sociology of the Negro Race* (New York: Holt, 1939); Raymundo Nina Rodrigues, *O animismo fetichista dos negros baianos*, facsimile ed. (Rio de Janeiro: Fundação Biblioteca Nacional/Editora da Universidade Federal do Rio de Janeiro, 2006); Fernando Ortiz, *Los negros brujos* (Miami: Ediciones Universales, 1973); Jean Price-Mars, *Ainsi parla l'oncle: Essais d'ethnographie* (Montreal: Mémoire d'Encrier, 2009).

12. E. Franklin Frazier, *The Negro Family in the United States* (Chicago: University of Chicago Press, 1939), 21.

13. Stephan Palmié, *The Cooking of History: How Not to Study Afro-Cuban Religion* (Chicago: University of Chicago Press, 2013), 122.

14. Melville J. Herskovits, "The Dilemma of Social Pattern, " *Survey Graphic* 6, no. 6 (1925): 677–78. Walter Jackson, "Melville Herskovits and the Search for Afro-American Culture," in *Malinowski, Rivers, Benedict, and Others: Essays on Culture and Personality*, ed. George W. Stocking Jr. (Madison: University of Wisconsin Press, 1986), 102.

15. Melville J. Herskovits, *The Myth of the Negro Past* (New York: Harper, 1941).

16. See David F. Garcia, *Listening for Africa: Freedom, Modernity, and the Logic of Black Music's African Origins* (Durham: Duke University Press, 2017), 94; Michael Iyanaga, "On Flogging the Dead Horse, Again: Historicity, Genealogy, and Objectivity in Richard Waterman's Approach to Music," *Ethnomusicology* 59, no. 2 (2015): 173–201; Margaret Wade-Lewis, "Lorenzo Dow Turner: Pioneer African-American Linguist," *Black Scholar* 21, no. 4 (1991): 10–24; and Richard A. Waterman, "On Flogging a Dead Horse: Lessons Learned from the Africanisms Controversy," *Ethnomusicology* 7, no. 2 (1963): 83.

17. Thornton and Heywood have made crucial contributions about the role of Africa and Africans in the Atlantic world and, reversely, the impact of the Atlantic system on Africa; see John K. Thornton, *Africa and Africans in the Making of the Atlantic World, 1400–1680*, 2nd ed. (Cambridge: Cambridge University Press, 1998); and Thornton and Heywood, *Central Africans, Atlantic Creoles*.

18. Mintz and Price wrote the essay in 1972, presented it in 1973, circulated it in typescript in 1976, and published it as a book in 1992. See Richard Price, "The Miracle of Creolization: A Retrospective," *New West Indian Guide/Nieuwe West-Indische Gids* 75, nos. 1–2 (2001): 35; and Sidney W. Mintz and Richard Price, *The Birth of African-American Culture: An Anthropological Perspective* (Boston: Beacon Press, 1992).

19. Gwendolyn Midlo Hall, *Africans in Colonial Louisiana: The Development of Afro-Creole Culture in the Eighteenth Century* (Baton Rouge: Louisiana State University Press, 1992); Thornton, *Africa and Africans*; Heywood, *Central Africans and Cultural Transformations*; Gwendolyn Midlo Hall, *Slavery and African Ethnicities in the Americas: Restoring the Links* (Chapel Hill: University of North Carolina Press, 2005); Ras Michael Brown, *African-Atlantic Cultures and the South Carolina Lowcountry* (Cambridge: Cambridge University Press, 2012); Jason R. Young, *Rituals of Resistance: African Atlantic Religion in Kongo and the Lowcountry South in the Eera of Slavery* (Baton Rouge: Louisiana State University Press, 2007); Pablo A. Gómez, "Transatlantic Meanings: African Rituals and Material Culture from the Early-Modern Spanish Caribbean," in *Materialities of Ritual in the Black Atlantic*, ed. Akinwumi Ogundiran and Paula Saunders (Bloomington: Indiana University Press, 2014), 125–42. See also Mintz and Price, *Birth of African-American Culture*; Michel-Rolph Trouillot, "Culture on the Edges: Creolization in the Plantation Context," paper presented at the colloquium "The Plantation System in the Americas," April 1989, Louisiana State University, Baton Rouge, revised and published in *Plantation Society in the Americas* 5, no. 1 (1998): 8–28; Paul E. Lovejoy, "Identifying Enslaved Africans in the African Diaspora," in *Identity in the Shadow of Slavery*, ed. Paul E. Lovejoy (London: Continuum, 2000), 1.

20. See, for example, David Scott, *Refashioning Futures: Criticism After Postcoloniality* (Princeton: Princeton University Press, 1999); Scott, "That Event, This Memory: Notes on the Anthropology of African Diasporas in the New World," *Diaspora: A Journal of Transnational Studies* 1, no. 3 (1991): 261–84; Stephan Palmié, "Creolization and Its Discontents," *Annual Review of Anthropology* 35 (2006): 433–56; Joseph C. Miller, "Retention, Reinvention, and Remembering: Restoring Identities Through Enslavement in Africa and Under Slavery in Brazil," in *Enslaving Connections: Changing Cultures of Africa and Brazil During the Era of Slavery*, ed. José C. Curto and Paul E. Lovejoy (Amherst, N.Y.: Humanity Books, 2004), 81–121.

21. José C. Curto and Renée Soulodre-LaFrance, *Africa and the Americas: Interconnections During the Slave Trade* (Trenton: Africa World Press, 2005); Kristin Mann and Edna G. Bay, eds., *Rethinking the African Diaspora: The Making of a Black Atlantic World in the Bight of Benin and Brazil* (London: Cass, 2001); Curto and Lovejoy, *Enslaving Connections*; Roquinaldo Ferreira, *Cross-Cultural Exchange in the Atlantic World: Angola and Brazil During the Era of the Slave Trade* (Cambridge: Cambridge University Press, 2012); and J. Lorand Matory, *Black Atlantic Religion: Tradition, Transnationalism, and Matriarchy in the Afro-Brazilian Candomblé* (Princeton: Princeton University Press, 2005). See also the much older Pierre Verger, *Flux et reflux de la traite des nègres entre le Golfe de Bénin et Bahia de Todos os Santos, du XVIIe au XIXe siècle* (Paris: Mouton, 1968), translated as Pierre Verger, *Trade Relations Between the Bight of Benin and Bahia from the Seventeenth to Nineteenth Century* (Ibadan, Nigeria: Ibadan University Press, 1976).

22. David Eltis et al. *The Trans-Atlantic Slave Trade: A Database on CD-ROM* (Cambridge: Cambridge University Press, 1999), compact disc; Gwendolyn Midlo Hall, *Databases for the Study of Afro-Louisiana History and Genealogy, 1699–1860* (Baton Rouge: Louisiana State University Press, 2000), CD-ROM. For earlier quantitative analysis, see also Philip D. Curtin, *The Atlantic Slave Trade: A Census*, ed. Societies American Council of Learned, ACLS Humanities E-Book (Madison: University of Wisconsin Press, 1969).

23. Eltis et al., Voyages.

24. Mintz and Price, *Birth of African-American Culture*, 50.

25. Robert W. Slenes, "'Eu venho de muito longe, eu venho cavando': Jongueiros cumba na senzala centro-africana," in *Memória do jongo: As gravações históricas de Stanley J. Stein Vassouras, 1949*, ed. Silvia Hunold Lara and Gustavo Pacheco (Rio de Janeiro: Folha Seca; Campinas: CECULT, 2007), 116–17; Jan Vansina, "Deep-Down Time: Political Tradition in Central Africa," *History in Africa* 16 (1989): 341.

26. Heywood, *Central Africans and Cultural Transformations*, 8.

27. Verger, *Flux et reflux de la traite*.

28. Arthur Ramos, *As culturas negras no Novo Mundo*, 4th ed. (São Paulo: Editora Nacional, 1979), 174, 233; Ramos, *O folclore negro do Brasil: Demopsicologia e psicanálise*, 2nd ed. (Rio de Janeiro: Livraria-Editora da Casa do Estudante do Brasil, 1954), 35.

29. Thompson, *Flash of the Spirit*, 164.

30. Edison Carneiro, *Religiões negras: Notas de etnografia religiosa; Negros bantos: Notas de etnografia religiosa e de folklore*, 3rd ed. (1936; repr., Rio de Janeiro: Civilização Brasileira, 1991), 62.

31. See, for instance, plate 6 in this volume, in which a xylophone is depicted in a Carlos Julião watercolor of a black king festival from eighteenth-century Brazil; Rogério Budasz, "Central-African Pluriarcs and Their Players in Nineteenth-Century Brazil," *Music in Art* 39, nos. 1–2 (2014): 11; Gerhard Kubik, *Angolan Traits in Black Music, Games, and Dances of Brazil: A Study of African Cultural Extensions Overseas* (Lisbon: Junta de Investigações Científicas do Ultramar, 1979), 23; Angela Lühning and Pierre Fatumbi Verger, "The Voyage of the Drums: From Africa to the Americas," *Art Music Review* 24 (2013), www.revista-art.com/the-voyage-of-the-drums-from-africa-to-the-americas/. While it might be possible to point to certain types of membrane drums, such as those seen in the central African photos in Lühning and Verger's essay (see caption for figure 8.1 in this volume), these are more difficult to trace, as membranes drums are part of so many different African musical cultures. Perhaps the least controversial example of a central African–derived drum still found today in the Americas is the Brazilian friction drum, known in Portuguese as a *cuíca*.

32. For examples of these so-called syncretisms in the prophetic Antonian movement or as part of the Kimpasi association in Kongo, see John K. Thornton, *The Kongolese Saint Anthony: Dona Beatriz Kimpa Vita and the Antonian Movement, 1684–1706* (Cambridge: Cambridge University Press, 1998); and Fromont, *Art of Conversion*.

33. See Fromont's chapter, in this volume.

34. Mary C. Karasch, *Slave Life in Rio de Janeiro, 1808–1850* (Princeton: Princeton University Press, 1987); Winifred Kellersberger Vass, *The Bantu Speaking Heritage of the United States*, vol. 2 (Los Angeles: Center for Afro-American Studies, University of California, 1979); Robert Farris Thompson and Joseph Cornet, *The Four Moments of the Sun: Kongo Art in Two Worlds* (Washington, D.C.: National Gallery of Art, 1981); Thompson, *Flash of the Spirit*; John K. Thornton, "I Am a Subject of the King of Kongo: African Political Ideology and the Haitian Revolution," *Journal of World History* 4 (1993): 181–214; Margaret Washington Creel, *A Peculiar People: Slave Religion and Community-Culture Among the Gullahs* (New York: New York University Press, 1988); Stuart B. Schwartz, *Slaves, Peasants, and Rebels: Reconsidering Brazilian Slavery* (Urbana: University of Illinois Press, 1992).

35. See Robert W. Slenes, "L'Arbre nsanda replanté: Cultes d'affliction kongo et identité des esclaves de plantation dans le Brésil du Sud-Est entre 1810 et 1888," *Cahiers du Brésil Contemporain* 67–68 (2007): 217–313; Marina de Mello e Souza, *Reis negros no Brasil escravista: História da festa de coroação do Rei Congo* (Belo Horizonte, Brazil: Editora da Universidade Federal de Minas Gerais, 2002); and Heywood, *Central Africans and Cultural Transformations*. See also Brown, *African-Atlantic Cultures*; Young, *Rituals of Resistance*; James H. Sweet, *Recreating Africa: Culture, Kinship, and Religion in the African-Portuguese World, 1441–1770* (Chapel Hill: University of North Carolina Press, 2003); Ferreira, *Cross-Cultural Exchange*; Bárbaro Martínez-Ruiz, *Kongo Graphic Writing and Other Narratives of the Sign* (Philadelphia: Temple University Press, 2013); and Christina Frances Mobley, "The Kongolese Atlantic: Central African Slavery and Culture from Mayombe to Haiti" (PhD diss., Duke University, 2015).

36. Heywood, *Central Africans and Cultural Transformations*. A veritable explosion of master's and doctoral theses on Afro-Brazilian topics, including religion and performance, has taken place in Brazil since the turn of the twenty-first century. This invaluable corpus of scholarship is available to researchers from the country's university portals.

37. The authors kindly mention Cécile Fromont, "Dancing for the King of Congo from Early Modern Central Africa to Slavery-Era

Brazil," *Colonial Latin American Review* 22, no. 2 (2013): 184–208; and Fromont, *Art of Conversion*.

38. Jeroen Dewulf, "Pinkster: An Atlantic Creole Festival in a Dutch-American Context," *Journal of American Folklore* 126, no. 501 (2013): 245–71.

39. Sylvia R. Frey and Betty Wood, *Come Shouting to Zion: African American Protestantism in the American South and British Caribbean to 1830* (Chapel Hill: University of North Carolina Press, 1998); Jon F. Sensbach, *A Separate Canaan: The Making of an Afro-Moravian World in North Carolina, 1763–1840* (Chapel Hill: University of North Carolina Press, 1998); Sensbach, *Rebecca's Revival: Creating Black Christianity in the Atlantic World* (Cambridge, Mass.: Harvard University Press, 2005); Edward E. Andrews, *Native Apostles: Black and Indian Missionaries in the British Atlantic World* (Cambridge, Mass.: Harvard University Press, 2013); John W. Catron, *Embracing Protestantism: Black Identities in the Atlantic World* (Gainesville: University Press of Florida, 2016).

40. See for instance, Mariza de Carvalho Soares, *People of Faith: Slavery and African Catholics in Eighteenth-Century Rio de Janeiro*, Latin America in Translation/En Traducción/Em Tradução (Durham: Duke University Press, 2011); Herman L. Bennett, *Africans in Colonial Mexico: Absolutism, Christianity, and Afro-Creole Consciousness, 1570–1640* (Bloomington: Indiana University Press, 2003); Sherwin K. Bryant, Rachel Sarah O'Toole, and Ben Vinson III, *Africans to Spanish America: Expanding the Diaspora* (Urbana: University of Illinois Press, 2012).

41. Diana Taylor, *The Archive and the Repertoire: Performing Cultural Memory in the Americas* (Durham: Duke University Press, 2003).

42. Joseph Roach, "Culture and Performance in the Circum-Atlantic World," in *Performativity and Performance*, ed. Andrew Parker and Eve Kosofsky Sedgwick (New York: Routledge, 1995), 59.

43. Ibid., 61. For bodily social memory, see also Suzel Ana Reily, "To Remember Captivity: The 'Congados' of Southern Minas Gerais," *Latin American Music Review* 22, no. 1 (2001): 4–30. For central African Atlantic performance, see Maureen Warner-Lewis, *Central Africa in the Caribbean: Transcending Space, Transforming Cultures* (Kingston: University of the West Indies Press, 2003); Monica Schuler, *"Alas, Alas, Kongo": A Social History of Indentured African Immigration into Jamaica, 1841–1865* (Baltimore: Johns Hopkins University Press, 1980); Bárbaro Martínez-Ruiz, "Kongo Atlantic Body Language," *Performance, art et anthropologie (Les actes de colloques du musée du quai Branly Jacques Chirac)*, December 8, 2009, http://actesbranly.revues.org/462; and Mamadou Diouf, *Rhythms of the Afro-Atlantic World: Rituals and Remembrances* (Ann Arbor: University of Michigan Press, 2010).

44. Reily, "To Remember Captivity," 4–30.

◇◇◇

PART 1

Ritual Battles from the Kongo Kingdom to the Americas

CHAPTER 1

Sangamentos on Congo Square?

Kongolese Warriors, Brotherhood Kings, and Mardi Gras Indians in New Orleans

JEROEN DEWULF

Henry Rightor famously described the Mardi Gras Indians' performances in 1900 as bands running along the streets of New Orleans on Fat Tuesday "whooping, leaping, brandishing their weapons and, anon, stopping in the middle of a street to go through the movements of a mimic war-dance, chanting the while in rhythmic cadence an outlandish jargon."[1] They are still today among the most enigmatic traditions of New Orleans's annual carnival celebration.

It is generally believed that this tradition started in the late 1880s, when Becate Batiste formed the Creole Wild West tribe in the Seventh Ward, a downtown neighborhood.[2] After part of the members of his tribe moved uptown, a new gang was established, the Yellow Pocahontas, and from there several other "tribes" or "gangs" developed in New Orleans's traditionally black neighborhoods. To this day these groups parade through the streets of their respective districts in "Indian" outfits on Fat Tuesday. Unlike second-line clubs, the Mardi Gras Indians are not a mass movement but rather a semi-underground phenomenon. During the Lent season, they reappear on Saint Joseph's Night (March 19) for what used to be a silent parade with lanterns and, since 1970, also on the third Sunday of March, known as Super Sunday. One of the earliest references to the Mardi Gras Indians can be found in Alice Moore Dunbar-Nelson's short story "A Carnival Jangle" (1899), which mentions how Washington Square was "filled with spectators masked and unmasked" to watch a "perfect Indian pow-pow" by "mimic Red-men," who "seemed so fierce and earnest."[3] This fascination for the "black Indians" is confirmed by Jelly Roll Morton, who recalls that during his childhood in downtown New Orleans at the turn of the twentieth century, "if the folks heard the sign of the Indians 'Ungai-ah!'—the crowd would flock to the Indians."[4]

The Mardi Gras Indians wear hand-sewn costumes called "suits" that are lavishly decorated with sequins, rhinestones, lace, ribbons, colored beads, and feathers. Their aprons and breastplates traditionally depict Native American war scenes, animals, and geometric figures. They also use feathered caps or "crowns" that look like Plains Indians' war bonnets. During parades groups of fifteen to thirty Mardi Gras Indians march as a militia, ready for battle. The "spy boy" is in the front and checks the area for other tribes. He is followed by the "flag boy," who sends out flag signals. Next comes the "wild man" or "medicine man," who is recognizable by his headpiece with horns, and he behaves in a "wild" fashion while holding back the crowds. Finally comes the "big chief," who carries a decorated lance. He is accompanied by his "queen" and protected by bodyguards, known as "scouts." Sympathizers from the neighborhood build a "second line" and help with the percussion and singing. They beat tambourines, cowbells, conga drums, snare drums, triangles, and pebble gourds and sometimes use umbrellas as dancing attributes. The big chief not only determines the route but also chooses the songs or chants that are performed in a call-and-response form and, while mostly in English, sometimes contain phrases that have remained undecipherable. The most famous of these chants is "Indian Red," a type of prayer song. Recurrent topics in Mardi Gras Indian songs are references to the bravery of the gang and its chief, accompanied by a refusal to "humbah" (humble) themselves by "bowing down" for the enemy.

The Mardi Gras Indians used to have a violent reputation, from the "humbug" between groups that could erupt when two enemy gangs would meet. While violence faded away since the 1930s, tribes still compete among one another today. To prepare for such a contest, gang members have weekly practices on Sunday afternoons and evenings, when they meet one another "in the circle" to rehearse dances and songs. As Allison "Tootie" Montana, then big chief of the Yellow Pocahontas, said in an interview in the 1960s, "we used to fight with knives and guns. . . . Now we compete by the beauty of our costumes."[5]

The lack of historical sources makes it tempting to relate the tradition to Buffalo Bill's touring Wild West shows that wintered in New Orleans in 1884–85 and presented a "Grand Performance" on Mardi Gras day in 1885.[6] There are good reasons to do so. Names of late nineteenth-century gangs such as the

Creole Wild West or the 101 Wild West confirm the impact of these shows on local performance culture. Moreover, the "Indian" outfit of the Mardi Gras Indians has nothing in common with how Native American tribes in the area used to dress. If, as some have argued, the Mardi Gras Indian performances developed out of mixed Native American and African American relationships and honor the heroism of these two historically oppressed groups in Louisiana, one would assume to find at least some traces of Natchez or Choctaw culture local to the area. But the Indian elements of the New Orleans's tradition clearly relate to the Cheyenne, Comanche, or Apache culture of Plains Indians that Buffalo Bill stereotyped and popularized in his shows.

Although there can be no denial that Buffalo Bill's shows are part of the stream of influences that shaped the Mardi Gras Indians, it can be doubted that the tradition started as a mere imitation of these circus-like attractions. There are two important reasons for this. One is that long before William Frederick "Buffalo Bill" Cody (1846–1917) was born, we find descriptions of street scenes in New Orleans that are remarkably similar to those of the Mardi Gras Indians today. A second reason is that similar performances have been observed in parts of the Americas where these Wild West shows were never performed. In mid-nineteenth-century Cuba, for instance, the French writer Léon Beauvallet observed how some blacks in a parade "had transformed themselves into South American savages, Red Skins or Apaches."[7] Thus, there are strong reasons to believe that the New Orleans's "black Indians" are not a uniquely Louisianan product but rather a specific variant of a broader phenomenon.

CONGO SQUARE

My point of departure is that the performances of the Mardi Gras Indians developed out of the dances that used to take place on New Orleans's Congo Square, a sort of common where the slave population organized a market and festivities on Sundays and religious holidays.[8] In his memoirs, published in 1880 as *My Southern Home*, the former slave William Wells Brown recalled that "the people that one would meet on the square many years ago" were "six different tribes of negroes, named after the section of the country from which they came," and that "the Minahs [*sic*] would not dance near the Congos, nor the Mandringas [*sic*] near the Gangas."[9]

Such rivalry among slave nations also existed in slave societies elsewhere in the Americas. Brown's observations correspond, for instance, to those of James Kelly, who wrote about Jamaica in the 1830s that "the Mandingos, the

Ebos, the Congoes, etc., formed into exclusive groups, and each strove to be loudest in the music and songs . . . peculiar to their country."[10] Also, in Uruguay and Argentina, it was common practice that slaves would gather on Sunday afternoons to dance, whereby "every 'nation' occupied its part of the designated space."[11]

The one group I focus on in this chapter is that of the Congos. When used in the context of transatlantic slavery, the word *Congo* relates to areas under the direct or indirect purview of the once powerful Kingdom of Kongo. Today scholars prefer to use the term *Kongo* to distinguish between the ancient kingdom and the later Belgian and French colonies in the region. The heartland of the Kongo Kingdom was located in the northwestern part of today's Angola and the western part of the modern Democratic Republic of Congo. Yet at the time when the transatlantic slave trade flourished, its influence extended as far as the Cabinda region, from where some of the earliest members of New Orleans's slave population originated. The prestige of the once mighty Kingdom of Kongo accounts for the fact that thousands of African slaves in the Americas identified themselves and their identity markers (dances, language, food, etc.) as "Kongo."

For several decades only a small minority of enslaved Africans in Louisiana were of Kongolese origin.[12] This changed when the originally French colony became Spanish in 1762. Under Spanish rule the slave population in Louisiana increased dramatically, and many of these new slaves originated from the Kongo region.[13] The number of people with Kongolese roots further increased in the aftermath of the 1791 slave rebellion in Saint Domingue, when some six thousand slaves and free persons of color arrived in Louisiana.[14]

Twenty-three years after the Louisiana Purchase of 1803, the missionary Timothy Flint provided the earliest extensive description of a "Congo dance" in New Orleans, when "hundreds of negroes, male and female, follow the king of the wake," who "for a crown he has a series of oblong, gilt-paper boxes on his head, tapering upwards, like a pyramid." "By his thousand mountebank tricks, and contortions of countenance and form, he produces an irresistible effect upon the multitude," Flint explains, and "all the characters that follow him . . . have their own peculiar dress, and their own contortions." "They dance," he writes, "and their streamers fly, and the bells that they have hung about them tinkle." Flint also mentioned that he had seen "groups of these moody and silent sons of the forest, following these merry bacchanalians in their dance, through the streets, scarcely relaxing their grim visages to a smile."[15] While it is unknown whether these "silent sons of the forest" were truly Native Americans or rather blacks in Native American attire, the behavior of the group is reminiscent of that of today's Mardi Gras Indians.

I recently discovered a new source on Congo Square, a story titled "The Singing Girl of New Orleans" (1849), which also refers to a "King of Congo" wearing "a crown, a great pyramid of painted paper boxes fastened together, which had the effect of nearly doubling his natural height." It also identifies a man "furnished with hoofs," another one "brandishing enormous horns," one who "displayed the tail of a monkey," and one who was covered with so many feathers that he reminded the author of a rooster and who "clapped his wings, crowing like a chantacleer [sic]." A lot of feathers were also to be seen in the case of yet another dancer, who was "stratting [sic] majestically, spreading behind him the plumes of the peacock." These dancers were "decked with all the colors of the rainbow," and "their necks, waists, arms and ankles literally bristled with innumerable little bells that jiggled and chimed as they moved, like millions of fairy tongues."[16]

The Kongo dance was also observed outside of New Orleans. In his *Journal of a Tour in America, 1824–1825*, Edward Stanley described a "negro fête" on a plantation situated about twenty-seven miles north of the city. There a "Congo dance" was performed, which Stanley defined as "chiefly a sort of shuffle, and a violent agitation of all the muscles of the body."[17] In the early 1830s, somewhere near the shores of the Ouachita River, Théodore Pavie observed how a slave overseer ordered his men to perform "the dance of the Congos." Following the order, "three old Negroes tuned their banjos, and three others began to beat the rhythm and a drum roll." Pavie expressed surprise about the "almost military movements of this African dance."[18]

Dances on Congo Square ceased in the 1850s.[19] Precisely at a time when Congo Square had lost its function as a gathering place for New Orleans's black population, however, Louis Gotschalk's composition *Bamboula* (1848) re-ignited interest in what had become a forgotten corner of the city. The fact that the cultural heritage of America's black population could be a source of inspiration for success in Paris—then still the mecca of culture—was a sensation and triggered what Ted Widmer has aptly called a wave of "Congomania."[20] Together with his fellow journalists George Washington Cable and Henry Castellanos, Lafcadio Hearn played a key role in the late nineteenth-century revival of interest in Congo Square. Their "witness reports" should be treated with caution, however, since they often relied on older sources, some of which were produced outside of Louisiana. Nevertheless, there are enough snippets of trustworthy information from earlier decades that allow us to characterize the "Kongo dance" as a male dance with violent gestures and high, acrobatic leaps. Recurring instruments were drums beaten with hands or sticks, animal jawbones scraped with a piece of metal, and caps with bells or nails attached to the legs or arms of the dancers. Banjos, violins, and triangles were also mentioned. The group leaders were known as kings and wore pyramid-shaped headwear that made them look taller. Some of the dancers wore an abundance of feathers.

THE KINGDOM OF KONGO

The most important performance tradition in the Kingdom of Kongo was known as *sanga(mento)*. Since the term was coined by the Portuguese, the first Europeans to establish contact with this African kingdom in 1483, it is tempting to relate its meaning to the Portuguese word *sangue*, blood. However, *sangamento* is derived from the verb *ku-sanga* in Kikongo, which evokes the spectacular and joyful leaps and jumps of the dancers.[21] The movements of this performance related to a war technique that the Jesuit Pêro Rodrigues in 1594 called *sanguar* and defined as "to leap from one side to another with a thousand twists and such agility that they can dodge arrows and spears."[22]

Sangamentos were, in fact, mock war performances. Their original meaning is uncertain but may relate to the mythical founding father of the Kongo Kingdom, a prince called Lukeni, who crossed the Congo River and conquered new land, thanks to his military skill and his command of iron technology. To the sound of drums, marimbas, scraping instruments called *cassutos*, and ivory horns, armed men in the Kongo Kingdom would show their agility in an imaginary war scene. The spectacular dodges, feints, and sudden leaps in these martial exercises served as a way to muster courage for battles but also provided young men with an opportunity to impress the community. In his *Report of the Kingdom of Congo* (1591), based on the writings by the Portuguese Duarte Lopez, the Italian explorer Filippo Pigafetta described the dress of Kongolese soldiers as "a cap ornamented with cock's, ostrich's, peacock's, and other feathers . . . which makes the men seem taller and very formidable" and "a belt . . . with bells attached to it . . . so arranged that when fighting with their enemies the sounds give them courage."[23] A seventeenth-century engraving discussed in Cécile Fromont's chapter in this volume illustrates the feathered headdress of central African warriors and military bands (see fig. 6.3). The abundant use of feathers by Kongolese warriors was also mentioned by the French abbot Liévin-Bonaventure Proyart, who in the 1770s observed that "those who depart for a military expedition never forget to paint their body red" and that "the majority of the soldiers wear feathers that are even larger and richer in color than those our ladies of the great world are nowadays wearing."[24]

The earliest description of a sangamento comes from the Portuguese chronicler Rui de Pina, who in his late fifteenth-century account mentions how "his Majesty [the king of Kongo] assembled all his nobles in court," whereupon he "took his bow and arrows and went to the square," where "as if in combat he played games."[25] A more extensive witness account has been provided by the Italian Capuchin Giovanni Francesco da Roma in the mid-seventeenth century:

> On these occasions, [the king] is richly dressed and wears a crown of great value on his head, similar to the one worn by emperors. In his left hand, he holds his big shield and in his right hand he holds his unsheathed sword. The nobles are also wearing their richest clothes, and even the soldiers do too, with the exception of those with a naked upper body, which helps them to remain agile with the sword and with the bow and arrow. On their heads, they attach lots of feathers of different colors. With the king in the middle, they start running in a group, holding unsheathed swords in their hands, shouting as if they were planning to loot the city. On the squares, they stop, and from opposite sides of the square some men come forward. . . . They start fighting and handle their shields, swords, bows and spears with such dexterity and agility that it is a pleasure to watch. They jump now and then, squat, straighten themselves up, and give horrifying looks while they shout and scream.[26]

These performances were of particular importance at a time of transition in power. Whenever a new *manikongo*, king of Kongo, was elected, sangamentos were performed as part of the delegation of power. It is no coincidence that formal investiture was accompanied by a mock war dance. Since successions were not hereditary but the result of an election process, local clans often resorted to violence to impose their candidate, and those who were elected depended heavily on rituals to demonstrate their power and ensure loyalty.[27]

It was precisely such a struggle for succession that brought great changes to the kingdom in the early sixteenth century. Following the death of the *manikongo* in 1506, a dispute over succession erupted between two of his sons. With Portuguese aid, Mvemba a Nzinga, better known under his Catholic baptismal name, Afonso, was able to defeat his half-brother in the Battle of Mbanza Kongo in 1506. In accordance with his faith, the new king dedicated his victory to a miraculous intervention by Saint James the Greater. It is likely that Afonso's vision, which was to become the foundation story of the Catholic kingdom of Kongo, was inspired by Portuguese missionaries. In the context of the battle for control over the Iberian Peninsula, Saint James the Greater, also known as Saint James the Apostle, had come to enjoy tremendous popularity among Catholic Iberians and came to be adopted as patron saint of the Spanish and Portuguese armies under the name Santiago Matamoros/São Tiago Matamouros, meaning Saint James, the Moor Slayer.[28]

Following Afonso's victory over his half brother, Saint James became the patron saint of Kongo. On Saint James's Day, July 25, nobles from all the provinces had to come to the capital, Mbanza Kongo, also called São Salvador, to pay tribute and taxes to the king. The solemnities in honor of the saint lasted for several days and included a banquet as well as a spectacular sangamento.[29]

Under King Afonso Portuguese culture became fashionable. The Kongolese aristocracy adopted Portuguese baptismal names, titles, coats or arms, banners, and styles of dress. Even after the Kongolese relationship with the Portuguese had soured in the mid-sixteenth century, and Portugal began to rival Kongolese control over the local slave trade from its fortified stronghold in Luanda, the influence of Portuguese religious and popular culture in the kingdom remained strong. Subsequent Kongolese kings continued to position themselves in the lineage of Afonso, using his coat of arms and Portuguese-style symbols of royalty such as the crown, sword, cape, throne, scepter, and, above all, religion to legitimate their claim to the throne.[30]

In consequence of the interaction with the Portuguese, a process of cultural syncretism set in that also affected sangamentos. The Capuchin Girolamo Merolla da Sorrento argues in his late seventeenth-century report that sangamentos in Soyo had two parts: one during which traditional clothes and weapons were used, followed by a second one with European dress and weaponry:

> Annually, every governor, or *Mani*, is required to appear with his people in the capital of Soyo at the Festival of St. James the Apostle and assist the first Mass. . . . Afterwards the Prince practices two acts of war; in one, according to the style of the country, he uses an arch and arrows, putting on top of his head a sheaf of very wide feathers made in the shape of a crown; in the other, he wears a hat, on top of which many feathers flutter, and a chain, a cross of gold, [with] strings of corals, pendants [hanging] from the neck all the way to the knee, and a small scarlet overcoat,

embroidered with gold thread, open from both sides for hunting so that arms can be stretched out and for other gallantries [such as] to use the harquebus.[31]

Both the cross and the red cape are direct allusions to the iconography of Saint James. One could, as such, argue that this "modern" form of sangamento combined the kingdom's two foundation stories: the traditional one in allusion to the hero Lukeni and the modern one in allusion to the first Catholic king Afonso.[32]

It may well be that the modern sangamento was also inspired by Portuguese mock war traditions, an example of which can be found in the 1620 celebrations in Luanda following the canonization of the Jesuit Francis Xavier. The festivities included not only a procession featuring "three giants," dances by "Creoles from São Tomé [with] their king," a march by the "brotherhoods of the city . . . all with their respective pennants," a "swordfight that was as well performed as the best one can see in Portugal," and a "dance with sticks" but also the performance of a "scene from the life of St. Francis Xavier about the time when he was preaching in Malacca and prophesized that the Portuguese would obtain a victory against those from Ache, which involved a great spectacle of war."[33]

Interestingly, honoring Saint James with a mock war dance was not only a Kongolese but also an Iberian tradition. Since Saint James was the patron saint of the soldiers, members of the military used to honor him with a mock war performance known in Spanish as *Moros y Cristianos* and in Portuguese as *Mouros e Cristãos* (*Moors and Christians*). *Moors and Christians* traditionally begins with a parade of the respective "embassies," which in reference to the Christian victory in the Battle of Lepanto in 1571 (dedicated to Our Lady of the Rosary) is sometimes anticipated by the arrival of the troops by boat. Modeled after Iberian medieval armies and courtly traditions, the embassies display a strong hierarchy, with a captain as leader, and furthermore include a spy, a flag bearer, a king and queen, a page, a buffoon, and so on. When the Moors (traditionally dressed in red, with capes and hats displaying half moons and Asian gemstones), are confronted by the Christians (traditionally dressed in blue), the Christian chief demands the Moorish chief to surrender and accept baptism. After a heated discussion, a mock fight sets in whereby the Moors initially seem to obtain victory but are eventually defeated and forced to bow to be baptized as Christians.[34]

The popularity of this tradition among Iberians, the fact that both the Kongolese and the Portuguese happened to honor Saint James with a mock war performance, and the fact that the Portuguese influence on Kongolese sangamento performances is undeniable make it possible that certain elements of *Moors and Christians* entered sangamentos. This assumption is all the more legitimate since Andrea da Pavia's seventeenth-century account on the Kingdom of Kongo mentions that, when questioned about the origin of the sangamento at the feast of Saint James, locals answered him that the Portuguese "taught and advocated this Feast of St. James. They themselves used to celebrate it very solemnly."[35]

Despite the rapid decline of the kingdom in the late seventeenth century, sangamentos continued to exist for a long time. During a trip to Kongo in 1816, the British explorer James Hingston Tuckey still witnessed a "sanga." "In the war dance," he explains, "the performer, with a sword, looks about from side to side as if expecting the enemy." At last he sees them and "flourishes his sword half a dozen times towards the quarter in which they are supposed to appear; advances; his eyes glowing fire; returns triumphant; while the spectators are clapping their hands and striking their breasts in turns; he then squats down."[36]

THE KONGOLESE DIASPORA

Evidence that sangamentos were introduced in the Americas can be found in the "visions" of Johannes King, written between 1864 and 1895 and bundled under the title *Skrekiboekoe* (Book of horrors). King was born in a maroon community in the Lower-Saramaka region of Suriname. Upon conversion to the Moravian Church, he became a missionary worker. His writings deal mostly with Christian topics but also contain information on daily life in maroon societies. At one point King describes a feast that erupted after a peace treaty had been signed with the Dutch:

> The next morning they took a piece of white cloth and raised the flag in the name of the Gran Gado [Great God] or the Masra Gado [Lord God] in heaven . . . and then they raised another flag with a piece of black cloth. This one they raised in the name of the former warriors who had fought the whites and won battles. Then they all gathered around this flag to give thanks to these warriors and honor them. They blew African trumpets, which in ancient times Africans had made out of wood in Africa. . . . When they blew their trumpets, they would also shoot their guns, beat the drums, sing, and dance while playing the *sanga* drums. The adults performed the *sanga* everywhere. The word *sanga* means that a lot of people

with guns, axes, and spears run around everywhere, acting just like the warriors used to fight in Africa, with a lot of battle noise.[37]

The parallels to sangamentos leave little doubt. This source can serve as proof that enslaved Kongolese did, in fact, bring the performance tradition with them to the Americas. The fact that King, as a nineteenth-century descendant of runaway slaves, still remembered the term *sanga* accounts for its continuous importance.

Performing armed mock war dances was obviously much more of a challenge for those who did not live in maroon communities. This may explain why, in many parts of Latin America, we observe how members of the Kongo nation became attached to *Moors and Christians* or developed a Kongolese variant of this Carolingian drama. These performances used to be organized in the context of sodalities, organizations, dedicated to a Catholic saint, that functioned as mutual-aid and burial societies. Sodalities had a strong hierarchal structure, for which European aristocratic titles were used, including the term *kings* for leaders.[38] One could suspect that the remarkable popularity of *Moors and Christians* relates to a policy of masking. In fact, the only way for sangamentos to survive outside of maroon communities was in the context of traditions that had the approval of the authorities. What at first view seems like the adoption of a purely Iberian tradition by slaves might thus contain a hidden symbolic meaning. After all, the ritual election and celebration of a king in Kongo required a mock war performance, which would explain why mutual-aid associations composed of members of the Kongo nation honored their elected kings with a performance of *Moors and Christians*. Precisely this symbolism could account for the attachment to a European chivalric performance that apparently has no connection whatsoever with African culture.

An example of this can be found in the Fiesta de Santiago Apostol in Loiza, Puerto Rico, which developed out of pantomimes representing battles between blacks dressed as Moors and as Spanish *caballeros*. Remarkably, local companies used to pay a financial tribute to the kings of the mutual-aid societies on this holiday, which corresponds to the tradition that nobles in the Kongo Kingdom would pay their taxes to the king on Saint James's Day.[39] In Brazil we find plenty of references to *Moors and Christians* in connection to Kongo mutual-aid associations, known as *congadas*. In some of these, dancers are dressed with feathered headwear, which makes them look like Native Americans. In 1843, for instance, Count Francis de la Porte de Castelneau witnessed the election of a king of Kongo in Sabará, Minas Gerais, and observed that "the court . . . was seated on either side of the king and queen; then came a long list of other characters, the most impressive of which were doubtless great captains, famous warriors, or ambassadors of distant authorities, all dressed up like Brazilian Indians, with huge feathered headdresses, cavalry sabers at their sides, and shields on their arms." He also noted that they "simulated battles and all kinds of somersaults."[40] Still today, *maracatu* parades in Brazil integrate several black dancers with such impressive feathered headwear. They are typical for Pernambuco, one of the historical centers of Kongolese culture in Brazil, and developed out of king parades, which explains why the sun umbrella, a traditional element to highlight the *king's* prestige, became an important element in these dances. *Maracatus* once functioned as sodalities and were famous for their *loas*, or Catholic veneration songs, during processions but have meanwhile become secularized in the context of carnival. Nevertheless, the connection to Kongo remains visible, as in the following carnival song: "Eu sou Rei! Rei do meu Reinado! Maracatu lá do Congo! Lá do Congo Nêle fui coroado! [I am king! King of my kingdom! *Maracatu* from Kongo. From Kongo, where I was crowned!]."[41] The presence of apparently Native American elements in what otherwise seems to be an ordinary Kongo king parade has long puzzled Brazilian scholars. Brazil's most eminent folklorist, Luís da Câmara Cascudo, confirms that "the Indian element converged, here and there, into *congadas*" but was unaware of the fact that Kongolese warriors used to wear feathered headdresses, similar to those of Native Americans, during sangamentos.[42]

A Kongolese variant of *Moors and Christians*, known as *cucumbi* in Brazil, used to involve several characters that recall Mardi Gras Indians as we know them from New Orleans. Nineteenth-century Brazilian descriptions speak of "Africans performing like Indians" and of black men "masquerading like Indians," who made "savage gestures" and were led by someone who, just like the Mardi Gras Indian spy men, "would occasionally put his ear to the ground to listen for approaching enemies."[43] *Cucumbis* also had a flag bearer, corresponding to the Mardi Gras Indian flag boy, and a "medicine man" who, just like the New Orleans's wild man or medicine man, would wear a headpiece with horns and behave in a "wild" fashion while holding back the crowds.[44] The tradition also existed in Cuba, where it was known under the name *bacumby* and was characterized by David Brown as "carnival figures dressed in feathers [who] were frequent participants in the . . . hierarchy of 'Kings and Queens' represented in carnival dramas."[45] These performances did not originate in the context of carnival, however, but used to be part of Kongolese sodality celebrations on major Catholic holidays. As Felipe Ferreira has shown, the performances of black men dressed like Native Americans during Brazilian carnival parades parallels that of "black Indians" or "wild Indians" during Corpus Christi and Epiphany celebrations in past centuries.[46] John Charles Chasteen claims that the presence of "black Indians" in Brazilian and other carnivals in the Americas are to be understood as relics of former dramatic dances by blacks on Catholic holidays, yet "no longer welcome in religious processions, black Indians found a nineteenth-century outlet at carnival."[47]

MARDI GRAS INDIANS

Several aspects of the Kongo dances recorded in New Orleans's Congo Square become clearer if related to sangamentos. The fact that they were known as male dances, with aggressive gestures and high leaps; that they honored a king; that men used feathered headwear to look taller; that they used jawbones to produce a scraping sound like that of the *cassuto*; and that dancers wore belts with bells attached to them all correspond to mock war performances in the Kingdom of Kongo.

The same applies to today's Mardi Gras Indians. While traditional interpretations hardly managed to make any sense of their behavior, interpreting their parades, songs, and mock war performances in connection to sangamentos and *Moors and Christians* clarifies much of the scenery. The military organization of the gangs; the strict hierarchy; the presence of the spy boy, flag boy, and medicine man; the importance of the pennant; the feathered headwear; the twirling of umbrellas by second-liners; and the modus operandi of the performance (the parade, meeting of the enemies, heated discussions, mock fights, the bowing of the defeated group) reveal striking parallels.

These parallels make it likely that the kings observed by Flint and others on New Orleans's Congo Square were not members of African nobility but leaders of local mutual-aid organizations who were being celebrated in accordance with African rituals. Congo Square must, in fact, have had a much deeper importance to the city's slave community than just entertainment. Rather, it was a space that allowed the black community to organize itself in groups that were vital in securing key functions in society, such as the provision of mutual aid to those in need, the election of community leaders, the honoring of the dead, and the transmission of cultural heritage to the new generation. Even after abolition, however, a mixture of poverty, discrimination, lack of opportunities, and suspicion of outsiders encouraged certain groups in New Orleans's black community to keep relying on one another rather than on others to secure a minimum of social protection, human dignity, and self-respect.

To this day New Orleans has a social-aid club, known as Zulu, that elects a "king." While Zulu is generally understood as a parody of the white Mardi Gras king Rex, one could speculate that both Zulu and the Mardi Gras Indians may have deliberately used a strategy of disguise. Since it was unimaginable in the segregated Louisianan society of the time to elect and honor a black king with African warrior dances without arousing fears of armed resistance, these mutual-aid societies needed a carnivalesque smoke-screen. What in normal circumstances would have aroused suspicion seemed harmless in the eyes of the authorities when it appeared to be only a form of humor or an "Indian" play.

Louis Armstrong's comment that "it was the dream of every kid in my neighborhood" to be chosen king of Zulu and that his election as king in 1949 was the realization of a "life-long dream" shows that this distinction meant more to the black community than just a parody.[48] That the Zulu king builds on older traditions can also be seen in reference to the Illinois Club, a social-aid society founded in New Orleans in 1895, which used to have black royal courts.[49] While the parallels between Kongo king–election rituals and the Krewe of Zulu are more obvious than with the Mardi Gras Indians, the prox-imity remains visible in references found in Mardi Gras Indian songs to the "the big chief of the Congo Nation" and to "kings" who have a "golden crown."[50] Moreover, already in the 1940s, Robert Tallant had pointed out that the Mardi Gras Indians were "formally organized," that they used to hold meetings "at regular intervals throughout the year," that "members pay dues," and that they "hold elections."[51] Later research by David Elliott Draper confirmed that gangs provide financial aid to members in need, assist those who are imprisoned, and cover funeral expenses. To adult members, he claims, the social entertainment of the gang is "of secondary importance in comparison with the instrumental qualities of being [a] member of the mutual-aid association."[52] The fact that both the Krewe of Zulu and Mardi Gras Indians used to begin their perfor-mance with a (Catholic) prayer clearly parallels ancient sodality procedures.[53] The reappearance of the Mardi Gras Indians around Saint Joseph's Day can be explained with reference to sodality traditions. This custom corresponds to the old Catholic tradition to conclude the carnival season on Laetare Sunday, a day of relaxation in the middle of Lent. As the "feast of light," Laetare was traditionally celebrated with festive night processions with lanterns, similar to big chief Harrison's record of Saint Joseph's night parades in New Orleans.[54]

Proof that the Mardi Gras Indians are a much older tradition than is traditionally assumed can be found in Henry Rightor's *Standard History of New Orleans* (1900). The author relates the "black Indians" to the city's "old carnival" and the typical revelries of a "half century ago" that still survived in "odd corners of the city," which confirms that this tradition already existed before the "new carnival" with the Mistick Krewe of Comus, established in 1856. Rightor explicitly writes that "oddly enough, it is the Negroes who preserve in its truest essence the primitive spirit of the carnival."[55]

I doubt, however, that these traditions were born in the context of carnival. My assumption rather is that both the Krewe of Zulu and the Mardi Gras Indians developed out of king-election ceremonies that used to be part of city parades during major Catholic holidays but, similar to what occurred in Latin America, were gradually pushed out of the church and ended up in carnival. We should not forget that New Orleans has a long (French and Spanish) Catholic history and used to have a well-established procession culture, in which blacks were enthusiastic participants.[56] Still, in 1822, long after the Louisiana Purchase, a reporter in *La Gazette* observed that, during processions, New Orleans looked "more like a Spanish . . . city than an American one."[57] However, under pressure by hardliners such as Father Borella and Archbishop Blanc, the Catholic Church had in the early nineteenth century become increasingly intolerant of Afro-Catholic performances.[58] As a result, these parades shifted from Epiphany and Corpus Christi to carnival.[59] This transition has been documented in nearby Mobile, where the history of carnival is traditionally explained as a feast that once upon a time used to begin on January 6 (Epiphany) with a festive parade that included a statue of the Virgin Mary.[60] In New Orleans January 6 still marks the official beginning of the carnival season, which accounts for a strong historical connection between Epiphany and Mardi Gras.

When Lyle Saxon, who had an Anglo-American background, had a chance to discover Mardi Gras in the company of a black man, he entered a world utterly foreign to him, not just because of the African elements but also because of elements rooted in folk Catholicism. In *Fabulous New Orleans* he describes how he witnessed "many Negroes in costume who seemed to be holding a Mardi Gras all their own," including "men wearing purple elephants' heads of papier-mâché; huge donkey's heads. Sometimes two men would combine in order to represent a comical horse or a violet-colored cow. A man passed by on stilts. . . . Two men were dressed in black tights, painted with white to imitate skeletons."[61] This scene is full of elements relating to ancient festive traditions in Iberian folk Catholicism. Men walking with stilts, dressing as oxen, riding hobbyhorses, wearing gigantic heads made of papier-mâché, and imitating skeletons are all typically associated with street animation during Iberian Epiphany and Corpus Christi processions.[62] Significantly, Saxon refers in the same passage to "masked yellow girls dressed as Spanish dancers" and the "Zulu king" and "negro men dressed as Indians with faces painted and feather headdresses."[63] The Spanish dancers, black kings, and "black Indians" all relate to traditions that must have once thrived in Afro-Iberian, Catholic performance culture but were eventually pushed out of the church. They lived on in the context of mutual-aid societies, however, and found a new home in carnival.

NOTES

Parts of this contribution have previously been published in my article "From Moors to Indians: The Mardi Gras Indians and the Three Transformations of St. James," *Louisiana History* 56, no. 1 (2015): 5–41; and in my book *From the Kingdom of Kongo to Congo Square: Kongo Dances and the Origins of the Mardi Gras Indians* (Lafayette: University of Louisiana at Lafayette Press, 2017). I thank the Louisiana Historical Association for its permission to republish part of these contributions in revised and amplified form in this article. Unless otherwise noted, all translations are my own.

1. Henry Rightor, ed., *Standard History of New Orleans* (Chicago: Lewis, 1900), 643.

2. Barbara Bridges, "Black Indian Mardi Gras in New Orleans," in *Caribbean Festival Arts: Each and Every Bit of Difference*, ed. John W. Nunley and Judith Bettelheim (Seattle: University of Washington Press, 1988), 156–63; Michael P. Smith, *Mardi Gras Indians* (Gretna, La.: Pelican, 1994), 21–148; Reid Mitchell, *All on a Mardi Gras Day: Episodes in the History of New Orleans Carnival* (Cambridge, Mass.: Harvard University Press, 1995), 114–54; Jason Berry, Jonathan Foose, and Tad Jones, "In Search of the Mardi Gras Indians," in *When Brer Rabbit Meets Coyote: African-Native American Literature*, ed. Jonathan Brennan (Urbana: University of Illinois Press, 2003), 197–217; Roger Abrahams, *Blues for New Orleans: Mardi Gras and America's Creole Soul*, with Nick Spitzer, John F. Szwed, and Robert Farris Thompson (Philadelphia: University of Pennsylvania Press, 2006), 51–78; George Lipsitz, "Mardi Gras Indians: Carnival and Counter-Narrative in Black New Orleans," in Brennan, *When Brer Rabbit Meets Coyote*, 218–40.

3. Alice Moore Dunbar-Nelson, "A Carnival Jangle" (1899), in *The Goodness of St. Rocque, and Other Stories* (New York: Dodd, Mead, 1899), 132–33.

4. Jelly Roll Morton, qtd. in Alan Lomax, *Mister Jelly Roll: The Fortunes of Jelly Roll Morton, New Orleans Creole and "Inventor of Jazz"* (New York: Duell, Sloan, and Pearce, 1950), 14–16.

5. Allison "Tootie" Montana, qtd. in Jason Berry, *The Spirit of Black Hawk: A Mystery of Africans and Indians* (Jackson: University Press of Mississippi, 1995), 108.

6. *Daily Picayune*, February 17, 1885.

7. Léon Beauvallet, *Rachel and the New World: A Trip to the United States and Cuba* (New York: Dix, Edwards, 1856), 364–66.

8. Jerah Johnson, "New Orleans's Congo Square: An Urban Setting for Early Afro-American Culture Formation," *Louisiana History* 32, no. 2 (1991): 117–57.

9. William Wells Brown, *My Southern Home; or, The South and Its People* (Boston: Brown, 1880), 121–24.

10. James Kelly, *Jamaica in 1831: Being a Narrative of Seventeen Years' Residence in That Island* (Belfast: Wilson, 1838), 20–21.

11. Vicente Rossi, *Cosas de Negros* (1926; repr., Buenos Aires: Librería Hachette, 1958), 68.

12. Gwendolyn Midlo Hall, *Africans in Colonial Louisiana: The Development of Afro-Creole Culture in the Eighteenth Century* (Baton Rouge: Louisiana State University Press, 1992), 60.

13. Ned Sublette, *The World That Made New Orleans: From Spanish Silver to Congo Square* (Chicago: Lawrence Hill Books, 2008), 107.

14. Paul Lachance, "The 1809 Immigration of Saint-Dominque Refugees," in *The Road to Louisiana: The Saint-Domingue Refugees, 1792–1809*, ed. Carl A. Brasseaux and Glenn R. Conrad (Lafayette: Center for Louisiana Studies, 1992), 247.

15. Timothy Flint, *Recollections of the Last Ten Years in the Valley of the Mississippi*, ed. George R. Brooks (1826; repr., Carbondale: Southern Illinois University Press, 1968), 103.

16. "The Singing Girl of New Orleans," *Barre Patriot*, September 21, 1849.

17. Edward Stanley, *Journal of a Tour in America, 1824–1825* (London: privately printed, 1930), 252–58.

18. Théodore Pavie, *Souvenir Atlantique: Voyage aux États-Unis et au Canada*, 2 vols. (Paris: Roret, 1833), 2:320.

19. Freddi Williams Evans: *Congo Square: African Roots in New Orleans* (Lafayette: University of Louisiana at Lafayette Press, 2011), 23.

20. Ted Widmer, "The Invention of Memory: Congo Square and African Music in Nineteenth-Century New Orleans," *Revue Française d'Études Américainnes* 98, no. 2 (2003): 72.

21. Cécile Fromont, *The Art of Conversion: Christian Visual Culture in the Kingdom of Kongo* (Chapel Hill: University of North Carolina Press, 2014), 21.

22. Jesuit Pêro Rodrigues, qtd. in António Brásio, ed., *Monumenta missionária Africana*, 15 vols. (Lisbon: Agência Geral do Ultramar, 1952–71 [vols. 1–11]; Lisbon: Academia Portuguesa da História, 1988 [vols. 12–15]), 4:563.

23. Filippo Pigafetta, *A Report of the Kingdom of Congo and the Surrounding Countries: Drawn Out of the Writings and Discourses of the Portuguese Duarte Lopez*, ed. Margarite Hutchinson (1591; repr., New York: Negro Universities Press, 1969), 36, 109.

24. Liévin-Bonaventure Proyart, *Histoire de Loango, Kakongo, et autres royaumes d'Afrique* (Paris: Berton, 1776), 163–64.

25. Rui de Pina, *Relação do Reino do Congo: Manuscrito inédito do Códice Riccardiano, 1910*, ed. Carmen M. Radulet (1492; repr., Lisbon: Imprensa Nacional, Casa da Moeda, 1992), 123.

26. Jean-François de Rome [Giovanni Francesco da Roma], *Brève relation de la fondation de la mission des Frères Mineurs Capucins du Séraphique Père Saint François au Royaume de Congo (1648)*, ed. François Bontinck (Louvain, Belgium: Nauwelaerts, 1964), 130–31.

27. John Kelly Thornton, *The Kongolese Saint Anthony: Dona Beatriz Kimpa Vita and the Antonian Movement, 1684–1706* (Cambridge: Cambridge University Press, 1998), 30–35; Fromont, *Art of Conversion*, 21–64.

28. Pigafetta, *Report of the Kingdom*, 70–89; Brásio, *Monumenta missionária Africana*, 1:256–59; António Brásio, ed., *História do Reino do Congo: Ms. 8080 da Biblioteca Nacional de Lisboa* (Lisbon: Centro de Estudos Históricos Ultramarinos, 1969), 77–80; Fromont, *Art of Conversion*, 47, 87, 91, 182.

29. Fra Luca da Caltanisetta, *Diaire congolais (1690–1701)*, ed. François Bontinck (Louvain, Belgium: Nauwelaerts, 1970), 5–6; Marcellino d'Atri, *L'anarchia Congolese nel sec. XVII: La relazione inedita di Marcellino d'Atri (1702)*, ed. Carlo Toso (Genova: Bozzi Editore, 1984), 2376–79; Fromont, *Art of Conversion*, 183–84.

30. António Custódio Gonçalves, "As influências do Cristianismo na organização política do Reino do Congo," in *Congresso Internacional Bartolomeu Dias e a sua época: Actas*, 5 vols. (Porto, Portugal: Universidade do Porto, 1989), 5:523–39; John K. Thornton and Linda M. Heywood, *Central Africans, Atlantic Creoles, and the Foundation of the Americas, 1585–1660* (Cambridge: Cambridge University Press, 2007), 135–43; Fromont, *Art of Conversion*, 47–59, 71, 128, 130, 143, 181.

31. Girolamo Merolla da Sorrento and Angelo Piccardo, *Breve e succinta relatione del viaggio nel regno di Congo nell' Africa meridionale* (Naples, 1692), 157.

32. Cécile Fromont, "Dance, Image, Myth, and Conversion in the Kingdom of Kongo: 1500–1800," *African Arts* 44, no. 4 (2011): 54–65.

33. Alfredo de Albuquerque Felner, *Angola: Apontamentos sobre a ocupação e início do estabelecimento dos portugueses no Congo, Angola, e Benguela extraídos de documentos históricos* (1620; repr., Coimbra, Portugal: Imprensa da Universidade, 1933), 531–43.

34. Michael J. Doudoroff, *Moros y Cristianos in Zacatecas: Text of a Mexican Folk Play* (Lawrence, Kans.: Amadeo Concha Press, 1981), vii; Max Harris, *Aztecs, Moors, and Christians: Festivals of Reconquest in Mexico and Spain* (Austin: University of Texas Press, 2000), 34–35; José Rivair Macedo, "Mouros e Cristãos: A ritualização da conquista no velho e no Novo Mundo," *Bulletin du Centre d'Etudes Médiévales d'Auxerre* 2 (2008): 2–10.

35. Louis Jadin, ed., "Voyages apostoliques aux missions d'Afrique du P. Andrea da Pavia, Prédicateur Capucin, 1685–1702," *Bulletin de L'Institut Historique Belge de Rome* 41 (1970): 451–52.

36. James Hingston Tuckey, *Narrative of an Expedition to Explore the River Zaire* (New York: Gilley, 1818), 207–8.

37. Chris de Beet, ed., *Skrekiboekoe: Boek der verschrikkingen; Visionen en historische overleveringen van Johannes King* (Utrecht: Bronnen Voor de Studie Van Afro-Suriname, Vakgroep Culturele Antropologie, Universiteit Utrecht, 1995), 247–49.

38. Jeroen Dewulf, *The Pinkster King and the King of Kongo: The Forgotten History of America's Dutch-Owned Slaves* (Jackson: University Press of Mississippi, 2017), 97–132.

39. Ricardo E. Alegría, "The Fiesta of Santiago Apostol (St. James the Apostle) in Loíza, Puerto Rico," *Journal of American Folklore* 69, no. 272 (April–June 1956): 123–34; Max Harris, "Masking the Site: The Fiestas de Santiago Apóstol in Loíza, Puerto Rico," *Journal of American Folklore* 114, no. 453 (2001): 358–69.

40. Fromont's chapter, in this volume; Count Francis de la Porte de Castelnau, qtd. in Luís da Câmara Cascudo, *Antologia do folclore brasileiro* (São Paulo: Martins Editora, 1965), 108.

41. Song lyrics qtd. in Luís da Câmara Cascudo, *Made in Africa* (1965; repr., São Paulo: Global Editores, 2001), 29–30.

42. Cascudo, *Antologia do folclore brasileiro*, 243–44.

43. Eric Brasil, "Cucumbis carnavalescos: Áfricas, carnaval, e abolição (Rio de Janeiro, década de 1880)," *Afro-Ásia* 49 (2014): 298.

44. Alexandre José de Mello Moraes Filho, *Festas e tradições populares no Brasil* (São Paulo: Editora da Universidade de São Paulo, 1979), 109–10; Luiz Edmundo, *Rio de Janeiro no tempo dos Vice-Reis*, 3 vols. (1936; repr., Rio de Janeiro: Conquista, 1956), 2:255–66.

45. David H. Brown, "The Afro-Cuban Festival 'Day of Kings': An Annotated Glossary," in *Cuban Festivals: A Century of Afro-Cuban Culture*, ed. Judith Bettelheim (Princeton: Wiener, 2001), 50.

46. Felipe Ferreira, *O livro de ouro do carnaval brasileiro* (Rio de Janeiro: Ediouro, 2004), 291–94.

47. John Charles Chasteen, *National Rhythms, African Roots: The Deep History of Latin American Popular Dance* (Albuquerque: University of New Mexico Press, 2004), 39, 96–98, 183.

48. Louis Armstrong, *Satchmo: My Life in New Orleans* (New York: Prentice-Hall, 1954), 127.

49. James Gill, *Lords of Misrule: Mardi Gras and the Politics of Race in New Orleans* (Jackson: University Press of Mississippi, 1997), 157–58.

50. Sublette, *World That Made New Orleans*, 308.

51. Robert Tallant, *Mardi Gras* (Garden City, N.Y.: Doubleday, 1948), 241.

52. David Elliott Draper, "The Mardi Gras Indians: The Ethnomusicology of Black Associations in New Orleans" (PhD diss., Tulane University, 1973), 23.

53. Lyle Saxon, Edward Dreyer, and Robert Tallant, *Gumbo Ya-Ya: A Collection of Louisiana Folk Tales* (Cambridge: Riverside Press, 1945), 7; Samuel Kinser, *Carnival, American Style: Mardi Gras at New Orleans and Mobile* (Chicago: University of Chicago Press, 1990), 174.

54. Al Kennedy, *Big Chief Harrison and the Mardi Gras Indians* (Gretna, La.: Pelican, 2010), 30, 71–72.

55. Rightor, *Standard History*, 631.

56. Charles E. Nolan, *A History of the Archdiocese of New Orleans* (New Orleans: Archdiocese of New Orleans, 2000), 9–20; Benjamin Henry Boneval Latrobe, *Impressions Respecting New Orleans: Diary and Sketches, 1818–1820*, ed. Samuel Wilson Jr. (New York: Columbia University Press, 1951), 35, 62, 94, 122–23, 164–65.

57. *La Gazette*, qtd. in Liliane Crété, *Daily Life in Louisiana, 1815–1830*, trans. Patrick Gregory (1978; repr., Baton Rouge: Louisiana State University Press, 1981), 151.

58. Randall M. Miller, "Slaves and Southern Catholicism," in *Masters and Slaves in the House of the Lord: Race and Religion in the American South, 1740–1870*, ed. John B. Boles (Lexington: University Press of Kentucky, 1988), 142; Roger

Baudier, *The Catholic Church in Louisiana* (New Orleans: privately printed, 1939), 254–55, 354–55.

59. Sublette, *World That Made New Orleans*, 113.

60. Kinser, *Carnival, American Style*, 108, 351; Rosary O'Neill: *New Orleans Carnival Krewes: The History, Spirit, amd Secrets of Mardi Gras* (Charleston, S.C.: History Press, 2014), 101.

61. Lyle Saxon, *Fabulous New Orleans* (1928; repr., New Orleans: Crager, 1952), 33–34.

62. Luís Chaves, *Danças, bailados, and mímicas guerreiras* (Lisbon: Ethnos, 1942), 9–23; Francis George Very, *The Spanish Corpus Christi Procession: A Literary and Folkloric Study* (Valencia, Spain: Moderna, 1962), 15, 37, 44–45, 91–99; Theophilo Braga, *O povo portuguez nos seus costumes, crenças, e tradições*, 2 vols. (Lisbon: Ferreira, 1885), 2:268–69.

63. Saxon, *Fabulous New Orleans*, 31.

FURTHER READING

Abrahams, Roger. *Blues for New Orleans: Mardi Gras and America's Creole Soul.* With Nick Spitzer, John F. Szwed, and Robert Farris Thompson. Philadelphia: University of Pennsylvania Press, 2006.

Chasteen, John Charles. *National Rhythms, African Roots: The Deep History of Latin American Popular Dance.* Albuquerque: University of New Mexico Press, 2004.

Dewulf, Jeroen. *From the Kingdom of Kongo to Congo Square: Kongo Dances and the Origins of the Mardi Gras Indians.* Lafayette: University of Louisiana at Lafayette Press, 2017.

Kinser, Samuel. *Carnival, American Style: Mardi Gras at New Orleans and Mobile.* Chicago: University of Chicago Press, 1990.

Mitchell, Reid. *All on a Mardi Gras Day: Episodes in the History of New Orleans Carnival.* Cambridge, Mass.: Harvard University Press, 1995.

Smith, Michael P. *Mardi Gras Indians.* Gretna, La.: Pelican, 1994

Sublette, Ned. *The World That Made New Orleans: From Spanish Silver to Congo Square.* Chicago: Lawrence Hill Books, 2008.

Williams Evans, Freddi. *Congo Square: African Roots in New Orleans.* Lafayette: University of Louisiana at Lafayette Press, 2011.

CHAPTER 2

Moros e Christianos
Ritualized Naval Battles
Baptizing American Waters with African Spiritual Meaning

KEVIN DAWSON

While on the Island of Itamaracá, in the Brazilian state of Pernambuco, in 1815, John Theodore Koster (ca. 1793–1820), an English coffee grower, traveler, and careful observer of slavery, watched as west-central African captives reenacted the Iberian tradition of *Moros e Christianos* in Spanish and *Mouros e Cristãos* in Portuguese (*Moors and Christians*) during an event he called the "christening of the king of Moors." In many important ways this mock ritualized battle followed the template of its more familiar terrestrial counterpart. Yet it also sharply diverged from it, as it was staged on coastal waterscapes that seamlessly merged water and adjoining lands into unified cultural spaces providing enslaved community members places of meaning and value. *Moros e Christianos* performances typically included choreographed dances. Scholarship since the 1990s as well as the chapters in this volume consider how west-central Africans in Kongo and Brazil "enacted a Christian discourse of triumph over heathenry honed in the *Reconquista*," pivoting on the Christian expulsion of Moslem rule from Iberia and often hinging on the mystical intervention of Saint James, a warrior saint. This chapter probes how Itamaracán slaves creatively reimagined *Moros e Christianos* to express west-central African freshwater and saltwater maritime traditions in Brazil's social and ecological environment.[1]

Itamaracá's population largely consisted of African-born, or saltwater, slaves, whom Koster labeled "Congo Negroes." Scholars have concluded that west-central Africans constituted the majority of Pernambuco's enslaved population, while those specifically from the Kingdom of Kongo figured prominently within them in terms of numbers and cultural influence.[2] Early one Monday morning, white and black residents "rose fresh and ready for action," thronging to Pilar Beach on the island's eastern shore to watch several hundred canoemen navigate dugouts constructed according to African design specifications to wage a mock naval battle during the "christening." All "the *jangadas* [rafts] and canoes were put on requisition; the owners of them and others of the inhabitants of the neighborhood were divided into two parties, Christians and Moors." An offshore platform had been constructed to represent a "Moorish fortress." Ashore "two high thrones" were erected, where the "Christian king" and "Moorish king" sat, "both of them being habited in fine flowing robes." The "Christian king" dispatched "his officers on horseback" to the Moorish ruler, demanding that he "undergo the ceremony of baptism, which he refused." War was declared, "the numerous *jangadas* and canoes of each party were soon in motion," and a naval battle ensued, with "much firing" of arrows, javelins, and spears, which presumably lacked sharp heads. The "Christian" navy drove the "Moorish" fleet back to the fort, which the "Christians" stormed and the "Moors" soon evacuated. Both sides executed amphibious beach landings, where they "fought hand to hand combat for a considerable time." Ultimately, "the Moorish king was taken prisoner, hurled from his throne, and forcibly baptized."[3]

The "christening of the king of Moors" possessed Portuguese-Catholic symbolism and meanings, as its name reflects. It occurred on Monday, February 6, 1815, during *intrudo*, also known as Shrovetide, Pre-Lenten Season, Carnival, or Mardi Gras. This was a three-day Christian period of revelry, which culminated in Fat or Shrove Tuesday, before the solemn observance of Lent commenced on Ash Wednesday.[4] Yet, it was west-central Africans who staged the festival, with seemingly no white input, the account suggesting that the event was constructed around an African dimension in addition to or in conjunction with its Portuguese Christian background.

Catholicism reached west-central Africa shortly after Portuguese interaction with the Kingdom of Kongo began in 1483. The monarch, Nzinga a Nkuwu (r. 1470–1509) converted to Catholicism and was baptized on May 3, 1491, taking the name João I after the Portuguese king. João's son and successor, Afonso I Mvemba a Nzinga (r. 1509–42), who remained a devout Christian, elaborated on his father's endeavors, imposing Catholicism as the official state religion while interlacing it into Kongo's "symbolic and historical fabric." He implemented broad cultural, religious, and technological reforms by drawing on Portuguese emissaries and Kongo men who had sojourned in Europe. Yet

Kongolese adoption of Christianity was mixed, ranging from earnest embrace to violent opposition. Still, the new religion gained traction.[5]

Because of this background, a large portion of west-central Africans arrived in Brazil with understandings of Catholic rituals and teachings. Beginning in the early sixteenth century, Catholic Portuguese visual and material culture coalesced with Kongo religious, cultural, social, and political customs to create Kongo-Catholic traditions. Churches were constructed, and stone and wooden crosses erected in urban centers, while depictions of Saint James symbolized Kongo political and spiritual power. Staffs, scepters, clothing, ivory and woodcarvings, jewelry, and other objects of material culture bore Catholic motifs. Scores of European priests proselytized in Kongo.[6]

Sustained historiographic debates circulate around what motivated Kongolese rulers to adopt Catholicism, whether Kongo-Catholicism was fundamentally an African or European religion, the extent to which Kongolese people embraced and internalized Catholic tenets, and captives' ability to recreate or reimagine Kongo-Catholicism in the Western Hemisphere. Some scholars argue that Kongo cosmology insinuated itself into and subsumed Catholicism. James Sweet posited, "Christianity and indigenous Kongolese religion operated in parallel fashion with the broad central African cosmology still being the dominant religious paradigm for most Kongolese, especially in the process of conversion to Christianity." He concluded that the Kongolese probably adopted "Christian symbols to represent their own deities, and they continued to worship them as they always had."[7] Others believe that, to varying degrees, Kongolese people embraced Catholicism according to church standards while adhering to their own valuations and interpretations of Christianity. For example, John Thornton argued that European priests "considered the Kongo form of Christianity, with its religious terminology borrowed from Kongo cosmology, as perfectly acceptable and normal." Despite changes, Kongo cosmology remained Kongolese, with Wyatt MacGaffey concluding that change "must be change in something that itself continues."[8]

Scholars also debate the predominance of "African retentions versus African creolizations in the Americas."[9] Historians of the African diaspora contend, as Jason Young stressed, that slaves "*remembered* Africa intentionally and deliberately" while "creating new and vibrant cultures informed by memories of Africa." They convincingly argue that the slave trade and slaveholders' purchasing preference congregated Africans from specific ethnic groups and regions, with Sweet asserting that bondpeople "were arriving in coherent cultural groupings that shared much in common," allowing many customs to cross "the Atlantic in nearly pure structure." Captives used "African culture," as Thornton noted, "to adapt to the Americas." While amalgamations routinely began in Africa, traditions were not "subsumed into a hazy cultural mist." Customs retained palpable textures, providing ethnic hallmarks while forging linkages with new communities.[10]

This chapter argues that the "christening of the king of Moors" was a Kongo maritime articulation, particularly informed by Kongo spiritual and cultural understandings despite—and including—its Christian name and meanings. Employing a broad Atlantic lens, it considers how Kongo cultural and spiritual meanings came to dwell in Itamaracá's waters as newly arrived water spirits, called *simbi*, informed this ritualized performance alongside and beyond the nominal presence of Catholic mysticism. During this ritualized performance, combatants crewed African-style dugout canoes that contained strong spiritual and secular links to the old continent, while the event as a whole, mirrored and recast an important type of military review, through which Kongolese expressed sacred and earthly connotations.

PARTING THE WATERS OF KONGO CULTURE

An examination of the king and his function provides a point of entry for considering this ceremony's Kongo dimensions, since the event occurred shortly before his coronation. Koster explained, "Congo negroes are permitted to elect a king or queen." In some regions of colonial Brazil, monarchs reigned for life, unless, as Koster noted, they "resigned" or were "displaced by [their] subjects." The selection of new kings and queens often coincided with the "festival of our Lady of Rosary," a ceremony elaborated on in several chapters of this volume. In March 1814 Itamaracá's king abdicated because of "old age," while the queen maintained her position. On the morning of his coronation, the successor visited the vicar to pay his respects, with the vicar saying, "in a jocular manner 'Well, sir, so to-day I am to wait upon you and be your chaplain.'" At about eleven o'clock a retinue of brightly clad "male and female Negroes" arrived at the church, with "flags flying and drums beating." The "king was dressed in an old fashioned suit of divers tints, green, red, yellow; coat, waistcoat, and breeches; his sceptre was in his hand, which was of wood, and finely gilt. The queen was in a blue silk gown, also of ancient make." The crowning occurred in the "principal chapel," with the vicar crowning the kneeling sovereign. Celebrations, consisting of "eating, drinking, and dancing," took place at Amparo, the plantation to which the "king belonged."[11] Some of Carlos Julião's late eighteenth-century watercolors as well as later images (discussed in Cécile Fromont's chapter within this book) visually document election festivals (figs. 6.1 to 6.2 and plates 4–9). Detailing revelers' use of bright regalia, African material culture, and African and European musical instruments, they enunciate how participants intentionally recreated and creatively reimagined the sights, sounds, and textures of west-central Africa in Brazil to infuse coronations with tangible cultural meaning and purpose.[12]

In Brazil many "Congo" communities elected kings to construct "ritual memory" that "symbolically link Afro-Brazilians to African political structures and to their African ancestors." Elizabeth Kiddy explained that lay religious confraternities dedicated to Our Lady of the Rosary routinely conducted elections. Brotherhoods afforded social and cultural spaces for African- and country-born slaves, as well as manumitted people, to reconstruct and reimagine communities predicated on shared African histories and Latin American experiences. Devotion to Our Lady of the Rosary emerged from the confluences of "Africans' appropriation of and adaptation of Christian mystic traditions" and is rooted in traditions cultivated in Portugal, transplanted to and nurtured in west-central Africa, then carried to Brazil. The first brotherhood of African membership in the Portuguese world was founded in Lisbon during the 1480s. During the sixteenth century nine brotherhoods, composed of enslaved and free Africans, were founded in Portugal, all "dedicated to Our Lady of the Rosary." This growth resulted, in part, from the use of the rosary as an ideal method for spreading the basic tenets of Christianity to illiterate peoples, allowing Africans "to re-form communities and rituals in the rosary brotherhoods because of similarities between their worldviews and the early modern layperson's relationship to the unseen world." A brotherhood was established in São Salvador, Kongo's capital, by 1610. By the 1690s Luanda, the capital of Portuguese Angola, had a church dedicated to Our Lady of the Rosary. In 1684 brotherhoods arrived in Brazil, where concepts "of being black in the rosary brotherhood" became based on two community-forming principles that bound them to Kongo. First, Our Lady of the Rosary became a patron of African-descended people. Second, festivals to her reinforced links to west-central Africa "through songs, drums, and ritual action and the calling of pretos velhos," who were ancestral spirits.[13]

West-central African bondpeople throughout Latin America performed terrestrial versions of *Moros e Christianos* that symbolized a "battle against" Islam during the Reconquista, in which Kongolese forces prevailed, often resulting from the "miraculous intercession of Saint James," a "warrior saint."

Sangamento dances were an important component of these rituals, which Itamaracáns reinvented to meet the geographic and hydrographic features that the island imposed on them, while apparently reflecting the maritime circumstances that precipitated their enslavement.[14] Sangamentos were, as Fromont elucidates, signifying performances that provided rhythms to public Kongo life while serving as preparatory martial-arts exercises for soldiers that allowed rulers to review their forces while projecting their strength and determination during formal declarations of war. They also accompanied "joyful celebrations of investitures, complemented courtly and diplomatic pageants, and lent their pomp to pious celebrations" on Catholic feast days. As expressions of west-central African martial arts, sangamentos contained two parts. Early in the routine dancers wore African garb while wielding African weapons before donning European attire and bearing European weaponry. Yet they were not always bifurcated, with performers also interlacing elements from both traditions.[15]

Relatedly, T. J. Desch-Obi traces the African roots and Atlantic routes of the martial-arts form called *ngolo* in west-central Africa and "*capoeiragem* or *capoeira Angola*," or simply capoeira, in Brazil, which included sangamentos. *Ngolo* was suited to Africans' fast-moving style of warfare that included "acrobatic evasions for defense," while kicks, combined with spiritual preparation, permitted combatants to cross the Kalunga and draw on supernatural powers, allowing them to injure opponents' bodies and souls. Brazilian authorities sought to suppress capoeira as expressions of what they deemed savage, heathen cultures that could, moreover, be used during acts of rebellion. Hence, it was routinely performed instead under the guise of dance.[16]

Beyond its ostensible Portuguese meaning, the "christening of the king of Moors" provided the opportunity for Itamaracá's new king to perform a review of his warriors in one of many gestures that, during the event, allowed the bonded community to articulate and perform a group identity informed by both African practices and Latin American circumstances. The "christening" occurred about eleven months after his coronation, and *intrudo* possibly provided the first festival that could facilitate it. Situating this large-scale military review in a manner acceptable for white authorities, captives reimagined Kongo traditions.

The christening's structure and contours cannot be fully understood without paying due attention to the maritime heritage of Itamaracá's slaves. Water covers some 75 percent of the earth's surface, and most people live near waterways. West-central Africa is no exception. It is a region defined by its many rivers, first among them was the eponymous Congo, which is the world's second largest. The region possesses a vast coastline and numerous lakes and rivers, while rains inundate the central Congo basin's floodplains twice per year, transforming the region into Africa's largest swamp. Here the cultural process was informed by human relationships with waterscapes, which created vast fertile places of meaning and value, where people cultivated deep social, cultural, and spiritual relationships with water and adjoining lands. West-central African waterscapes equally shaped most people's work and recreational lives, providing many with fresh- and saltwater maritime expertise as they fished, engaged in canoe-born trade, and swam to cool off, relax, and enjoy their bodies in the company of friends and relatives. It is incorrect to bifurcate west-central African societies as discretely terrestrial or maritime. Most societies can be treated as amphibious, as many of their members were fishing farmers and farming fishermen who fished one season, cultivated another, used dugouts to convey goods to market, and were proficient in maritime and terrestrial warfare. Concurrently, oligarchs regularly conscripted free and enslaved dependents to paddle their trade dugouts and man war canoes. For instance, when Ndobo, a ruler on the upper Congo River, prepared for a long-distance commercial voyage during the 1880s, he impressed 125 of "the hardiest men," who were fishing farmers, to crew "five large canoes." During the early modern period, the region was home to numerous professional canoe makers capable of crafting war, trade, and fishing dugouts that could exceed eighty feet in length and carry several tons of cargo. Nonprofessionals carved smaller canoes ranging from about six to twenty feet in length.[17]

Many west-central Africans were skilled in naval and amphibious warfare, with polities possessing navies capable of defending home waters and protecting maritime commerce while often projecting military, political, and economic power. It is seemingly incorrect to treat west-central African military forces as discrete armies and navies. Instead of regarding warriors as land-bound soldiers, we should consider them as *marines*, capable of crewing dugouts, executing naval maneuvers, fighting in canoes (which possess limited lateral stability, rendering them vulnerable to capsizing), making amphibious landings to fight ashore, and disembarking from riverbanks while being barraged by enemy arrows, spears, and javelins.[18]

Historian Robert Harms concludes that piracy was the greatest danger faced by those residing in the Congo River basin. During the nineteenth century some riparian villages plundered passing dugouts, while some fishermen, merchants, and farmers augmented their incomes by attacking trade canoes and launching amphibious raids against waterside settlements. Predatory villages could be avoided by sneaking along rivers, while the power of mariners' firearms was "always supplemented by the power of magic charms," which could produce concealing rainstorms or transform their dugouts into innocuous floating clumps of river vegetation.[19] Still, maritime warfare produced many slaves skilled in the art of canoeing and canoe making. For example, Zamba, who was raised along "the river Congo," about a five-day paddle from its mouth, before being kidnapped into South Carolinian bondage in 1800, recalled that his slave-trading father employed numerous canoemen to deliver hundreds of people down the Congo. These voyages presented opportunities for raiding riverside villages, which, in one instance, yielded "a hundred and thirty" captives.[20]

KONGOLESE CULTURAL CURRENTS IN THE DIASPORA

The Atlantic slave trade created cultural watersheds that funneled traditions into the waters of the Western Hemisphere, informing Brazilian slaves' ability to as they recreated Kongo maritime fluencies. To this end, historian Roquinaldo Ferreira explains that the Atlantic, Angola, and Brazil formed a "social and cultural continuum" with slave ships, affording the "physical mobility" necessary for bondpeople to remain culturally connected to ancestral lands while becoming members of new communities of meaning and purpose. Other scholars have examined how captives intertwined similar, yet distinct, traditions in slave ships' holds. Still, the Atlantic and all the rivers emptying into it were more than cultural highways. Waterscapes of the Western Hemisphere afforded immense spaces that African-descended peoples culturally and intellectually colonized, transforming them into conduits for deities and ancestral spirits to voyage to the Americas and for departed slaves to transmigrate across the Kalunga to the spirit world.[21]

Brazilian enslavers failed to impose Western cultural meanings on Itamaracá's waters, which once possessed indigenous values, making them fertile spaces for slaves to recreate and reimagine African traditions. On the island, as elsewhere, plantations were constructed along navigable waters to facilitate the shipment of slave-produced cash crops to market. Incessant waves of saltwater canoe makers, canoemen, and canoewomen broke on the shores of the Americas, forming cultural beachheads, where they recreated and reconceptualized maritime traditions. Slaves imposed Kongo valuations onto waterscapes they populated with deities. Using dugouts as cultural and spiritual anchors, they bound themselves to homelands and spirit worlds.[22]

Water figured prominently in west-central African perceptions of natural and spiritual worlds and their intersections. It was an important sacred space, and many believed the realm of the dead lay at the bottom of the ocean or a large body of water. Kongolese peoples believed the Kalunga, which "literally means ocean or large body of water," was an intermediary crossed during voyages to the land of the dead, providing inland and littoral peoples with aquatic spiritual understanding.[23]

Water simbi were prominent west-central African deities who arrived in the Americas with their enslaved believers. As primordial nature deities, they resided in objects that linked the living and spirit worlds and were pervasive and central to aquatic spiritual understandings. Inhabiting streams, rivers, lagoons, ponds, and marshes, they were especially prevalent in distinctive waterways, like waterfalls, hot springs, and rapids, where the "roar of water crashing over cataracts sounded like simbi crying out." Those residing along the Congo River's north bank near the river port of Boma said simbi cried, "'Kill, Kill,' (vonda, vonda)," warning how a perplexity of eddies threatened to sink dugouts and nineteenth-century European steamboats. Simbi demanded and rewarded respect and punished disobedience; hence, sacrifices could ensure successful fishing, commercial, and naval endeavors. Though not ancestral spirits, simbi represented the original inhabitants of a particular place, deeply rooting communities to a region while legitimizing their claims to it. The arrival of the simbi in the Americas permitted captives to intellectually and spiritually colonize waterscapes, making them existential extensions of west-central African communities.[24]

West-central African slaves used aquatic spiritual understandings to help make sense of their new environments and circumstances. There was seemingly a conscious choice to situate this christening in Pilar's waters as opposed to Itamaracá's mainland-facing side. Prior to the Middle Passage, most Kongo slaves did not interact with the ocean; hence, Pilar's waters conceivably provided the distinguishing setting simbi preferred while facilitating their function of linking the here and now to the spirit world. Though large waves do not break in Pilar's waters, small waves and storm-generated surf could have been simbi voices. Pilar faces eastward, into the rising sun—across the Kalunga and toward Africa—providing multiple meanings while affording deities and simbi direct access to ancestral waters and lands, as well as to the realm of the dead.[25]

Traditional watercraft the world over represented more than modes of transport. They were social maps expressing cultural understandings, spiritual beliefs, aesthetic values, and personal and collective identities.[26] Sharing an archetypical design, African dugouts crafted by members of discrete ethnicities drew on time-tested canoe-making methods and designs. Canoe making was widely regarded as a sacred profession, with dugouts treated as secular and spiritual items. The tall canopy trees needed for crafting large dugouts were routinely regarded as sacred, connecting the earth and heavens. A canoe's value was measured by its ability to produce income and return mariners ashore, as well as by social, cultural, and spiritual valuations.[27] Eighteenth- and nineteenth-century sources indicate that spirituality was deeply engrained into canoe making and canoeing in west-central Africa. Before trees were felled, homage was paid to them and the spirits residing within them. Canoe makers along the upper Congo River did not drink water while constructing a dugout, believing that "it would leak." Charms were used to prevent cracking, "ward off evil influences from spoiling it," and guard against theft and piracy. Dugouts possessed a soul, which could be male or female, with their gender determining how they rode. Sacrifices were made to a canoe's spirit to ensure successful fishing and commercial voyages, as their soul communicated with those of the deep. Canoes' timber and the waters they plied connected mariners and their societies to ancestral spirits and aquatic deities.[28]

Enslaved community members collaborated to construct African-style dugouts for personal use, while slaveholders commanded others to do so. Regardless, these ubiquitous watercraft permitted African-born slaves to interact with their world as they had done in west-central Africa. Facing forward to paddle, they knelt or sat on the hull, observing the world as they and their ancestors had in Africa rather than be seated backward while rowing Western-style boats. Viewing waterscapes at eye level and peering beneath its surfaces, they felt water pulsating against hulls while cooling breezes carried the smell of African-informed cuisine seaward into their nostrils. Enslaved canoemen used call-and-response paddling songs, many of which were sung in African languages, to set the rhythms of their work to a steady, manageable African pace rather than the relentless tempos desired by their enslavers. After hours of paddling, they plunged into Itamaracá's waters to wash away the sweat of their labors and cool and relax taxed muscles. Granted, slavery transformed canoes from African craft used to generate income and comfort for canoemen, fishermen, and market-bound farmers into mechanisms of exploitation. But, even when paddling slave-produced cash crops to market, canoeing largely remained an African sensory experience, permitting many to see, feel, and hear familiar maritime traditions.[29]

While sources do not document Itamaracáns' aquatic spiritual beliefs, amateur naturalist John Luccock reported on the vibrancy of west-central African beliefs near Rio de Janeiro. In 1816 Luccock embarked on a boat excursion up Guanabara Bay with a Portuguese sailor and "four stout [saltwater] negroes." On an islet Luccock found the skeletal remains of a "porpoise." He precipitated a work stoppage by putting the skull, which possessed spiritual meaning for the bondmen, into the boat, dismissing their convictions as "superstitious dread." The boatmen were already uneasy about plying Guanabara's sacred waters and voyaging past the burning of "spiral" seashells used to produce lime. Many west-central Africans believed seashells, especially spiral-shaped ones, possessed spiritual significance, as they represented the circular travels of one's soul. The slaves were deeply aggrieved when their entreaties to jettison the skull were ignored, and the sailor escalated the situation by tossing "it into the lap of one of them." This proved the breaking point, and the bondmen ceased working until the skull was "thrown overboard."[30]

Many members of Itamaracá's largely African-born population undoubtedly arrived with canoeing skills honed on African waters. Even though canoes are prone to capsizing, planters possessed many for shipping sugar across the roughly half-mile wide Canal de Santa Cruz to the mainland and to ships lying at anchor. They simultaneous bent slaves' African expertise to meet their needs, employing them to load and unload, balance, and paddle heavily loaded canoes, trusting they would not deposit the perishable wealth of plantation slavery into the blue.

CHARTING THE CULTURAL WATERS OF BONDAGE

Too often we, as scholars, stand with our backs to rivers, lakes, and seas, confining our examinations to dry spaces—to islands and continents—even as most studies of the Atlantic world and African diaspora consider waterside locations. Terrestrial approaches have contributed mightily to our understanding of slave experiences. Still, some one hundred years after first recognizing slavery as a field worthy of intellectual deliberation, we know very little about how captives understood and engaged with the waterscapes that adjoined many slaveholdings and formed important elements of their alternate physical and cultural "territorial system[s]." Standing on Itamaracá's beach, John Koster was forced to face seaward to watch west-central African cultural traditions transpire afloat. Beaches invite scholars to step out of their shoes, to curl their toes in the sand, and to embark on intellectual voyages that chart the cultural waters of bondage, as we consider how aquatic pursuits informed terrestrial circumstances.[31]

Itamaracá's ritualized battle gives voice to participants' circumstances, allowing us to ponder their lived experiences at a granular level. It illustrates how slaves deployed their cultural heritage to provide waterscapes and their lives with palpable west-central African meanings. Large numbers of dugout "canoes were put on requisition," permitting canoe makers to publicly demonstrate their craftsmanship. The several hundred marines *conscripted* into the Moorish and Christian forces showcased their muscular seminude bodies, which were gifts from the creator, while demonstrating their maritime proficiencies to throngs of spectators. Indeed, they performed coordinated naval maneuvers, stood in dugouts while wielding mock weapons, and disembarked at the fort and beach. Landsmen and novices surely would have been incapable of such actions; precipitating the mass baptism of Christians and Moors would have undoubtedly capsized their canoes.[32]

Importantly, this battle had to be presented in a nonthreatening manner to whites, who seemingly did not understand its complexity of west-central African meanings. Koster states that kings "exercise a species of mock jurisdiction over their subjects which is much laughed at by the whites," while portraying the battle and other *intrudo* events as buffoonery and uncivilized diversions. As Elizabeth Kiddy explains, such minimalizing conclusions reflected white perceptions gained "from the outside. The veneer of insignificance allowed" captives to project west-central African beliefs onto Brazilian society, even after martial arts and the electing of kings were outlawed, permitting monarchs to hold sway over white and black Brazilians while conspicuously displaying military abilities.[33]

Many of Itamaracá's African-born observers and combatants probably began voyages into slavery during warfare, including naval and amphibious battles and piracy, infusing the christening with numerous meanings. The ritualized battle surely provided a recognizable setting for men to obtain and enunciate honor and masculinity in nonlethal manners that remained strikingly similar to lethal methods employed during African warfare. The battle conceivably represented Kongolese achievements as constructed memories blurred into myths and historical memory, allowing warriors to bask in past glories or compensate for defeats. Like horse races, swimming, foot races, and aquatic blood sports, the christening undoubtedly strengthened community bonds, affording participants and observers with dignity, self-respect, and a sense of "Congo" pride.[34]

"Christian" naval supremacy undoubtedly enhanced the king's authority by harnessing Kongo-Christian mysticism. Several Kongo rulers integrated Portuguese Christian beliefs into their historical narratives to advance claims of divine monarchy while inserting themselves into Portuguese lines of dynastic succession. To this end, oral, literary, and artistic representations of Saint James figured prominently. This line of understanding transformed Kongo warriors into Christian knights, while using sangamentos to project monarchs' military might through "African mythology" enhanced by Christian powers. During traditional, land-bond renditions of *Moros e Christianos*, Iberian forces often prevailed only after Saint James intervened.[35]

Even while employing Kongo-Catholic beliefs, Itamaracá's king apparently consolidated his power around Kongo traditions. Kings of Congo retained many of the same political and spiritual authority in Brazil as those of the Kingdom of Kongo—albeit they could exercise them only to a much lesser degree. Both linked the here and now to the unseen realm of deities and ancestors, merging religious and political functions "into a single, multifaceted power complex on which the health of the community rested." By the late eighteenth century, kings in Brazil were regularly called "Kings of Congo," a title used in an "extraethnic sense" for leaders of communities composed of enslaved and freedpeople.[36]

Even as slavery dishonored and disrespected Africans, kings enjoyed the right to respect, with Itamaracá's monarchy receiving the vicar's begrudged deference while his owner hosted a coronation party attended by slaves from across the island. Planters invested significant money in the coronation and christening, granting slaves time off to construct the "Moor's" fort and to participate in both events. Whites loaned the king and his retinue formal clothing for both occasions, as well as valuable horses, canoes, and real and mock weapons. Importantly, these loaned objects, including captives' commodified bodies, represented the potential loss of significant wealth through the injury or death of a slave or horse. Many kings also wielded influence among whites, often serving as intermediaries between them and slaves.[37]

The power of Itamaracá's king undoubtedly increased as most of the island's white and black population gazed seaward to witness his military prowess. Many others apparently arrived from the mainland, swelling the numbers of observers. Whether out of respect for the king, to dress in accord with the event, or both, "all were in best clothing." Like Kongo kings, he invoked Kongo-Christian mystic traditions to an extent but abstained from conjuring saintly intervention to subjugate his Moorish opponent. He more likely made sacrifices to and invoked simbi and other aquatic deities, whose influences in the deep made them more logical maritime allies on waters possessing west-central African meanings than a land-bound knight whose armor was a liability in an unstable dugout.[38]

Koster invites readers to conclude that Itamaracá's slaves articulated Catholic understandings, albeit imperfect ones, during their enactment of the Reconquista and the king's coronation. By situating the christening in an Atlantic context, we can peer beneath its Catholic surface waters to trace west-central African traditions across the diaspora and consider how slaves recreated and reimagined Kongolese maritime traditions that were constrained by the fetters of bondage. Dugout canoes were an African, not European, watercraft, and the style of warfare mirrored those of west-central Africa. Dugouts provided recognizable African spaces of social, cultural, political, and spiritual meaning and purpose. Many of the African participants and observers were conceivably captured by pirates or maritime slave raiders, as members of defeated naval or amphibious forces. Kongolese cosmology probably figured prominently. Simbi and ancestral spirits traversed the Kalunga, projecting Kongo spiritual meanings onto Brazilian waters. Koster focused on Catholic traditions throughout his travelogue yet did not mention Saint James's presence at this ritualized performance. True, he did not intervene in all *Moros e Christianos*, but his absence allows us to speculate on the intervention of simbi, as well as other deities and ancestral spirits.

NOTES

1. For quotes, see Henry Koster, *Travels in Brazil* (London: Longman, Hurst, Rees, Orme, and Brown, 1816), 332–33; and Cécile Fromont, "Dancing for the King of Congo from Early Modern Central Africa to Slavery-Era Brazil," *Colonial Latin American Review* 22, no. 2 (2013): 188, 197. For *Moros e Christianos* performed throughout the Atlantic world, see Cécile Fromont, *The Art of Conversion: Christian Visual Culture in the Kingdom of Kongo* (Chapel Hill: University of North Carolina Press, 2014), 25–38, 47, 53, 57, 63, 70; Jeroen Dewulf, *From the Kingdom of Kongo to Congo Square: Kongo Dances and the Origins of the Mardi Gras Indians* (Lafayette: University of Louisiana at Lafayette Press, 2017), 25, 38–40, 54, 58, 62, 87, 89–91, 96, 180–81; Jeroen Dewulf's chapter, in this volume; Malgorata Oleszkiewicz-Peralba, *The Black Madonna in Latin America and Europe: Tradition and Transformation* (Albuquerque: University of New Mexico Press, 2007), 54; 188; Aurelio M. Espinosa, *The Folklore of Spain in the American Southwest: Traditional Spanish Folk* (Norman: University of Oklahoma Press, 1990), 23, 214–19; Michael J. Doudoroff, *Moros y Cristianos in Zacatecas: Text of a Mexican Folk Play* (Lawrence, Kans.: Amadeo Concha Press, 1981); and Max Harris, *Aztecs, Moors, and Christians: Festivals of Reconquest in Mexico and Spain* (Austin: University of Texas Press, 2000). For other works that consider the function of African kings in slave communities, see Cécile Fromont's, Michael Iyanaga's, and

Lisa Voigt's chapters, in this volume. See also Joseph C. Miller, "Retention, Reinvention, and Remembering: Restoring Identities Through Enslavement in Africa and Under Slavery in Brazil," in *Enslaving Connections: Changing Cultures of Africa and Brazil During the Era of Slavery*, ed. José C. Curto and Paul E. Lovejoy (Amherst, N.Y.: Humanity Books, 2004), 99.

2. Herbert S. Klein and Francisco Vidal Luna, *Slavery in Brazil* (Cambridge: Cambridge University Press, 2010), esp. 155; Joseph C. Miller, "Central Africa During the Era of the Slave Trade, c. 1490s–1850s," in *Central Africans and Cultural Transformations in the American Diaspora*, ed. Linda M. Heywood (Cambridge: Cambridge University Press, 2002), 21–69; James H. Sweet, *Recreating Africa: Culture, Kinship, and Religion in the African-Portuguese World, 1441–1770* (Chapel Hill: University of North Carolina Press, 2003). In this chapter *Kongo* and *Kongolese* refer to all Kikongo-speaking peoples, in addition to those from the Kingdom of Kongo. *Congo* reflects historical usage of this term as Brazilians applied it to a diverse group of enslaved and free people connected to west-central Africa. For differences in African and Amerindian canoe designs, see Kevin Dawson, *Undercurrents of Power: Aquatic Cultures in the African Diaspora* (Philadelphia: University of Pennsylvania Press, 2018), 143–63.

3. Koster, *Travels in Brazil*, 331–33.

4. Ibid., 331. Ash Wednesday was February 8, 1815.

5. Jason R. Young, *Rituals of Resistance: African Atlantic Religion in Kongo and the Lowcountry South in the Era of Slavery* (Baton Rouge: Louisiana State University Press, 2007), 46; Fromont, *Art of Conversion*, 2–5.

6. Young, *Rituals of Resistance*, 43–76, esp. 76; Fromont, *Art of Conversion*.

7. James H. Sweet, "'Not a Thing for White Men to See': Central African Divination in Seventeenth-Century Brazil," in Curto and Lovejoy, *Enslaving Connections*, 143.

8. John Thornton, "The Development of an African Catholic Church in the Kingdom of Kongo, 1491–1750," *Journal of African History* 25, no. 2 (1984): 152; Wyatt MacGaffey, "Europeans of the Atlantic Coast of Africa," in *Implicit Understandings: Observing, Reporting, and*

Reflecting on the Encounters Between Europeans and Other Peoples in the Early Modern Era, ed. Stuart B. Schwartz (Cambridge: Cambridge University Press, 1994), 255; Sweet, *Recreating Africa*, 113–17; Anne Hilton, *The Kingdom of Kongo* (Oxford: Clarendon Press, 1985), 62–66; Fromont, *Art of Conversion*, esp. 13–14; Young, *Rituals of Resistance*, 43–76; Wyatt MacGaffey, *Religion and Society in Central Africa: The Bakongo of Lower Zaire* (Chicago: University of Chicago Press, 1986).

9. Sweet, "Not a Thing," 143.

10. Young, *Rituals of Resistance*, 1–20, esp. 3, 9–10; Sweet, *Recreating Africa*, esp. 116, 123; Michael A. Gómez, *Reversing Sail: A History of the African Diaspora* (Cambridge: Cambridge University Press, 2005), 1–2; John K. Thornton, *Africa and Africans in the Making of the Atlantic World, 1400–1800*, 2nd ed. (Cambridge: Cambridge University Press, 1998), 320; Gwendolyn Midlo Hall, *Slavery and African Ethnicities in the Americas: Restoring the Links* (Chapel Hill: University of North Carolina Press, 2005), esp. 164–72. See also Roquinaldo Ferreira, *Cross-Cultural Exchange in the Atlantic World: Angola and Brazil During the Era of the Slave Trade* (Cambridge: Cambridge University Press, 2012), 242; and Heywood, *Central Africans and Cultural Transformations*.

11. Koster, *Travels in Brazil*, 273–76; Elizabeth W. Kiddy, *Blacks of the Rosary: Memory and History in Minas Gerais, Brazil* (University Park: Pennsylvania State University Press, 2005).

12. Fromont's chapter, in this volume; Fromont, *Art of Conversion*, 60–62, plate 9.

13. Koster, *Travels in Brazil*, 273; Elizabeth W. Kiddy, "Who Is the King of Congo? A New Look at African and Afro-Brazilian Kings in Brazil," in Heywood, *Central Africans and Cultural Transformations*, 153–55; Kiddy, *Blacks of the Rosary*.

14. For the quote, see Fromont, "Dancing for the King," 188, 197. See also Kiddy, *Blacks of the Rosary*, esp. 46–47, 77–78; Kiddy, "King of Congo," in Heywood, *Central Africans and Cultural Transformations*, 172; and Koster, *Travels in Brazil*, 136, 159–60. Other subaltern groups similarly staged *Moros e Christianos* rituals; see Carolyn Dean, *Inka Bodies and the Body of Christ: Corpus Christi in Colonial Cuzco, Peru*

(Durham: University of North Carolina Press, 1999).

15. Fromont, *Art of Conversion*, 21–63.

16. Thomas J. Desch-Obi, "Combat and Crossing the Kalunga," in Heywood, *Central Africans and Cultural Transformations*, 353–70, esp. 357, 359, 361–62; Desch-Obi, *Fighting for Honor: The History of African Martial Art Traditions in the Atlantic World* (Columbia: University of South Carolina Press, 2008), esp. 17–51. See also Robert Farris Thompson, foreword to *Ring of Liberation: Deceptive Discourse in Brazilian Capoeira*, by John Lowell Lewis (Chicago: University of Chicago Press, 1992), xii–xiv; Robert Farris Thompson, *Dancing Between Two Worlds: Kongo-Angolan Culture and the Americas* (New York: Caribbean Cultural Center, 1991); and C. Daniel Dawson, *Capoeira Angola and Mestre João Grande: The Saga of a Tradition, the Development of a Master* (New York: Rosen, 1993). Desch-Obi used *ngolo* to consider numerous west-central African cognates; see Obi, "Combat and Crossing the Kalunga," in Heywood, *Central Africans and Cultural Transformations*, 357n14.

17. E. J. Glave, *In Savage Africa; or, Six Years of Adventure in Congo-Land* (New York: Kessinger, 1892), 128. For considerations of how water shaped west-central Africa's human experience, see Robert W. Harms, *River of Wealth, River of Sorrow: The Central Zaire Basin in the Era of the Slave and Ivory Trade, 1500–1891* (New Haven: Yale University Press, 1981); Harms, *Games Against Nature: An Eco-cultural History of the Nunu of Equatorial Africa* (New Haven: Yale University Press, 1987); and Joseph C. Miller, *Way of Death: Merchant Capitalism and the Angolan Slave Trade, 1730–1830* (Madison: University of Wisconsin Press, 1988). For maritime warfare, see John K. Thornton, *Warfare in Atlantic Africa, 1500–1800* (London: Routledge, 1999); and Robert S. Smith, "Canoe in West African History," *Journal of African History* 11, no. 4 (1970), 515–33. For Africans' maritime expertise and captives' ability to transmit these skills to the Americas, see Dawson, *Undercurrents of Power*.

18. Dawson, *Undercurrents of Power*, 136–37.

19. Harms, *River of Wealth*, 97.

20. Zamba, *The Life and Adventures of Zamba, an African Negro King; and His Experience of Slavery in South Carolina*, ed. Peter Neilson (London: Smith, Elder, 1847), 2, 17, 35, 50–56, 82.

21. Ferreira, *Cross-Cultural Exchange*, 159–63; esp. 245; Alexander X. Byrd, *Captives and Voyagers: Black Migrants Across the Eighteenth-Century British World* (Baton Rouge: Louisiana State University Press, 2008); Marcus Rediker, *The Slave Ship: A Human History* (New York: Penguin Books, 2007); Sean M. Kelley, *The Voyage of the Slave Ship Hare: A Journey into Captivity from Sierra Leone to South Carolina* (Chapel Hill: University of North Carolina Press, 2016); Sidney W. Mintz and Richard Price, *The Birth of African American Culture: An Anthropological Perspective* (Boston: Beacon Press, 1976), 42–51.

22. Dawson, *Undercurrents of Power*.

23. Hilton, *Kingdom of Kongo*, 9, 23, 94; Obi, "Combat and Crossing the Kalunga," in Heywood, *Central Africans and Cultural Transformations*, 353–70; MacGaffey, *Religion and Society*, 7–8, 72–73, 43–55.

24. Ras Michael Brown, *African-Atlantic Cultures and the South Carolina Lowcountry* (Cambridge: Cambridge University Press, 2012), 1–2, 99, 115–23, esp. 117; John H. Weeks,

25. Brown, *African-Atlantic Cultures*, 126–34; Young, *Rituals of Resistance*, 1–2, 84–85.

26. For examples of traditional boats' societal values, see Greg Dening, *Islands and Beaches: Discourse on a Silent Land; Marquesas, 1774–1880* (Honolulu: Dorsey Press, 1980), 142; Erik Gilbert, *Dhow and the Colonial Economy of Zanzibar, 1860–1970* (Athens: Currey, 2004), esp. 1–2, 38–39, 41, 46, 48; and Dawson, *Undercurrents of Power*, 99–250.

27. Harms, *River of Wealth*, esp. 59–60, 69, 169–70; Smith, "Canoe in West African History," 520–21.

28. John H. Weeks, *Among the Congo Cannibals* (London: Lippincott, 1913), 94–95; Charles Kingsly Meek, *A Sudanese Kingdom: An Ethnographical Study of the Junkan-Speaking People of Nigeria* (London: Negro Universities Press, 1931), 427; Dawson, *Undercurrents of Power*, 99–118.

29. Dawson, *Undercurrents of Power*, 99–142. For canoeing in west Central Africa, see

Mary H. Kingsley, *Travels in West Africa: Congo Français and Cameroons* (London: Macmillian, 1897), 165, 180–81, 239; and Weeks, *Among the Congo Cannibals*, 92–93, 96–99, 160, 171, 244–45, 263–64, 267.

30. John Luccock, *Notes on Rio de Janeiro, and the Southern Parts of Brazil: Taken During a Residence of Ten Years in That Country* (London: Leigh, 1820), 334, 335, 344, 364–66; Robert W. Slenes, "The Great Porpoise-Skull Strike: Central African Water Spirits and Slave Identity in Early-Nineteenth-Century Rio de Janeiro," in Heywood, *Central Africans and Cultural Transformations*, 183–209; MacGaffey, *Religion and Society*, 96–99, 121.

31. Rhys Isaac, *Transformation of Virginia, 1740–1790* (Chapel Hill: University of North Carolina Press, 1982), 52–53.

32. Koster, *Travels in Brazil*, 332–33.

33. Kiddy, *Blacks of the Rosary*, 128.

34. Kevin Dawson, "Enslaved Swimmers and Divers in the Atlantic World," *Journal of Social History* 47, no. 1 (2013): 1340–43.

35. Fromont, *Art of Conversion*, 25–38, 47, 53, 57, 63, 70; Fromont, "Dancing for the King," 188, 197.

36. Kiddy, *Blacks of the Rosary*, esp. 46; Kiddy, "King of Congo," in Heywood, *Central Africans and Cultural Transformations*, esp. 169.

37. Kiddy, *Blacks of the Rosary*, esp. 46; Kiddy, "King of Congo," in Heywood, *Central Africans and Cultural Transformations*, esp. 169.

38. Koster, *Travels in Brazil*, 333–34.

FURTHER READING

Barcia, Manue. *West African Warfare in Bahia and Cuba: Soldier Slaves in the Atlantic World, 1807–1844*. Oxford: Oxford University Press, 2014.

Curto, José C., and Paul E. Lovejoy. *Enslaving Connections: Changing Cultures of Africa and Brazil During the Era of Slavery*. Amherst, N.Y.: Humanity Books, 2004.

Graham, Richard. *Feeding the City: From Street Market to Liberal Reform in Salvador, Brazil, 1780–1860*. Austin: University of Texas Press, 2010.

Hawthorne, Walter. *From Africa to Brazil: Culture, Identity, and the Atlantic Slave Trade, 1600–1830*. Cambridge: Cambridge University Press, 2010.

Nishida, Mieko. *Slavery and Identity: Ethnicity, Gender, and Race in Salvador, Brazil, 1808–1888*. Bloomington: Indiana University Press, 2003.

CHAPTER 3

A Mexican *Sangamento?*

The First Afro-Christian Performance in the Americas

MIGUEL A. VALERIO

In February 1539 recently colonized Tenochtitlan (the future Mexico City) was the stage of a lavish two-day festival meant to commemorate the Truce of Nice, signed the year before between Emperor Charles V and King Francis I of France at Aigues-Mortes.[1] This armistice ended the second of the three Italian Wars (1521–26, 1536–38, and 1542–46), sparked by Charles's election as Holy Roman Emperor.[2] This ceasefire was significant for New Spain (as colonial Mexico was then known) because the emperor's war with France had caused instability in the viceroyalty. For example, New Spain's first alleged black rebellion plot the previous year (1537) had been blamed on the war.[3] So when the news of the détente arrived in Mexico-Tenochtitlan in September 1538, the recently installed viceroy, Antonio de Mendoza (r. 1535–50), and the Audiencia (or Royal Court)—the two government bodies most closely linked to the victorious monarch Charles V—ordered the staging of great festivities, whose planning took more than four months.[4] The celebrations in Mexico City mirrored those held at Aigues-Mortes and other parts of the empire, with one particular exception: surprisingly, given the 1537 alleged black rebellion plot, it included a procession of "more than fifty" blacks "wearing great riches of gold and precious stones and pearls and silver."[5]

Bernal Díaz del Castillo, one of the foot soldiers of Hernán Cortés, the Iberian man who lead the Spanish overtake of the Aztec Empire, was among those who witnessed the festival. Writing some thirty years later, he described Mexico City's celebrations in chapter 201 of his *Historia verdadera de la conquista de la Nueva España* (*The True History of the Conquest of New Spain* [ca. 1575]). According to his recollections, the festivities consisted of several parts: a mock hunt, a *Moros y Cristianos* (*Moors and Christians*) choreography (see Kevin Dawson and Jeroen Dewulf, in this volume), a mock naval battle reenacting the siege of Rhodes, dramatic plays, a banquet at the end of each day (one hosted by Mendoza at the viceregal palace and the other by Cortés in his own palace), speeches, and the procession of "more than fifty" blacks. The reenactment of the siege of Rhodes, a common theme in Renaissance festivals, was itself a restaging of Cortés's offensive against the island city of Tenochtitlan in 1521, which explains why Cortés, then out of favor, was elected to perform the prominent role of "captain general" in the mock battle. In this performance Cortés, who had been dismissed from his post of governor of New Spain in 1535, when Antonio de Mendoza was named the region's first viceroy, symbolically returned to his former role.

The procession of the "more than fifty" blacks took place on the first day in a life-size forest set up in the city's main square. The forest had been the setting of the mock hunt, wherein indigenous performers hunted Mesoamerican animals, but Díaz del Castillo writes that "it was nothing compared to the performance of horseback riders made up of negroes and negresses who were there with their king and queen, and all on horses; they were more than fifty, wearing great riches of gold and precious stones and pearls and silver, and then they went against the savages, and they had another hunt, and it was something to be seen, the diversity of their faces, of the masks they were wearing, and how the negresses breastfed their little negroes and how they paid homage to the queen."[6] Scholars, such as Jerry Williams and Max Harris, have struggled to explain this performance. Williams, unable to account for the blacks' performance, wonders if the blacks' rich regalia and diversity of masks was a parody or imitation of the Spaniards' own lavish clothing, for according to Díaz del Castillo, the Spanish women were richly dressed in "red and silk dresses and gold and silver jewelry with precious stones."[7] Taking up Williams's question, Harris argues that the blacks' performance was a parody of the next day's main event, the reenactment of the siege of Rhodes. According to Harris, "the blacks' own purpose was to parody their indulgently overdressed Spanish rulers."[8] I contend that this assessment a priori underplays the blacks' agency and propose instead in this chapter a line of inquiry that seeks on the contrary to underscore their previously ignored role.

Díaz del Castillo's text leaves open several major questions about the performance. Was this a particular type of festival performance? Who were the performers? How were they allowed to perform so soon after the alleged 1537 black rebellion plot? In light of that plot, what does their inclusion in the festivities mean? In this chapter I would like to explore possible, and thus far unexplored, avenues for answering these questions. To identify the performers, I explore the demography of New Spain's black population at the time, which consisted of two groups: *ladinos* and *boçales*. Ladinos were Christianized, Spanish-speaking, mostly free blacks, while boçales were slaves newly arrived from the African continent itself. I contend here that the performers were ladinos, and that the plot, if it took place, was led by boçales. To identify the performance itself, I traced the journey ladinos made from Africa to New Spain via the Iberian Peninsula. I consider the possibility that it could be the first American instance, or at least a precedent, of a central African festival performance that became widespread in the African diaspora in the Iberian Atlantic. It is important to look at this performance from an Afrocentric perspective because it highlights cultural continuity in the diaspora. In other words, it underscores how Africans took and adapted their culture to their new Iberian lives. In the case of Latin America, as the historian Herman Bennett has called for, this approach allows the telling of the African diaspora story from a perspective other than that of the institution of slavery.[9]

Perhaps scholars who have looked at Díaz del Castillo's text have struggled to understand the blacks' performance because they have not looked to Africa or the African-derived festive practices of colonial Latin America. Although those practices are recorded only in later sources, a range of hints amply warrant wondering about their connection with the one Díaz del Castillo describes. Starting in 1570s, for instance, the *actas* (minutes) of Mexico City's *cabildo* (city council) record payments for black performances for some of the city's major annual celebrations, such as Corpus Christi.[10] Because of the little scholarship on Afro-Christian festivals available to them at the time they wrote about Díaz del Castillo's text, it is easy to understand why scholars' may have overlooked this aspect of the performance. Moreover, the black performance was not the focus of their analysis, and it is precisely because they looked at the black performance through the lens of the European performance (the reenactment of the siege of Rhodes) that they offered a Eurocentric explanation of its staging. My approach, in contrast, proposes to analyze the elusive mentions of black festival performances like the one offered by Díaz del Castillo by bringing them together with core components of other festive manifestations across times and geographies. This broad comparative method, I posit, brings to the fore new possibilities to interpret festive traditions heretofore overlooked or misunderstood.

While the paucity of sources means that my analysis remains speculative, pursuing this line of inquiry has significant implications for the scholarship on Afro-Christian festivals and, more generally, on the diaspora. This inquiry invites scholars to look further into the often overlooked sixteenth century and thus push back the timeline of our research on manifestations of black social and religious life in the Americas. New Spain is key in attempts to write a full history of the black festive tradition in the Americas. Not only did its Afro-Christian festive history begin the earliest but, even if it has not received much scholarly attention, it also had arguably the most vibrant festive culture of early modern America, a culture that, what is more, regularly incorporated black festive practices.[11] While most scholarship on the topic has focused on Brazil's eighteenth century, New Spain's sixteenth and seventeenth centuries, recorded in many manuscript and printed volumes (post 1570s), can help us construct a clearer history of Afro-Christian festivals in the Americas. This approach, moreover, enriches our understanding of the black Atlantic by underlining the role New Spain/Mexico played within it.

THE TWO GROUPS OF AFRICANS IN NEW SPAIN IN 1539

In 1539 there were two groups of Africans in Mexico City: boçales and ladinos.[12] Boçales were mostly West Africans (i.e., from regions between Senegambia and the Bight of Biafra) brought as slaves to the Americas starting in 1501. Colin Palmer estimated in the 1970s that there were ten thousand boçales in New Spain in 1537.[13] This high estimate has since been called into question. Indeed, Voyages: The Trans-Atlantic Slave Trade Database, the authoritative source for Middle Passage demography, does not record more than one thousand African slaves in New Spain in 1537. Nonetheless, this is still a significant number of boçales in the former Aztec capital, only recently seized by Spain. Ladinos, on the other hand, were Africans who had lived on the Iberian Peninsula, where they had been Christianized before coming to the Americas. Many of these ladinos were central Africans who had traveled or been taken to the Iberian Peninsula after the Portuguese reached the region south of the Congo River in the 1480s. The slave trade database shows that central Africans did not reach the Americas directly between 1501 and 1538, but rather through the Iberian Peninsula.

Ladinos came to the Americas as personal servants of the invading Spaniards. Cortés himself is said to have had at least three ladinos in his service.[14] Ladinos, who fought alongside their Spanish employers, were rewarded for the part they took in the colonization of Mexico and gained a considerable degree of social and economic agency in the new territory. This knowledge allows us to distinguish between two very distinct groups of Africans in Mexico City at the time of the performance Díaz del Castillo describes. One was ladinos, with an Iberian itinerary and therefore Iberian cultural exposure, most of whom were free albeit employed as personal servants. The other was boçales, newly arrived from West Africa, with little exposure to European culture. Thus, ladinos were better poised to build the alliances that would have allowed them to stage the performance. Newly enslaved in a foreign land, boçales, on the other hand, would have been keener to resist their European oppressors. I thus argue that it is likely that it was boçales slaves, without connections to central Africa, who led the alleged 1537 plot, again, if it did indeed take place.

In his report for the year 1537, Viceroy Mendoza informed Charles V, the king of Spain, that "the blacks had elected a king and plotted to kill all the Spaniards and take over the land."[15] Labeling the leaders of slave revolts as kings would become the norm in the Americas. When slaves revolted in Veracruz in 1570, for example, the leader, Gaspar Yanga, was said to have crowned himself king on the symbolic date of January 6, feast of the Epiphany, popularly known as Three Kings' Day.[16] Similarly, the 1579 truce between the Spanish government and Luis Mazambique, the leader of the maroons of Portobelo, refers to him as a king.[17] Thus when later colonial documents associated black festive kings, such as the one in Díaz del Castillo's text, with rebel kings, it was a move that shed negative light on the practice of electing and crowning kings among black confraternities.[18] Given this dynamic, it would seem unlikely that the same group who led the alleged rebellion plot would have been invited to perform in the festival, especially since the supposed leaders of the plot had been executed. Instead, I contend that the city's ladinos, many of whom lived as free persons and served the viceroyalty's wealthy Spaniards, including the viceroy, were the ones invited to perform in the festival.

Narratives of the Spanish colonization of Mexico illustrate the status of ladinos in early colonial society. The Codex Azcatitlan, created toward the end of sixteenth century, recounts the history of the Mexica or Aztec people from their migration from their ancestral home, Aztlan, to the Spanish colonization of Mexico from an indigenous perspective. One of its images chronicling the early colonial period shows Juan Cortés, one of Hernán Cortés's black servants, in Spanish clothing (plate 1 in color insert). The codex's best-known image of the meeting between Hernán Cortés and Mexica emperor Moctezuma depicts the Spaniards wearing armor from head to toe, leaving exposed and identifiable only the heads and faces of the two Cortéses. In the case of the Codex Durán (ca. 1581), which is a literary narrative of the colonization of Mexico authored by the Spanish Dominican friar Diego Durán (ca. 1537–1588), with illustrations by indigenous artists, there is no mention of ladinos; yet Juan Cortés appears in two illustrations. As in the Codex Azcatitlan, these images are very telling. In the illustration of Hernán Cortés meeting the lords of Tlaxcala, Juan Cortés stands behind the Spaniard as richly dressed as he appeared in the Codex Azcatitlan (plate 2 in color insert). These depictions of Juan Cortés suggest that ladinos enjoyed some degree of social status in early colonial society. His attire, especially in the Codex Azcatitlan, is comparable to that of a Spanish *señor* (gentleman). That ladinos could attain such status is also recorded in the story of Juan Garrido, who, for his role in the colonization of Mexico, was given a plot of land outside the city. He later became the porter of the city council, for which he was given a lot within the city's *traza* (limits), making him a *vecino* (citizen).[19] Garrido's case illustrates the social mobility ladinos could enjoy in early colonial society. That mobility would have positioned them to stage the performance described in Díaz del Castillo's text.

An anonymous sixteenth-century Dutch painting also illustrates the occasional high social standing of Afro-descendants in the Iberian Peninsula.[20] The painting shows a black knight wearing a black cape with the cross of the knightly order of Saint James in one of Lisbon's central squares, the Chafariz d'El-Rey, or the King's Fountain (plate 3 in color insert). Two black characters, perhaps knights themselves or the knight on horseback's companions, walk in front of him. To his left, there is maybe another black knight, also on horseback; however, we cannot discern for sure, since his back is to us. The rest of the painting shows many other Afro-descendants engaged in a host of other activities, from playing the tambourine in the foreground to dancing with a European some distance from the black knight of Saint James. According to Didier Lahon, around 1550 Lisbon had a black population of ten thousand.[21] This Iberian precedent could explain why the performers in Mexico-Tenochtitlan appeared as a cavalry. Horses were a rare commodity in New Spain in 1539; Mendoza himself reported in 1537 that there were only 620 horses in the whole viceroyalty. Given this scarcity, we can imagine the significance of seeing ladinos riding horses they likely borrowed from the city's elite.

The painting also bears witness to the festive practices of Afro-Iberians (*ethiopes*) in its depiction of music playing and dancing. Afro-Iberians held their own communal celebrations and were included in public festivities in both Portugal and Spain, starting in the fourteenth century.[22] In Lisbon, in 1451, for example, Afro-Iberians performed their own unique dances for the wedding of Leonor of Portugal and Holy Roman Emperor Frederick III, Charles V's grandparents.[23] Africans preserved and adapted their festive traditions in the peninsula, and later ladinos, be it those Africans themselves or their descendants, brought them to the Americas.

THE FIRST SANGAMENTO IN THE AMERICAS?

Ladinos brought to the Americas their Afro-Christian culture, including the formation of confraternities and the staging of festivals. Black confraternities had existed in the slave ports of the Mediterranean since the fourteenth century.[24] Seville was home to what is considered the oldest black confraternity, Our Lady of the Angels, known as "Los Negritos," believed to have been founded toward the end of the fourteenth century for infirmed blacks by the city's archbishop.[25] In 1455 a group of free blacks in Barcelona received royal approval for their confraternity's charter.[26] In 1472 a group of free blacks in Valencia received the same royal approval.[27] In Lisbon blacks were admitted to the city's rosary confraternity in 1460 and "soon formed an independent entity that outsiders could already recognize in the last decades of the 1400s."[28]

Afro-Iberian confraternities held their own festivals and participated in public performances in the Iberian Peninsula. But there is no record of these practices before 1539. Nonetheless, later documents sketch how Afro-Iberians practiced a syncretic mix of African and European Christian customs.[29] This makes Díaz del Castillo's text the earliest description of an Afro-Christian performance in the Iberian world. Because no other contemporaneous source exists about similar events, I turn to understand the festivities in Díaz del Castillo's text to a comparison with later, better-known, practices. I argue that, considered from this angle, the performance indeed took the form of an identifiable Afro-Christian festival. Because of the paucity of contemporary sources, my hypothesis is highly speculative, but it is sustained by an analysis of how Afro-Christian festive practices developed in the Iberian Peninsula and how they could have been then taken to the Americas by ladinos.

Specifically, one custom central Africans took to the Iberian Peninsula, and eventually to the Americas, was what became known as a sangamento after the Portuguese arrived in the Kongo in 1483. Mexico City's black performance bears many similarities with the form this dance took in the diaspora. Thus, I propose looking at this dance as the possible form the black performance in Díaz del Castillo's text took. As Cécile Fromont points out, the Christian

Kongo sangamento consisted of two acts: "In the first act, the dancers dressed 'in the way of the country,' wearing feathered headdresses and using bows and arrows as weapons. In the second act, the men changed their outfits, donning feathered European hats, golden crosses, necklace chains, knee-length strings of corals, and red coats embroidered with gold thread."[30] This description already shows how the dance had incorporated European elements in Africa and illustrates, as John K. Thornton has argued, that "beginning in the fifteenth century [central Africans] were quick to adapt elements of European culture, including religion and aspects of material culture."[31]

As Fromont notes, the two parts of sangamento reenacted the two foundations of the Kongo, one mythological and the other Christian. The first act of the dance reenacted the founding of the Kongo by Lukeni, "the original civilizing hero of the Kongo's creation myth." The second act of the dance reenacted the founding of the Christian Kongo by king Afonso I Mvemba a Nzinga (r. 1509–42) in 1509. As Fromont asserts, Afonso "imposed Christianity as the kingdom's state religion and integrated it into the symbolic and historical fabric of the Kongo."[32]

After rising to power, through several letters to the kingdom's elite, Afonso recast his victory over his main challenger, his brother Mpanzu a Kitima, as a Christian miracle. As Fromont points out, while the Portuguese recognized Afonso, the defunct king's firstborn, as his father's legitimate successor, Kongo law recognized him only "as one of several eligible successors." Mpanzu opposed his brother's rule because he did not want to convert to Christianity. He led an army of followers who also rejected Christianity. According to the legend, during what seemed the final battle, greatly outnumbered and about to be defeated, Afonso's soldiers began shouting the name of Saint James, the saint whose name Iberians called on in battle against the Moors during the Reconquista (711–1492). Afonso's army's shouts caused Mpanzu's men to panic, which cost them the battle and the war. According to the narrative formulated by Afonso in his letters, those who survived from Mpanzu's army later said that "an army of horsemen led by Saint James himself appeared in the sky under a resplendent white cross and struck scores dead."[33]

In her analysis of how sangamento was transformed in the diaspora, Fromont argues that Afro-Iberians added ceremonial royalty to the dance.[34] Indeed, the 1565 charter of Lisbon's black rosary confraternity called for the election of "kings and queens, princes and princesses, dukes and duchesses, counts and countesses, marquises and marchionesses, cardinals, and any other dignity."[35] This provision became the norm among black confraternities. Didier

Lahon, for example, cites an undated election by a black confraternity from the city of Vila Viçosa, Évora, Portugal, indicating that it took place before 1639.[36] A black confraternity of the rosary was founded in the city of Évora in 1518 and another one in Vila Viçosa in the first decades of the seventeenth century.[37] Furthermore, Isidoro Moreno posits that black confraternities may have held elections in Seville as early as 1477.[38] In the nineteenth century João Ribeiro Guimarães suggested that blacks performed with their king and queen in Lisbon in 1484.[39]

Scholars assert that the practice of electing ceremonial royalty existed before it was formulated in confraternity charters. As Fromont writes in chapter 6 of this volume, "Men and women of African origins and descent, leaving in freedom or enslaved first in Europe and later in the Americas, have chosen and celebrated leaders they hailed as their kings and queens since the fifteenth century." Taken to the Iberian Peninsula, sangamento may have been adopted and adapted by Afro-Iberians regardless of their African origin.

Given this trajectory, I would like to suggest, first, that Díaz del Castillo's text could very well describe the first sangamento with ceremonial royalty in the Americas. While scholars have struggled to explain the performance, its true nature may come to light when viewed from the perspective of the sangamento as delineated earlier. Newly arrived from the Iberian Peninsula (either Seville or Lisbon), ladinos could have brought the festive practice to New Spain.[40] If that is the case, this would be the first example of a sangamento being performed in the Americas; many years before it was recorded in Brazil.[41] Even if that were not the case, the events still formed a significant precedent, against the backdrop of which Afro-Christian festivals would later develop in Mexico and elsewhere in the Americas.[42]

The sangamento dimension would also add another layer of meaning to the battle between the black and indigenous performers. In his analysis of the festival, Harris argues that this mock battle came from the Renaissance tradition of battles between wild men.[43] But when viewed from the perspective of a sangamento, this battle gains a new significance. As Fromont points out, in the Christian Kongo the second part of sangamento was formulated as a battle between (victorious) Christian and (defeated) heathens. In the Americas indigenous people took the place of the heathens in the performance.[44] The battle between the black and indigenous performers could suggest that the black performers coordinated the battle with the indigenous performers. This would underscore the black performers' agency in the planning of the festivities, which has been neglected by former analyses of the festival.[45] The blacks' performance stands on its own and is not dependent on the Spaniards' performance and attire for meaning.

I would also like to consider the possibility that the performers were members of a confraternity. Mexico City's first rosary confraternity was founded in 1538 in the city's Dominican convent, just a year before the festival.[46] Dominicans had been instrumental in the establishment of black rosary confraternities in the Iberian Peninsula as well as in central Africa.[47] Lisbon's black rosary confraternity, for example, was under the protection of the city's Dominican convent. According to Clara García Ayluardo and Nicole von Germeten, membership in Mexico City's rosary confraternity "was open to all."[48] Moreover, according to Fray Agustín Dávila y Padilla, the first chronicler of the Dominican order in Mexico, "within a few days there was hardly any man or woman in the city who was not a member" of the city's rosary confraternity.[49] This panorama makes it likely that blacks, especially ladinos, were admitted to the confraternity, as they had been in Lisbon before they branched off in 1565. As the Lisbon case shows, in the absence of black confraternities, Afro-Iberians joined mixed confraternities and may have done the same in Mexico City before its first black confraternity was founded in the mid-1500s.[50]

IMPORTANCE OF THE 1539 PERFORMANCE

In our current state of knowledge, it is unclear whether the black performers in Díaz del Castillo's text either performed a sangamento or belonged to a confraternity, nor can we ascertain who they were individually. Strong evidence, however, indicates that they were ladinos who had lived as members of African and Afro-descendant communities in the Iberian Peninsula. There they had the opportunity to become members of confraternities and to take part in festive celebrations independently or within broader civic or religious occasions. The performance described in Díaz del Castillo's text is the earliest reference to the participation of Africans in festival celebrations in the Americas. As such, it could be the earliest evidence of a sangamento in the diaspora and in any case provides us the background against which the American versions of the Kongo martial dance should be considered. Seen as an African-designed event rather than an act of mimicry, the 1539 festival provides an important demonstration of uninterrupted—but neither simple nor unchanging—cultural continuity between African and diasporic celebrations, even with a detour through the Iberian Peninsula. It underscores how Africans and their descendants took and adapted their culture in their new lives. At a minimum this performance remains an important early moment in the archive of Afro-Christian festivals to be considered alongside the other manifestations discussed elsewhere in this volume. It constitutes an important early example of Africans using European Christian rituals as a medium to express their identity. Later on in the colonial period, central Africans themselves would stage this performance, as other chapters in this volume show. But New Spain was always an exception, as enslaved men and women were brought directly to the viceroyalty only between 1580 and 1640, during the union of the Portuguese and Spanish Crowns.[51]

NOTES

I am indebted to Cécile Fromont for her patience and hard work in seeing this chapter through and to Lisa Voigt, Dorothy Noyes, the participants of the Symposium on Afro-Christian Festivals in the Americas at Yale in February 2015, and anonymous reviewers for their comments on previous versions.

1. Patricia Lopes Don, "Carnivals, Triumphs, and Rain Gods in the New World: A Civic Festival in the City of México-Tenochtitlán in 1539," *Colonial Latin American Review* 6, no. 1 (1997): 17.

2. David Porter, *Renaissance France at War: Armies, Culture and Society, c. 1480–1560* (Woodbridge, Suffolk: Boydell and Brewer, 2008), 30–37.

3. Antonio de Mendoza y Pacheco, "Asuntos de gobierno de México," reg. 27, sec. 184, Patronato Real, General Archive of the Indies (AGI), Seville.

4. Bernal Díaz del Castillo, *Historia verdadera de la conquista de la Nueva España (manuscrito "Guatemala")*, ed. José Antonio Barbón Rodríguez (ca. 1575; Mexico City: Colegio de Mexico/Universidad Nacional Autónoma de México, 2005), 754; Lopes Don, "Carnivals, Triumphs, and Rain Gods," 17–18. *Historia verdadera* was also published posthumously in 1632 in Madrid. That edition was based on what became known as the "Madrid" manuscript. I cite from the "Guatemala" manuscript, which is believed to be Díaz del Castillo's first draft (see Barbón Rodríguez's introduction). Abridged English editions of this text have been published under the title

of *The Discovery and Conquest of Mexico* (e.g., 1928; repr., Oxford: Routledge, 2014). For an unabridged English edition, see *The True History of the Conquest of New Spain*, ed. Janet Burke and Ted Humphrey (London: Hackett, 2012).

5. Díaz del Castillo, *Historia verdadera*, 755. Unless otherwise noted, all translations are my own. Aigues-Mortes's festival is narrated in the anonymous *Relación muy verdadera sobre las pazes y concordia que entre Su Magestad y el Christianísimo Rey de Francia passaron, y las fiestas y reçibimiento que se hizo a Su Magestad en la Villa de Aguas Muertas, a XIV y XV de Julio de MDXXXVIII*, Royal Library of Spain, El Escorial. For an analysis of other commemorations of the truce in the viceroyalty of New Spain, of which Mexico City was the capital, see Max Harris, *Aztecs, Moors, and Christians: Festivals of Reconquest in Mexico and Spain* (Austin: University of Texas Press, 2000), chaps. 13, 14.

6. "No fue nada para la inbençión que ovo de xinetes hechos de negros y negras con su rey y reina, y todos a cavallo, que eran más de çinquenta, y de las grandes riquezas que traían sobre sí, de oro y piedras ricas y aljófar y argentería; y luego van contra los salvajes y tienen otra quistión sobre la caça, que cosa era de ver la diversidad de rostros que llebavan las máscaras que traían, y cómo las negras daban de mamar a sus negritos y cómo hacían fiestas a la reina" (Díaz del Castillo, *Historia verdadera*, 755).

7. Jerry M. Williams, *El teatro del México colonial: Época misionera* (New York: Lang, 1992), 65; Harris, *Aztecs, Moors, and Christians*, chap. 13; Díaz del Castillo, *Historia verdadera*, 755.

8. Harris, *Aztecs, Moors, and Christians*, 130.

9. Herman L. Bennett, *Colonial Blackness: A History of Afro-Mexico* (Bloomington: Indiana University Press, 2011), 5–7.

10. Ignacio Bejarano, ed., *Actas del cabildo de la Ciudad de México*, 51 vols. (Mexico City: Aguilar e Hijos, 1889–1911), 17:180, 335; 18:79, 296.

11. See my "Kings of the Kongo, Slaves of the Virgin Mary: Black Religious Confraternities Performing Cultural Agency in the Early Modern Iberian Atlantic" (PhD diss., Ohio State University, 2017), chaps. 2, 3; as well as Linda A. Curcio-Nagy, *The Great Festivals of Colonial Mexico City: Performing Power and Identity* (Albuquerque: University of New Mexico Press, 2004), 58–63.

12. See Matthew Restall, "Black Conquistadors: Armed Africans in Early Spanish America," *Americas* 57, no. 2 (2000): 171–205.

13. Colin A. Palmer, *Slaves of the White God: Blacks in Mexico, 1570–1650* (Cambridge, Mass.: Harvard University Press, 1976), 133.

14. See Restall, "Black Conquistadors."

15. "Los negros tenian helegido un rrey y concertado entrellos de matar a todos los espanoles y aserse con la tierra" (Mendoza y Pacheco, "Asuntos de gobierno").

16. Patrick J. Carroll, *Blacks in Colonial Veracruz: Race, Ethnicity, and Regional Development* (Austin: University of Texas Press, 2001), 90–92.

17. Carol Farrington Jopling, *Indios y negros en Panamá en los siglos XVI y XVII: Selecciones de los documentos del Archivo General de Indias* (Antigua: Centro de Investigaciones Regionales de Mesoamérica, 1994), 378–79.

18. Luis López de Azoca, "Carta de López de Azoca, alcalde del crimen de la Audencia de México," doc. 4, reg. 1, sec. 73, Audiencia de México, AGI; "Relacion del alçamiento que negros y mulatos libres y cautivos de la Ciudad de Mexico de la Nueva España pretendieron hazer contras los españoles por Quaresma del año de 1612, y del castigo que se hizo de los caveças y culpados," MS-2010, National Library of Spain, Madrid, fols. 158–64.

19. Restall, "Black Conquistadors," 177.

20. See Kate Lowe, "The Lives of African Slaves and People of African Descent in Renaissance Europe," in *Revealing the African Presence in Renaissance Europe*, ed. Joaneath Spicer (Baltimore: Walters Art Museum, 2012), 19–20; and Isabel Castro Henriques, *Os africanos em Portugal: História e memória, séculos XV–XXI* (Lisbon: Comité Português do Projecto Unesco "A Rota do Escravo," 2011), 25–36.

21. Didier Lahon, "Da redução da alteridade a consagração da diferença: As irmandades negras em Portugal (séculos XVI–XVIII)," *Projeto História* 44 (2013): 54.

22. See Lahon, "Da redução da alteridade"; Didier Lahon, "Esclavage, confréries noires, sainteté noire et pureté de sang au Portugal (XVIème XVIIIème siècles)," *Lusitana Sacra* 2, no. 15 (2003): 119–62; and Isidoro Moreno, "Plurietnicidad, fiestas, y poder: Cofradías y fiestas andaluzas de negros como modelo para la América colonial," in *El mundo festivo en España y América*, ed. Antonio Garrido Aranda (Cordoba: University of Cordoba, 2005), 169–88.

23. Kate Lowe, "The Global Population of Renaissance Lisbon: Diversity and Its Entanglements," in *The Global City on the Streets of Renaissance Lisbon*, ed. Annemarie Jordan Gschwend and Kate Lowe (London: Holberton, 2015), 58.

24. Isidoro Moreno, *La antigua hermandad de "Los Negritos" de Sevilla: Etnicidad, poder, y sociedad en 600 años de historia* (Seville: University of Seville/Government of Andalucia, 1997), 25–56. On Afro-Iberian confraternities, see Iván Armenteros Martínez, "De hermandades y procesiones: La cofradía de esclavos y libertos negros de Sant Jaume de Barcelona y la asimilación de la negritud en la Europa premoderna (siglos XV–XVI)," *Clío: Revista de Pesquisa Histórica* 29, no. 2 (2011); Debra Blumenthal, "La Casa dels Negres: Black African Solidarity in Late Medieval Valencia," and Aurelia Martín Casares, "Free and Freed Black Africans in Granada in the Time of the

Spanish Renaissance," both in *Black Africans in Renaissance Europe*, ed. Thomas Earle and Kate Lowe (Cambridge: Cambridge University Press, 2005), 225–46, 247–60; António Brásio, *Os pretos em Portugal* (Lisbon: Agência Geral das Colônias, 1944); Lahon, "Redução da alteridade"; Lahon, "Esclavage, confréries noires"; and William D. Philips, *Slavery in Medieval and Early Modern Iberia* (Philadelphia: University of Pennsylvania Press, 2014), 91–97. For a relatively comprehensive list of early modern Afro-Iberian confraternities, see Patricia Ann Mulvey, "The Black Lay Brotherhoods of Colonial Brazil: A History" (PhD diss., City University of New York, 1976), 283–86.

25. Karen Graubart contests this narrative, arguing that there were too few sub-Saharans in Seville at the time to support the existence of this confraternity before the sixteenth century (conversation with the author, electronic source, May 30, 2017).

26. Próspero Bofarull y Mascaré, ed., *Colección de documentos inéditos de la Corona de Aragón*, 41 vols. (Barcelona: Monfort, 1847–1910), 8:466.

27. Miguel Gual Camarena, "Una cofradía de negros libertos en el siglo XV," *Estudios de Edad Media de la Corona de Aragón* 5 (1952): 457–66.

28. Cécile Fromont, "Dancing for the King of Congo from Early Modern Central Africa to Slavery-Era Brazil," *Colonial Latin American Review* 22, no. 2 (2013): 185; Jorge Fonseca, *Religião e liberdade: Os negros nas irmandades e confrarias portuguesas (séculos XV à XIX)* (Lisbon: Humus, 2016), 23–37.

29. See Fromont, "Dancing for the King"; and Marina de Mello e Souza, *Reis negros no Brasil escravista: História da festa de coroação de Rei Congo* (Belo Horizonte, Brazil: Editora da Universidade Federal de Minas Gerais, 2002).

30. On the meaning of sangamento, see Cécile Fromont, *The Art of Conversion: Christian Visual Culture in the Kingdom of Kongo* (Chapel Hill: University of North Carolina Press, 2014), 21.

31. John K. Thornton, "Central Africa in the Era of the Slave Trade," in *Slaves, Subjects, and Subversives: Blacks in Colonial Latin America*, ed. Jane G. Landers and Barry M. Robinson

(Albuquerque: University of New Mexico Press, 2006), 84.

32. Fromont, *Art of Conversion*, 23–53, 24, 4.

33. Ibid., 27.

34. Fromont, "Dancing for the King," 185.

35. "Principe, reys, duque, condes, marquezes, cardeal, e quaes quer outras dignidades," Compromisso da Irmandade de Nossa Senhora do Rosário dos Homens Pretos, 1565, MS-151, National Library of Portugal, Lisbon, fols. 9v–10r.

36. Lahon, "Esclavage, confréries noires," 142–43.

37. Fonseca, *Religião e liberdade*, 43–58

38. Moreno, "Plurietnicidad, fiestas y poder," in Aranda, *Mundo festivo*, 176.

39. João Ribeiro Guimarães, *Summario de varia história: Narrativas, lendas, biographias, descripções de templos e monumentos, statisticas, costumes civis, politocos e religiosos de outras eras*, 5 vols., Lisbon: Sousa Neves, 1875), 5:148.

40. On blacks' trajectory from Africa to the Iberian Peninsula and the Americas, see Karen B. Graubart, "'So color de una cofradía': Catholic Confraternities and the Development of Afro-Peruvian Ethnicities in Early Colonial Peru," *Slavery and Abolition* 33, no. 1 (2012): 43–64.

41. See Fromont, "Dancing for the King."

42. See Souza, *Reis negros no Brasil escravista*.

43. Harris, *Aztecs, Moors, and Christians*, 128.

44. Fromont, "Dancing for the King," 188, 196–200.

45. Lopes Don, "Carnivals, Triumphs, and Rain Gods"; Williams, *Teatro del México colonial*, 64–65; Harris, *Aztecs, Moors, and Christians*, 123–11.

46. Agustín Dávila y Padilla, *Historia de la fundación y discurso de la provincia de Santiago de México de los Predicadores* (Brussels: Ivan de Meerbeque, 1625), 354–57; Juan Bautista Méndez, *Crónica de la provincial de Santiago de México de la Orden de Predicadores*, ed. Justo Alberto Fernández Fernández (ca. 1650; repr., Mexico City: Porrua, 1993), 80–81.

47. Elizabeth W. Kiddy, "Congados, Calunga, Cadombe: Our Lady of the Rosary in

Minas Gerais, Brazil," *Luso-Brazilian Review* 37, no. 1 (2000): 47–61.

48. Clara García Ayluardo, "Confraternity, Cult, and Crown in Colonial Mexico City, 1700–1810" (PhD diss., University of Cambridge, 1989), cited in Nicole von Germeten, *Black Blood Brothers: Confraternities and Social Mobility for Afro-Mexicans* (Gainesville: University Press of Florida, 2006), 22.

49. Dávila y Padilla, *Historia de la fundación*, 357.

50. Bejarano, *Actas del cabildo*, 14:227; Martín Enríquez, "Carta del virrey Martín Enríquez," 1572, Mexico City, doc. 82, sec. 19, Audiencia de México, AGI, fols. 1v–2r. On Afro-Mexican confraternities, see Germeten, *Black Blood Brothers*.

51. Nicole von Germeten, "Juan Roque's Donation of a House to the Zape Confraternity, Mexico City, 1623," in *Afro-Latino Voices: Narratives from the Early Modern Ibero-Atlantic World, 1550–1812*, ed. Kathryn Joy McKnight and Leo J. Garofalo (Indianapolis: Hackett, 2009), 84.

FURTHER READING

Fogelman, Patricia, and Marta Goldberg, eds. "'El rey de los congos': The Clandestine Coronation of Pedro Duarte in Buenos Aires, 1787." In *Afro-Latino Voices: Narratives from the Early Modern Ibero-Atlantic World, 1550–1812*, edited by Kathryn Joy McKnight and Leo J. Garofalo, 155–73. Indianapolis: Hackett, 2009.

Heywood, Linda M. *Central Africans and Cultural Transformations in the American Diaspora*. Cambridge: Cambridge University Press, 2002.

Sweet, James H. *Recreating Africa: Culture, Kinship, and Religion in the African-Portuguese World, 1441–1770*. Chapel Hill: University of North Carolina Press, 2003.

Thornton, John K. *Africa and Africans in the Making of the Atlantic World, 1400–1800*. 2nd ed. Cambridge: Cambridge University Press, 1998.

Valerio, Miguel A. "The Queen of Sheba's Manifold Body: Creole Afro-Mexican Women Performing Sexuality, Cultural Identity, and Power in Seventeenth-Century Mexico City." *Afro-Hispanic Review* 35, no. 2 (2016): 79–98.

Walker, Tamara J. "The Queen of *los Congos*: Slavery, Gender, and Confraternity Life in Late-Colonial Lima, Peru." *Journal of Family History* 40, no. 3 (2015): 305–22.

◇◇◇

PART 2

America's Black
Kings and Diplomatic
Representation

CHAPTER 4

Representing an African King in Brazil

LISA VOIGT

The representation of African kings and queens was, and still is, a common feature of public festivals in the Americas. As Kevin Dawson's and Cécile Fromont's chapters in this volume discuss, one of its longest-running manifestations in Brazil is the coronation and procession of African sovereigns practiced by the enslaved and free black members of the Irmandade de Nossa Senhora do Rosario dos Pretos (Black Brotherhood of Our Lady of the Rosary) on feast days, also known as the congado. Other chapters in this volume—by Jeroen Dewulf, Junia Furtado, Michael Iyanaga, and Miguel A. Valerio—use the rosary coronation festival in Brazil to draw connections to or make comparisons with Afro-Catholic celebrations elsewhere in the Americas, and even (in Furtado's case) the Kingdom of Dahomey in West Africa. The coronation festival involves what performance studies scholar Diana Taylor calls the *repertoire* of embodied practice (i.e., performance, song, dance, gestures), in contrast to the enduring materials of the *archive* (i.e., permanent visual and textual records, such as texts and buildings), according to Taylor's demarcation of these two spheres of knowledge and representation.[1] It would be unwise to draw too sharp a distinction, however, since the repertoire of African sovereigns in Christian festivals was both governed by and represented in the archive: documents that prescribe its organization and structure as well as narratives that recount specific celebrations. This chapter focuses on archival representations of the act of representing African kings in Brazil, not only because these texts are, for the most part, our only access to the festive repertoire of earlier periods, but also because they show how this repertoire was performed beyond the rosary festival in other, secular venues—how it was representedb elsewhere—as well as how it was represented to other audiences besides those present for the performance (e.g., readers). An analysis of these representations can help illuminate what it meant for various performers and publics—those of European and of African descent—to represent African kings in colonial Brazil, which in turn can help us understand the multivalence of congados and the agency available to crowned African sovereigns in Christian festivals, as described in the other chapters of this volume.

Among the best-known archival sources representing African kings in Brazil are the illustrations produced by foreign travelers, such as the lithograph by the Bavarian artist Johann Moritz Rugendas, *Feast of Saint Rosaly, Patroness of the Blacks* (1835), analyzed by Furtado and especially Fromont in their contributions to this volume (plate 4; fig. 6.1). But we also know about the African king repertoire through the documents produced by the members of the black confraternities themselves, such as the 1715 *compromisso* (statutes) from Vila Rica, Minas Gerais, which mandates the yearly election of a king and queen, who are obliged to "attend with their government the festivities of Our Lady."[2] The black brotherhoods' *compromissos* are an example of how African agency can be found not only in the repertoire but also in the archive—in representations on paper as well as on the street. Even in late nineteenth-century Lisbon we can read of a case in which the legitimacy of a claim to the festive Congo throne was based on a rosary brotherhood's *compromisso* and other documents, indicating how closely intertwined the repertoire and archive were for the African king ceremonies.[3] Elsewhere I have discussed another case of the Black Brotherhood of the Rosary's intervention in the archive—its sponsorship of the account of a festival in Vila Rica, Minas Gerais, titled *Triunfo eucharístico* (1734)—which, I have argued, was just as significant and performative as its participation in the festival itself.[4] Although the accounts analyzed here are not the product of black authorship or sponsorship in the same way, the references to texts and the control over their meaning point to the ways in which real African kings, and their representatives, valorized and used not only the domain of the repertoire (performance, ritual, and ceremony) but also the archive of written texts to pursue their own agendas. Uncovering this agency requires careful attention to textual representations—in particular, the published accounts of festivals and ceremonies—using the tools of literary analysis.

The levels of mimesis quickly multiply when we look for representations of African kings in the early modern Iberian world. Indeed, this repertoire was already so well known in eighteenth-century Brazil that it was imitated by other groups in civic festivals. For example, a group of *pardos* (people of mixed African and European ancestry) performed a mock African king ceremony during the 1762 celebrations in Rio de Janeiro of the birth of Dom José, prince of Beira, the heir apparent to the Portuguese throne. In effect, the pardos— who often had their own confraternities and were thus unlikely to be members of the black brotherhood associated with the "real" king of Congo ceremony— performed a representation-of-a-representation of an African king during a festival commemorating the birth of a future Portuguese monarch.[5] Of course, like all festivals from this period, we know about it only through yet another, archival layer of representation: in this case, two anonymous accounts published in Lisbon in 1763, *Epanafora festiva, ou relaçaõ summaria das festas, com que na cidade do Rio de Janeiro capital do Brasil se celebrou o feliz nascimento do serenissimo principe da Beira nosso senhor* [Festive Epanaphora, or summary relation of the festivities with which the city of Rio de Janeiro, capital of Brazil, celebrated the fortunate birth of the most serene prince of Beira, our lord] and *Relação dos obsequiosos festejos, que se fizerão na cidade de S. Sebastião do Rio de Janeiro, pela plausivel noticia do nascimento do serenissimo senhor principe da Beira o Senhor D. Joseph no anno de 1762* [Account of the obsequious festivities that were done in the city of Saint Sebastian of Rio de Janeiro for the praiseworthy news of the birth of our most serene lord prince of Beira and Sir Dom Joseph in the year of 1762]. The latter text describes in more detail the courtly procession, including a king, a prince, two ambassadors, and seven *sobas* (or African chiefs), among others.[6] The first of the subsequent ten dances involves a variety of exotic African animals (lion, camel, monkey, elephant), while the final dance is described as a royal *baile do Congo* (dance of the Congo) involving performers richly dressed in silks of gold, silver, and other colors and adorned with many diamonds. The royal court is preceded by a group of *cabundás* (fugitive slaves) bedecked in feathers, who hack open a path for them to proceed.[7] While the costumes do not appear to be ethnographically specific, the presence of feathers is common to the festive repertoire of African sovereigns throughout the Atlantic, from the Kingdom of Kongo to Brazil to New Orleans, as Dewulf's and Fromont's chapters in this volume point out.

If the *Relação dos obsequiosos festejos* emphasizes the exotic, fanciful dimensions of the representation of African kings by the pardos, *Epanafora festiva* is even more generalizing, and comments explicitly on the strangeness of the performance: "The mixed men (a natural result of two opposite colors), who incorrectly but for convenience's sake we call *pardos*, also came out on one of those days, with a farce in imitation of the state and ceremony of the king of Congo. The gestures, music, instruments, dance, and costume all had much in the manner of those Africans, displeasing to good sense but entertaining because of their strangeness."[8] The narrative circumscribes the performance's import to an entertaining farce depicting strange and different (read: barbarous) customs, concluding, "Beauty is different there; good singing is very distinct."[9] The narrator also emphasizes the fictive dimension of the representation by highlighting the skill of the performers and the applause they elicited: "our *pardos* did it, then, with all propriety, and they earned the applause that can be granted to an imitation."[10] However "properly" it was carried out, the narrator suggests, the "imitation" was in no way confused with the real "state and ceremony."

One of the effects of the text's emphasis on its mimetic dimension is to create more distance between the signifier and the signified (as it were), between the mock African king and real black sovereignty. By contrast, the African kings crowned in the rosary brotherhood festivals often enjoyed the authority and respect of real sovereigns, as we can a glean from a complaint of a priest from Mariana, Minas Gerais, in a petition to the governor in 1771: "All that feigned ostentation did not produce any effect other than persuading the same blacks and some of the populace that the one *who was called king was a real king,* spending with drinks and abominable dances what they had raised through alms for the purposes of praising God and Our Lady" (my emphasis).[11] Just over a half-century earlier, the Jesuit André João Antonil had argued in favor of slaveowners allowing their slaves to celebrate the rosary festival with crowned kings, singing, and dancing "honestly."[12] By 1771 the dances that Antonil qualified as "honest" were deemed "abominable" by the priest from Mariana because of the real authority assumed by the feigned kings—even over nonblack residents—and the resulting disruption of the social order. The 1771 petition gives numerous examples of black "insolence" and "aggression" provoked by the crowned African kings, such as a fight that broke out when two white shoemakers failed to take off their hats in the presence of the king and his court or an instance in which two "distinguished men" had to give up their seats in church for the black king and his officials. The priest, Father

Leonardo de Azevedo Castro, writes that in his parish "the blacks recognize the reelected king as a *true king*; they hold him as an oracle, render him obedience, and treat him as their king even outside the functions of the church" (my emphasis).[13] The authors of the 1763 festival accounts preclude any such interpretation of the mock African king ceremony by insisting on its imitative, entertaining dimensions. The performance is represented in the text as not only strange and different but also distant from the realm of real social interaction (and upheaval) that we can glimpse in the 1771 petition from Mariana.

THE DIPLOMATIC REPRESENTATION OF AFRICAN KINGS

The 1771 petition mentions that African king ceremonies in Lisbon and other parts of Portugal are no longer permitted "because of their affronts," and it refers to their earlier prohibition by the viceroy in Bahia.[14] Although the bans surely proved at least to some degree ineffective, there was also another way in which African kings continued to be represented in colonial Brazil: the diplomatic missions of ambassadors representing real African heads of state. Pierre Verger describes four embassies to Bahia from the kings of Dahomey between 1750 and 1811 and several more from other African kings in this period; even earlier—perhaps the first—was the one sent by the rulers of the Kingdom of Kongo and of Soyo to Recife in 1642, while the city was under Dutch rule.[15] As historian Silvia Hunold Lara has argued, these representations of African kings in Brazil happened on the same streets and before the same publics as the ones carried out by the Black Brotherhood of the Rosary (and the other groups that imitated their celebrations of African kings).[16] Music historian José Ramos Tinhorão goes even further in suggesting a direct connection between the rosary brotherhood's coronation ceremonies and royal embassies from the Kingdom of Kongo, such as the one planned by King Manuel I to be sent to the pope in 1512.[17] Lara is rightly skeptical of this claim and more reasonably argues for the resonance between the two types of spectacles for both black and white viewers.[18]

It is not hard to project such a similarity when we read, in Caspar Barlaeus's *Rerum per octennium in Brasilia* (1647), a history of the Dutch colony in Brazil, of the spectacular, mimetic performance of an African king receiving African ambassadors during the diplomatic mission to Recife in 1642: "We also saw the scene of their king sitting on the throne and attesting to their majesty through an unyielding silence, then of the ambassadors coming from abroad and adoring the king, according to the ceremonies used in their nations, and their performances and imitation of their courtesies and signs of obedience, things that they showed for our recreation, somewhat merry after drinking."[19] It seems unlikely that these scenes were intended merely to serve as entertainment for a white audience, as Barlaeus presents it. Clearly this is not an imitation in the same way as that of the pardos in Rio, given the proximity between the performers and the characters they are representing: they are, after all, African ambassadors representing African ambassadors to an African king. Besides performing the diplomatic repertoire expected at African courts, the ambassadors of Kongo and Soyo also reveal their familiarity with European, archival codes of representation, for they present letters from their rulers to the Count of Nassau and the Dutch Company directors.[20]

Over a century after the embassy to the Count of Nassau, in 1750, an ambassador representing the king of Dahomey arrived in Salvador on a diplomatic mission to ease tensions and reestablish trade after his people had attacked and destroyed the Portuguese fort of Ajudá on the Mina Coast. The embassy's representation of the African king in Brazil was in turn represented in an account written by the Portuguese writer and periodical editor José Freire Monterroio Mascarenhas: *Relaçam da embayxada, que o poderoso rey de Angome, Kiay Chiri Bronco senhor dos dilatadissimos sertoens de Guiné mandou ao illustrissimo e excellentissimo senhor D. Luiz Peregrino de Ataíde* [Account of the embassy, which the powerful king of Angome, Kiay Chiri Bronco, lord of the vast backlands of Guiné sent to the most illustrious and excellent lord Dom Luís Peregrino de Ataíde; 1751]. Mascarenhas concludes this brief, nine-page account of the reception of the Dahomean ambassadors in Salvador by calling for "ampler news of the government of this king, and of the commerce that can be done there, to satisfy the desire of those curious about history and geography."[21] Despite ending with this call for "ampler news," Mascarenhas implicitly presents his narrative as a fulfillment of those desires and a corrective to the confusion and uncertainty surrounding west African realms that he decries in the *Relaçam*'s introduction.[22] There he writes that, although Africa is one of three parts of the ancient world and long known to cosmographers, "one cannot speak of the [African realms] without the danger of falling into many errors."[23] For Mascarenhas, texts, not only individuals, can serve as ambassadors of other lands to correct such misrepresentations and contribute to the global spread of knowledge.

Mascarenhas does not, however, avoid falling into many errors himself. As Pierre Verger indicates, his description of the geographic location of Dahomey is rather fanciful, and he mistakenly renders King Tegbessu's name as Kiay Chiri

Bronco.[24] He also misrepresents the reason for the embassy, omitting any reference to the prior hostilities against the Portuguese fort and attributing the king's initiative to the desire for a commercial treaty—the renewal of the exchange of African slaves for Brazilian tobacco, euphemistically described as a "treaty of friendship and commerce"—with the Portuguese Crown.[25] The omission of the previous events gives his account a fundamentally different cast than Viceroy Luís Peregrino de Ataíde's own report on the embassy, as several scholars, including Verger, Lara, and Kirsten Schultz, have pointed out.[26] Crucially for a diplomatic mission, the differences between the viceroy's and Mascarenhas's accounts of the embassy revolve around matters of representation and recognition.[27]

For his part, Mascarenhas portrays the embassy to have been received with the consummate respect and hospitality. The Jesuits, who (as the viceroy also reports) hosted the ambassador and his retinue at their college, receive him as they do the viceroys returning from a period of governing in India or other people of "great distinction"; such a reception reflects the congruence between the role of ambassador and that of viceroy, both representatives of their kings abroad.[28] Indeed, Mascarenhas portrays the ambassador—whom he calls (perhaps just as fancifully) Churumá Nadir—as a person of great distinction, praising his "noble figure" and the grandeur of his retinue and reiterating the Jesuits' desire to communicate "how much they recognized the distinction of his character."[29] Mascarenhas also shows the ambassador to be self-conscious about the dignities owed to him "in honor of his monarch, whom he represented in Brazil."[30] According to his own report, by contrast, the viceroy refused to even recognize the ambassador's legitimacy: "Since Dahomey had violated with such scandal the good faith that the Portuguese nation had with it, this viceroy could not trust his protestations, nor even less receive messengers from his part, *nor recognize these messengers as his ministers*, and the only reception he did was nothing more than a simple demonstration of hospitality that Your Majesty orders to treat all foreigners who through some incident or business come to their ports" (my emphasis).[31] Alleging a prior breach of trust on the part of the African kingdom, the viceroy asserts that he treated the ambassador only as he would any foreigner, not as the representative of the king of Dahomey. Yet this claim is presented with its own share of bad faith, since it is belied by the viceroy's subsequent acknowledgment to have participated in the exchange of gifts and messages between the sovereigns whom he and the ambassador represent.[32]

In Mascarenhas's account the roles are in effect reversed, and it is the Dahomean ambassador who is quite literally unable to recognize the viceroy when he is first brought to meet him. The description of the encounter is worth quoting at length for the way it juxtaposes the viceroy's almost indiscernible presence with the ambassador's assertive display of both Portuguese- and African-derived ceremonial greetings:

> The ambassador entered the hall with great confidence, making curtsies on one side and another, displaying gravity without affectation, until arriving at the place where the count viceroy was, and not distinguishing his person among the magnificence that he saw in all of them, he asked his interpreter which one it was, and then, without losing the sovereignty of his appearance, he bowed first in the Portuguese way with three curtsies, putting on great airs, and immediately following, in the manner of his country, prostrating himself to the ground with his arms extended and hands one on top of the other and snapping his fingers like castanets: the ceremony with which they are accustomed to venerating their kings in Angome.[33]

In Mascarenhas's narrative of this meeting—unlike the viceroy's—the ambassador is clearly the protagonist. He introduces African diplomatic protocols while also demonstrating his familiarity with European ones, and he further imposes an African imprint on the encounter when he refuses the viceroy's offer to sit down next to him, saying that to be seated would imply a long conversation, and "this was not done to the ambassadors in his court, because the ambassador's message was always brief."[34] Earlier, the ambassador had similarly rebuffed the viceroy's offer to have sumptuous Portuguese clothing made for him and his companions, saying that he came well provisioned in this regard and "nor should he present the embassy dressed in the Portuguese manner, but according to the customs of his country, in order to represent the king of whom he was minister."[35] In Mascarenhas's version, the ambassador is careful to ensure that both he and his brief message properly represent the Dahomean king—in effect, to diminish the distance between the sovereign and his representative.

By contrast, the viceroy's attempt to shape the encounter to better represent his own sovereign has anachronistic results. The viceroy orders a delay in the ambassador's reception for it to coincide with the celebration of the Portuguese king's birthday: "the reason for this delay being, to give an occasion for [the ambassador] and his retinue to judge the extent of the grandeur of this monarch, by the magnificence in which the birthday of our sovereign was celebrated in such distant parts."[36] Mascarenhas quickly points out that

King João V was already dead by the time the festivities in Salvador occurred; the news had just not yet arrived to "such distant parts." Silvia Hunold Lara argues that the remark on the bad timing is part of Mascarenhas's ironic, critical portrayal of the viceroy.[37] Just as remarkable about the passage, I would add, is the way in which it turns the Dahomeans from exotic performers—as in the mock African king ceremony held by the pardos in Rio—into spectators, even putting them in the position of "judging" the grandeur of the Portuguese king.[38]

This depiction is very far indeed from the representation of blacks in a contemporary festival account, printed in the same year and by the same publisher: Mathias Antonio Salgado and Manoel Joseph Correa e Alvarenga's *Monumento do agradecimento . . . relação fiel das reais exéquias* [Monument of the gratitude . . . true relation of the royal exequies; 1751], an account of the funeral ceremonies for João V in São João del-Rei, Minas Gerais. Here the author describes the black slaves who mourned João V's death as "little intelligent in things of public utility, not knowing how to weigh the scepter's downfall on the scale of their understanding."[39] The characterization underscores slaves' exclusion from literacy, education, and the public sphere.[40] By contrast, the presence of slaves in Mascarenhas's account has an entirely different function and serves in another way to highlight the African ambassador's agency and protagonism. When his Brazilian hosts protest after he insists on offering twenty gold coins to the blacks who had carried his sedan chair, the ambassador once again calls attention to his sovereignty as a royal representative: "no one had jurisdiction to limit the actions of princes."[41] Transatlantic distance may be the reason that the Portuguese king's birthday was mistakenly celebrated in Salvador after he was already dead, but that same distance does not, apparently, limit the jurisdiction of the African king's representative.

In sum, Mascarenhas depicts the African ambassador as a far more successful representative of his king than the viceroy was of his Portuguese sovereign. Surely this is in part the result of Mascarenhas's goal of portraying the viceroy in a bad light, as Lara has argued by reading the account in the political context of the Portuguese elite.[42] After all, the author ultimately controls the representation of the African king narrated in his text, and we cannot overlook his motives for representing both sovereign representatives (the viceroy and the ambassador) in the way that he does. Nevertheless, attending to the ambassador's control over the diplomatic message within the account offers a way to think beyond the white author's motivations and to imagine the possibility of black interventions in the archive.

Near the end of the pamphlet Mascarenhas transcribes what was pre-sumably the ambassador's "brief message" from the king, relayed to the viceroy with the assistance of not one but two interpreters, a Portuguese and a mulatto.[43] Through all this mediation and different layers of representation we cannot, of course, assume to hear the "voice" of the Dahomean ambassador or his king, even if it is offered as such. Nevertheless, the speech holds a key to reading this and other representations of African kings in Brazil. In the speech the ambassador in fact distinguishes between two "representations": his oral report of the king's wishes, which he calls "this rugged representation," and the letter that—like the 1642 ambassadors of Congo and Soyo to Recife—the king of Dahomey wrote to his Portuguese counterpart, which the ambassador offers as "proof" of what he has expressed: "Your Excellency will see *the proof of the truth of my expressions* signed with the royal stamp of his grandeur. Then he took a letter out of his breast, and gave it to the count, commending it to secrecy; and he continued by saying, '*May Your Excellency receive this repre-sentation from that great monarch, who elected [the ambassador] to occupy this place*'" (my emphasis).[44] Yet this representation, written by the African king—the "proof of the truth" of the other one, the embassy—is never revealed to readers: the ambassador orders that "the secret, which Your Excellency will see in the letter, will not be made public nor manifest, without the express order of your sovereign monarch and of my great king of Angome."[45] Indeed, Mascarenhas reports that the letter's content was never revealed.[46]

In the *Relaçam da embayxada*, the message at the heart of the represen-tation, its "truth"—and, even more important, its publication or circulation among a Brazilian or Portuguese public—is controlled not by the white author or narrator but by the African king and his ambassador. At some level, of course, this secret belongs to Mascarenhas as the author of a text that is ultimately more literary than historical; as J. Hillis Miller writes, an "essential feature of literature is to hide secrets that may not ever be revealed."[47] Yet it also resembles the secrets that readers are not permitted to know because of an active refusal on the part of an informant, as Doris Sommer has highlighted in the case of Mayan activist Rigoberta Menchú's testimonial.[48] By keeping this secret, the ambassador delivers the ultimate challenge to the faith in the transparency of representations of African kings. Rather than simply ascribing it to the insufficiency of European languages to represent the other—as a result of insurmountable distance and difference—we should allow his gesture to remind us that sometimes obfuscation on the part of the one being represented is purposeful.

PLATE 1 Anonymous, *Juan Cortés*, in the Codex Azcatitlan, Mexico, mid-sixteenth to early seventeenth century. MS Mexicain 59–64, Bibliothèque nationale de France, fol. 22v. Photo: BnF.

PLATE 2 Diego Durán, *Juan Cortés*, in the Codex Durán, Mexico, sixteenth century. Detail, MSS/1980–MSS/1982, Biblioteca Nacional de España, fol. 207r. Photo: BNE.

PLATE 3 Anonymous, *Chafariz d'El-Rey*, Netherlandish School, sixteenth century. Berardo Collection, Lisbon. Photo: The Berardo Collection.

FÈTE DE Sᵀᴱ ROSALIE, PATRONE DES NÈGRES.

PLATE 4 Johann Moritz Rugendas, *Feast of Saint Rosaly, Patroness of the Blacks*, in *Voyage pittoresque dans le Brésil* (Paris: Engelmann et Cie, 1835), division 4, book 16, plate 19. Photo courtesy of Oliveira Lima Library, Catholic University of America.

PLATE 5 Carlos Julião, *Black King Festival*, Brazil, last quarter of the eighteenth century. Watercolor on paper. In Julião, *Riscos illuminados*. Iconografia C.I.2.8, in the collections of the Fundação Biblioteca Nacional, Rio de Janeiro. Photo: Acervo Fundação Biblioteca Nacional do Brasil.

PLATE 6 Carlos Julião, *Black Queen Festival*, Brazil, last quarter of the eighteenth century. Watercolor on paper. In Julião, *Riscos illuminados*. Iconografia C.I.2.8, in the collections of the Fundação Biblioteca Nacional, Rio de Janeiro. Photo: Acervo Fundação Biblioteca Nacional do Brasil.

PLATE 8 View from the rooftop of Nossa Senhora da Conceição toward the Church of Santa Efigênia on the hilltop, Ouro Preto, Brazil. Photo: Rubens Chaves / Pulsar Imagens.

PLATE 9 Augusto Riedel, *Congado dos pretos em Morro Velho, Provincia de Minas, Brazil*, 1868–69. Black and white albumen print, 21.8 × 27.9 cm, in the collections of the Fundação Biblioteca Nacional, Rio de Janeiro. Photo: Acervo Fundação Biblioteca Nacional do Brasil.

PLATE 10 Beatriz da Conceição samba dancing in front of an altar of Saint Anthony at a domestic *reza* in Cachoeira, Bahia, Brazil, on June 12, 2011. Photo © Michael Iyanaga.

Just as purposeful—at the other extreme—was the choice of the members of the Black Brotherhood of the Rosary to sponsor a publication, *Triunfo eucharistico*, recounting the festivities surrounding the transfer of the Eucharist from its temporary placement in their chapel to a new parish church in Vila Rica, Minas Gerais. The Black Brothers' role in publishing this text is often overlooked in favor of its Portuguese author, Simão Ferreira Machado, even though their sponsorship is highlighted on the title page.[49] But the dedication signed by "os Irmãos Pretos," the members of the Black Brotherhood of the Rosary, clearly reveals a consciousness of the utility of print—the domain of the archive—to shape and preserve a public image: "This consideration obliged us to solicit this public writing, in which our affection will always be referred in perpetual memory, and such magnificent solemnity in all of its order will be continuously narrated to those in the present and the future."[50] Even if the festival described in *Triunfo eucharistico* did not (as far as we know) involve the coronation of an African king, the account may have aided in the brotherhood's efforts to continue the controversial practice in the context of the feast day of Our Lady of the Rosary, by reassuring readers of their Catholic devotion and submission to Portuguese, not African, figures of authority.

Mascarenhas's account of the Dahomean embassy offers no such assurances. However much the diplomatic mission may have been intended to restore and promote the slave trade, the account of it unsettles the racial hierarchy on which the slave trade was based, by showing the African ambassador to have greater authority and control over the diplomatic encounter and communication than the Brazilian viceroy. If the king of Dahomey's representative is "both a facilitator of contact between nations and a marker of their difference from each other," as Timothy Hampton describes ambassadors by drawing on a sixteenth-century diplomatic manual, the *Relaçam da embayxada* does not reduce that difference to the "entertaining strangeness" of the scene of African diplomacy displayed for the Dutch government in Recife in 1642 or the mock African king ceremony performed in the 1762 celebrations in Rio de Janeiro.[51] Instead, the ambassador embodies the authority that many African slaves in Brazil—even, perhaps, the 834 subsequently brought from Dahomey as a result of his mission—attributed to the crowned African kings of Catholic festivals, much to the consternation of white officials and observers.

Indeed, as many chapters of this volume reveal, Africans and Afro-descendants in Brazil found occasions to represent themselves and their interests in positive and productive ways—both in secret and in public, in the archive and the repertoire—despite the oppression and restrictions of slavery.

Attending to their self-representations in performance and print challenges accounts of not only the "social death" imposed by slavery but also of the emergence of an exclusionary, bourgeois public sphere.[52] Scholars have suggested several ways of revising or expanding the notion of the public sphere: by turning our attention from print to performance or embodied representation, and by pointing out the many ways in which diasporic Africans used written and print technologies to negotiate, alleviate, or resist their oppression or to strengthen communities and "counterpublics."[53] Texts such as the *Relaçam da embayxada*—the textual representation of a public performance that includes a private, secret textual representation at its core—require us to think about black interventions in, and especially their control over, these multiple spheres of representation at the same time.

NOTES

1. Diana Taylor, *The Archive and the Repertoire: Performing Cultural Memory in the Americas* (Durham: Duke University Press, 2003), 19.

2. "Assystir com o seu estado ás festividades de Nossa Senhora." Francisco Antônio Lopes, *Os palácios de Vila Rica: Ouro Preto no ciclo do ouro* (Belo Horizonte, Brazil, 1955), 195–96. The *compromisso* goes on to specify that the elected judges may, but are not obliged to, meet the king and queen at their houses and accompany them to the church—and if they do, that they should not delay the festival too much—suggesting that disputes over authority and precedence within the brotherhood were common. An amended version in 1745 continues to insist that the king and queen "will come to the said church only with their State, without a larger company of Brothers in order to avoid sowing discord and holding the festivities too late, as always happens [virão para a dita Igreja só com o seu Estado, sem maior acompanhamento de Irmãos para se evitarem discordias e fazer festividades fora de horas como sempre tem acontecido]" (doc. 40, cx. 45, Arquivo Histórico Ultramarino-Minas Gerais). Unless otherwise noted, all translations are my own.

3. In a semisatirical vignette, "O Congo em Lisboa [The Congo in Lisbon]," the narrator relates a case in which the legitimacy of Princess Sebastiana Julia, "regent of the kingdom of the empire of Congo [regente do reino do imperio do Congo]," was challenged and defended at a festive ball; see João Ribeiro Guimarães, *Summario de varia historia* (Lisbon: Rolland e Semoind, 1872), 5:147–49, 147. The legal defense of her claims is based on "the statutes of the brotherhood of the Lady of the Rosary, established in the convent of Saint Joan, with their licenses, petitions, and reports [o compromisso da irmandade da Senhora do Rosario, estabelecida no convento de Santa Joanna, e suas licenças, petições e informações]"; Guimarães, *Summario de varia historia*, 148. In a parallel move that mitigates the effect of the tale's satire, the narrator concludes by marshaling his own historical (textual and artistic) evidence that supports the claims of the antiquity of the brotherhood. Here and throughout this chapter, I use "Kongo" to refer to the Kingdom of Kongo in Africa and "Congo" to refer to members of the ethnic group known by that name in the Americas and Europe.

4. Simão Ferreira Machado, *Triunfo eucharistico, exemplar da christandade lusitana na publica exaltaçaõ da fé na solemne trasladaçaõ do Divinissimo Sacramento da Igreja da Senhora do Rosario, para hum novo Templo da Senhora do Pilar em Villa Rica, Corte da Capitania das Minas* (Lisbon: Officina da Musica, 1734); Lisa Voigt,

Spectacular Wealth: Festivals in Colonial South American Mining Towns (Austin: University of Texas Press, 2016), chap. 4.

5. On pardo brotherhoods, see Antonia Aparecida Quintão, *Lá vem o meu parente: As irmandades de pretos e pardos no Rio de Janeiro e em Pernambuco (século XVIII)* (São Paulo: Annablume/Fapesp, 2002).

6. I cite from Sonia Gomes Pereira's transcription of portions of this account in "A representação do poder real e as festas públicas no Rio de Janeiro colonial," in *Barroco: Actas do II Congresso Internacional* (Porto, Portugal: Universidade do Porto, 2004), 663–78, 669n26.

7. Pereira, "Representação do poder real," 669n26, 667n20.

8. "Sahiraõ tambem em hum destes dias, com huma farça á imitaçaõ do estado, de que em ceremonia se serve o Rey dos Congos, esses homens mixtos (natural resulta de duas cores oppostas) a quem com impropriedade, mas por convivencia chamamos *Pardos*. Os gestos, a musica, os instrumentos, a dança, e o traje tudo muito no uso daquelles Africanos, descontentando ao bom senso, naõ deixavaõ de diverter o animo por estranhos"; *Epanafora festiva, ou relacaõ summaria das festas, com que na cidade do Rio de Janeiro capital do Brasil se celebrou o feliz nascimento do serenissimo principe da Beira Nosso Senhor* (Lisbon: Miguel Rodrigues, 1763), 27.

9. "He outra lá a formosura; muito diverso o bom canto"; ibid.

10. "Fizeraõ-o pois os nossos Pardos com toda a propriedade, e agencearaõ com ella o applauso, que pode franquear-se a huma imitação"; ibid.

11. "Todo aquele fingido aparato não produzia mais efeito que o de persuadirem-se os mesmos negros e alguns do povo que *o intitulado rei o era na realidade*, gastando-se com bebidas e abomináveis danças o que tiraram de esmolas a título de louvarem a Deus e à Senhora" (my emphasis). I cite from the transcription of this petition in Carlos Drummond de Andrade, "Rosário dos homens pretos," *Drummond, testemunho da experiência humana*, Projeto Memória, March 5, 2016, www.projeto memoria.art.br/drummond/obra/prosa_en saios-e-cronicas.jsp.

12. Antonil writes that slaves should be allowed to "create their kings and sing and dance honestly for a few hours, after celebrating in the morning their festival of Our Lady of the Rosary [crearem seus Reys, cantar, e bailar por algumas horas honestamente . . . depois de terem feito pela manhã suas festas de Nossa Senhora do Rosário]"; André João Antonil, *Cultura e opulencia do Brasil por suas drogas e minas* (Lisbon: Deslandesiana, 1711; repr., Recife: Imprensa Universitária da Universidade Federal de Pernambuco, 1969), 28.

13. "Ao rei reeleito o reconhecem os pretos por *verdadeiro rei*, o têm por oráculo, rendem-lhe obediência, tratam-no pelo seu rei ainda fora das funções da igreja" (my emphasis); Andrade, "Rosário dos homens pretos." The petition includes fifteen examples of the authority wielded by elected black kings: "Experience has shown that, after some slave has been king, his presumption is such that he no long serves his master with satisfaction—let alone if they are freedmen; all the blacks continue always treating them as old kings [Tem mostrado a experiência que, depois de ser rei algum escravo, é tal a sua presunção que não servem mais a seu senhor com satisfação, o que será sendo forros: todos os pretos os ficam tratando sempre como reis velhos]"; Andrade, "Rosário dos homens pretos." See Furtado's chapter in this volume for further discussion of this document, as well as Valerio's for examples of the involvement of elected kings in rebellions in New Spain. Silva describes the eighteenth century as a time of passage from the "baroque festival" to "Enlightenment intolerance," ending in the repression of the black brotherhoods and their festivals because of suspicions that the elected kings fomented rebellion; Luiz Geraldo Silva, "Da festa barroca a intolerância ilustrada: Irmandades católicas e religiosidade negra na América portuguesa (1750–1815)," *Repensando el pasado, recuperando el futuro*, ed. Verónica Salles-Reese (Bogota: Editorial Pontificia Universidade Javeriana, 2005), 271–87. On the prohibition in Brazil of black festivals in general and of the coronation of African kings in particular, see Quintão, *Vem o meu parente*, 114–21.

14. The twelfth item reads, "In Lisbon or in those parts of Portugal it is known that they no

longer use such kings because of their insults, and at least in Bahia, for many years until now they are prohibited by the governor or vice-roy, because of the same insults [Em Lisboa ou nessas partes de Portugal consta que já se não usam os tais reis pelos seus insultos; e pelo menos na Bahia há muitos anos até agora estão proibidos pelo governador ou vice-rei, por causa dos mesmos insultos]"; Andrade, "Rosário dos homens pretos." Lara cites and discusses several such prohibitions of the coronation ceremony issued in 1728, which concluded that the elected judges of the rosary brotherhoods could only "do their festivals in their church [fazer na sua igreja as suas festas]"; see Silvia Hunold Lara, *Fragmentos setecen-tistas: Escravidão, cultura, e poder na América portuguesa* (São Paulo: Companhia das Letras, 2007), 212. See also Marina de Mello e Souza, *Reis negros no Brasil escravista: História da festa de coroação de Rei Congo* (Belo Horizonte, Brazil: Editora da Universidade Federal de Minas Gerais, 2002), 234–36.

15. Pierre Verger, *Fluxo e refluxo do tráfico de escravos entre o Golfo do Benin e a Bahia de Todos os Santos dos Séculos XVII a XIX*, 4th ed. (Salvador, Brazil: Corrupio, 2002). On these embassies, and in particular the correspondence sent with the Dahomean ambassadors in 1805 and 1811, see also Ana Lucia Araujo, "Dahomey, Portugal and Bahia: King Adandozan and the Atlantic Slave Trade," *Slavery and Abolition* 33, no. 1 (2012), 1–19.

16. Lara, *Fragmentos setecentistas*, 216–18.

17. José Ramos Tinhorão, *Os negros em Portugal: Uma presença silenciosa* (Lisbon: Editorial Caminho, 1988), 140–41.

18. Lara writes, "Parading on the streets or in colonial squares, the courts of Congo kings in public dynastic festivals could recall other black kings, in faraway Africa or much closer, leaders of many brothers in the black confraternities [Desfilando em ruas e praças coloniais, os reinados de congos das festas públicas dinásti-cas podiam rememorar outros reis negros, na longínqua África ou bem mais próximos, líderes de muitos irmãos e confrades pretos]"; *Fragmentos setecentistas*, 217–18.

19. "Etiam scenam sedentis in solio Regis sui et majestatem pertinaci silentio testantis.

inde Legatorum peregrè venientium et Regem ritibus gentium suarum adorantium, habitum et ficta obsequia ac venerationem, quae recreandis nostratibus post pocula hilariores exhibebant"; Caspar Barlaeus, *Rerum per octennium in Brasilia et alibi nuper gestarum . . . historia* (Amsterdam: Ioannis Blaev, 1647), 245. I thank Cesar Lopes Gemelli for his assistance with the translation of this passage.

20. Barlaeus, *Rerum per octennium in Brasilia*, 244. On the 1642 embassy and the portraits of the ambassadors by Albert Eckhout, see Cécile Fromont, *The Art of Conversion: Christian Visual Culture in the Kingdom of Kongo* (Chapel Hill: University of North Carolina Press, 2014), 115–21. Fromont explains how the envoys display a combination of European and Kongo Christian elite regalia ("with a possible nod to the regional fashion of Soyo" in the use of shells as adornment), parallel to their enact-ment of a mix of European and central African diplomatic practices in Barlaeus's text; *Art of Conversion*, 116.

21. "Noticias mais amplas do Estado deste Rey, e do comercio, que nelle se póde fazer, para satisfazermos o dezejo dos curiozos da Historia, e da Geographia"; José Freire Monterroio Mascarenhas, *Relaçam da embayxada, que o poderoso rey de Angome, Kiay Chiri Bronco senhor dos dilatadissimos sertoens de Guiné mandou ao illustrissimo e excellentissimo senhor D. Luiz Peregrino de Ataíde* (Lisbon: Francisco da Silva, 1751), 11.

22. Mascarenhas, *Relaçam da embayxada*, 3.

23. "Se naõ póde fallar nelles sem o perigo de tropeçar em muitos erros"; ibid.

24. Verger points out that Mascarenhas locates the Gulf of Benin to the west of the kingdom, when it was in fact to the south; *Fluxo e refluxo*, 258. Some of the other geographic referents seem to refer to more distant locales, including a river in Mozambique (Rio dos Bons Sinaes), an Indian kingdom (Reyno de Bonsoló), and a Japanese island (Tanixuma), where Fernão Mendes Pinto reported having been shipwrecked; see his *Peregrinaçam* (Lisbon: Crasbeeck, 1614), 164r–166v.

25. "Hum tratado de amizade, e comercio"; Mascarenhas, *Relaçam da embayxada*, 4. Araujo describes how the embassy returned

to Dahomey with more than eight thousand rolls of tobacco in April 1751 and went back to Bahia in June 1752 with 834 slaves; "Dahomey, Portugal and Bahia," 3.

26. Verger, *Fluxo e refluxo*; Lara, *Fragmentos setecentistas*; Kirsten Schultz, "News of the Conquests: Narrating the Eighteenth-Century Portuguese Empire," *Hispanic Review* 86, no. 3 (2018): 329–51.

27. On the complexity of "representation" in early modern diplomacy—one of the three principal actions of diplomatic activity, along with negotiation and mediation—see Timothy Hampton, *Fictions of Embassy: Literature and Diplomacy in Early Modern Europe* (Ithaca: Cornell University Press, 2009), 8.

28. Mascarenhas, *Relaçam da embayxada*, 5.

29. "Quanto reconheciaõ a distinçaõ do seu character"; ibid., 11.

30. "Em obsequio do seu Monarcha, a quem elle representava no Brasil"; ibid., 6.

31. "Como o Daomé tinha violado com tanto escândalo a boa fé em que vénia com este a naçaõ Portugueza, nem este Vice Rey podia fiarse nos seus protestos, nem menos receber mensageyros da sua parte, *ou reconhecer a estes mensageiros por seus Ministros*, e que todo o acolhimento que lhes fizera não vinha a ser outra couza mais de que hum mero efeito do hospitalidade com que V. Mage. mandava tratar aos Estrangeiros que por algum incidente, ou negocio vem aos seus portos"; Luís Peregrino de Ataíde, Count of Atouguia, "O Conde de Atouguia Vice Rey do Brazil da conta a S. Mage. de que o regulo Damoé o mandara comprimentar por dois mensageyros seus pedindolhe juntamente a continuação do comercio da Costa da Mina, e demais que com eles passara," June 29, 1751, Bahia, Códices, Arquivo Histórico Ultramarino, fols. 245–46v, 246r.

32. The viceroy reports on the exchange of gifts as well as his delivery of the embassy's message to the king: "It seemed to him appropriate that they take some present in compensation for the one that they brought, and he ordered prepared for [the ambassador] some clothes proportionate to the custom of his country, which were delivered when they were about to embark . . . which seemed to him

to be the obligation of this Viceroy to *represent to His Majesty*, so that it would be clear what happened with the said messengers and the objective of their visit [Que lhe parecia nesse ponto levassem algum prezente em recompença do que trouxeraõ, e lhe mandara preparar huns vestidos proporcionados ao costume do seu paîz os quaes se entregaraõ quando estavaõ para embarcar . . . o que lhe parecia da obrigação deste ViceRey fazer presente a Vossa Mage. para lhe ficar patente o que asy se passara com os ditos mensageiros e objecto da sua hida]"; Ataíde, "O Conde de Atouguia Vice Rey," 246v.

33. "Entrou o Embayxador na sala com grande confiança, fazendo cortezias para huma, e outra parte, observando huma gravidade sem affectaçaõ, até chegar ao lugar, que o Conde Vice-Rey ocupava; e naõ distinguindo a sua pessoa entre a magnificência, que divisava em todos, perguntou pelo seu interprete qual era, e logo, sem perder a soberania do seu aspecto, o cortejou primeiro á Portugueza com três cortezias, feitas com muito ar, e imediatamente, ao modo do seu Paiz, prostrando-se por terra com os braços estendidos, e as mãos huma sobre outra, e trincando os dedos, como castanhetas: ceremonia com que em Angome costumaõ venerar aos seus Reys"; Mascarenhas, *Relaçam da embayxada*, 9.

34. "Assim não dava na sua Corte aos Embayxadores, cujo recado he sempre breve"; ibid.

35. "Nem elle a [embaixada] devia dar vestido á Portugueza, mas ao uso do seu Pais, para representar o Rey, de quem era Ministro"; ibid., 7.

36. "Sendo o fundamento desta demora, dar-lhe ocasião para que elle, e a sua comitiva ajuizassem, pela magnificencia com que em parte taõ distante festejava o anniversario do nosso Soberano, qual he a grandeza deste Monarcha"; ibid., 6.

37. Lara explains that, for Mascarenhas, "the initiative to associate the two events only served to emphasize the clumsiness of [the Count of] Atouguia. It was one more element to be exploited rhetorically in favor of a (political) reading of the figure and actions of the viceroy [a iniciativa de associar os dois acontecimentos apenas servia para marcar a falta de jeito de Atouguia. Era mais um elemento a ser

explorado retoricamente em prol de uma leitura (política) da figura e da atuação do vice-rei]"; *Fragmentos setecentistas*, 198.

38. Mascarenhas, *Relaçam da embayxada*, 6.

39. "Pouco inteligentes da pública utilidade, e que não sabem pesar a ruína do cetro na balança do entendimento"; Mathias Antonio Salgado and Manoel Joseph Correa e Alvarenga, *Monumento do agradecimento, tributo da veneração, obelisco funeral do obséquio, relação fiel das reais exéquias, que à defunta majestade do ridelíssimo e augustíssimo Rei o Senhor Dom João V dedicou o Doutor Matias António Salgado, vigário colado da matriz de Nossa Senhora do Pilar de São João del-Rei oferecida ao muito alto, e poderoso Rei Dom José I Nosso Senhor* (Lisbon: Silva, 1751), repr., *Movimento academicista no Brasil, 1641–1820/22*, vol. 3, pt. 2, ed. José Aderaldo Castello (São Paulo: Conselho Estadual de Cultura, [1969–]), 225–56, 227.

40. On the exclusion of Africans from the public sphere and "forced a-literacy," see, for example, Elizabeth Maddock Dillon, *New World Drama: The Performative Commons in the Atlantic World, 1649–1849* (Durham: Duke University Press, 2014), 14–20.

41. "Ninguem tinha jurisdição para limitar as acçoens dos Principes"; Mascarenhas, *Relaçam da embayxada*, 11.

42. Lara, *Fragmentos setecentistas*, 161.

43. Mascarenhas, *Relaçam da embayxada*, 10.

44. "Esta tosca representação"; "*A prova da verdade das minhas expressoens* verá Vossa Excellencia firmada com o Signete Real da sua grandeza. A este tempo tirou do seyo huma Carta, e a entregou ao conde, recomendan-do-lhe o segredo della; e continuou dizendo: *Receba Vossa Excellencia esta reprezentação da parte daquelle grande Monarcha, que o elegeo para occupar este lugar*" (my emphasis); ibid.

45. "O segredo, que Vossa Excellencia verá na sua Carta, naõ será publico, nem manifesto, sem expressa Ordem do seu Soberano Monarcha, e do meu grande Rey de Angome"; ibid.

46. Mascarenhas writes, "It was never divulged what the letter contained, nor what the caskets enclosed [Naõ se divulgou nunca, nem o que a Carta continha, nem o que os cayxoens encerravaõ]"; *Relaçam da embayxada*,

11. The contents of the letter may not have been disclosed, but we do know the contents of the boxes: the viceroy's report revealed that they enclosed "cloth from that coast [panos daquela costa]", which were remitted to Lisbon along with three of the four black women sent as gifts from the king of Angome; the fourth lost her sight and was not "in a condition that could be sent [em termos de poder enviarse]"; Ataíde, "O Conde de Atouguia Vice Rey," 246r.

47. J. Hillis Miller, *On Literature* (London: Routledge, 2002), 40. Timothy Hampton highlights the analogy between literature and diplomacy, with its concern over matters of representation and signification, in his analysis of ambassadorial writing and literary representations of embassies in the early modern period; see *Fictions of Embassy*, 10.

48. Doris Sommer explains, "Her techniques include maintaining the secrets that keep readers from knowing her too well. One conclusion to draw is that parties to productive alliances respect cultural distances among members. Like the rhetorical figure of metonymy, alliance is a relationship of contiguity, not of metaphoric overlap. To reduce the distance between writer and readers would invite false identifications that make one of those positions redundant"; see *Proceed with Caution, When Engaged by Minority Writing in the Americas* (Cambridge, Mass.: Harvard University Press, 1999), 116.

49. For example, in a 2009 book on *Triunfo eucharistico*, Luciano de Oliveira Fernandes mistakenly attributes the text's dedication to Simão Ferreira Machado instead of the Black Brotherhood of the Rosary; see *Alegorias do fausto: O Triunfo eucharistico e a Igreja Matriz de Nossa Senhora do Pilar de Ouro Preto* (Ouro Preto: Universidade Federal de Ouro Preto, 2009), 19. *Triunfo eucharístico*'s title page refers to how the book was "dedicated to the Sovereign Lady of the Rosary by the Black Brothers of her Brotherhood and at their insistence exposed to public notice by Simão Ferreira Machado, native of Lisbon and resident of Minas [Dedicado á Soberana Senhora do Rosario pelos Irmãos Pretos da sua Irmandade, e a instancia dos mesmos exposto á publica noticia por Simam Ferreira Machado natural de Lisboa, e morador nas Minas]"; Simão Ferreira Machado, *Triunfo eucharistico, exemplar da christandade lusitana*

na publica exaltaçaõ da fé na solemne trasladaçaõ do Divinissimo Sacramento da Igreja da Senhora do Rosario, para hum novo templo da Senhora do Pilar em Villa Rica, Corte da Capitania das Minas (Lisbon: Officina da Música, 1734). For a fuller analysis of *Triunfo eucharistico* and a development of the argument in this paragraph, see Voigt, *Spectacular Wealth*, chap. 4.

50. "Esta consideraçaõ nos obrigou a solicitar esta publica escriptura, em que sempre o nosso affecto esteja referindo em perpetua lembrança, e continua narraçaõ aos presentes, e futuros toda a ordem de taõ magnifica solemnidade"; Machado, *Triunfo eucharistico*, 138–39.

51. Hampton, *Fictions of Embassy*, 8.

52. See Orlando Patterson, *Slavery and Social Death: A Comparative Study* (Cambridge,

Mass.: Harvard University Press, 1982); and Jürgen Habermas, *The Structural Transformation of the Public Sphere: An Inquiry into a Category of Bourgeois Society* (Cambridge, Mass.: MIT Press, 1989).

53. On performance and embodied representation, see Taylor, *Archive and the Repertoire*; and Dillon, *New World Drama*; on blacks' use of writing in colonial Peru, see José R. Jouve Martín, *Esclavos de la ciudad letrada: Esclavitud, escritura, y colonialism en Lima (1650–1700)* (Lima: Instituto de Estudios Peruanos, 2005); on black "counterpublics," see Joanna Brooks, "The Early American Public Sphere and the Emergence of a Black Print Counterpublic," *William and Mary Quarterly*, 3rd ser., 62, no. 1 (2005): 67–92.

FURTHER READING

Primary Sources

Epanafora festiva, ou relacaõ summaria das festas, com que na cidade do Rio de Janeiro capital do Brasil se celebrou o feliz nascimento do serenissimo principe da Beira Nosso Senhor. Lisbon: Miguel Rodrigues, 1763.

Machado, Simão Ferreira. *Triunfo eucharistico, exemplar da christandade lusitana na publica exaltaçaõ da fé na solemne trasladaçaõ do Divinissimo Sacramento da Igreja da Senhora do Rosario, para hum novo templo da Senhora do Pilar em Villa Rica, Corte da Capitania das Minas.* Lisbon: Officina da Música, 1734.

Mascarenhas, José Freire Monterroio. *Relaçam da embayxada, que o poderoso rey de Angome, Kiay Chiri Bronco senhor dos dilatadissimos sertoens de Guiné mandou ao illustrissimo e excellentissimo senhor D. Luiz Peregrino de Ataíde.* Lisbon: Francisco da Silva, 1751.

Secondary Sources

Fromont, Cécile. "Dancing for the King of Congo from Early Modern Central Africa to Slavery-Era Brazil." *Colonial Latin American Review* 22, no. 2 (2013): 184–208.

Kiddy, Elizabeth W. *Blacks of the Rosary: Memory and History in Minas Gerais, Brazil.* University Park: Pennsylvania State University Press, 2005.

Lara, Silvia Hunold. *Fragmentos setecentistas: Escravidão, cultura e poder na América portuguesa.* São Paulo: Companhia das Letras, 2007.

Mello e Souza, Marina de. *Reis negros no Brasil escravista: História da festa de coroação de Rei Congo.* Belo Horizonte, Brazil: Editora da Universidade Federal de Minas Gerais, 2002.

Voigt, Lisa. *Spectacular Wealth: Festivals in Colonial South American Mining Towns.* Austin: University of Texas Press, 2016.

CHAPTER 5

Black Ceremonies in Perspective

Brazil and Dahomey in the Eighteenth Century

JUNIA FERREIRA FURTADO

Between 1796 and 1798 two Brazilian Catholic priests, Cipriano Pires Sardinha and Vicente Ferreira Pires, made a trip to Dahomey, in the Bight of Benin. Both had been appointed ambassadors of Portugal and sent by the prince regent Dom João, the future Dom João VI, to convert this African kingdom to Catholicism.[1] They were also tasked with producing an account of the journey, describing the parts of the continent through which they traveled.[2] The result was a manuscript now held in the Ajuda Palace in Lisbon, titled "Viagem de África em o Reino de Dahomé" (African voyage in the Kingdom of Dahomey).[3]

The aim of this chapter is to discuss the ways in which the two priests described the festivals and ceremonies they witnessed in Dahomey in the late eighteenth century from their perspective as men from Brazil and, at least for one of them, of African descent. A jumping-off point in drawing comparisons between these sorts of ceremonies on both sides of the Atlantic may be found in the descriptions of the black festivals held by the rosary confraternities in Minas Gerais, as well as certain manifestations of African culture in the same captaincy. Since in Brazil both men lived in cities with huge populations of black African slaves, they were certainly familiar with many of the customs and rites that they later witnessed in Africa. How did they react to what they observed, and how did they describe it?

Back in Brazil, Vicente and Cipriano lived in two cities. The former resided in the city of Salvador in the captaincy of Bahia, the first capital of the State of Brazil, in a zone dominated by sugar plantations. The latter was a resident of the village of Tejuco, located in the northeastern portion of the captaincy of Minas Gerais, which happened to be the administrative center of the diamond-producing region, the so-called Diamond District. Vicente was a foundling, subject to suspicions of being of mixed race despite the fact that orphans were legally considered free whites.[4] Cipriano, according to his baptismal record, had been born to Francisca Pires, a black woman and former slave who had been freed by the time he was born.[5] He was registered as the son of an unknown father, but during his life he claimed that his father was his mother's owner—the Portuguese doctor Manoel Pires Sardinha. Though the doctor never recognized the boy as a son, he did name Cipriano as one of his heirs.[6]

During his childhood Cipriano came into contact with African culture in the streets of Tejuco as well as in the slave quarters (*senzala*) of his father's house, where he lived for quite some time with his mother, despite having been born free. There his father's captives of different African origins lived in cramped proximity, sharing their ancestral values, preserving a multiplicity of African cultures and passing them on to their descendants. Slaves who arrived in Brazil, having established affinities during the Middle Passage, often found them "cemented in their captivity, through their work, or even within families."[7] After the death of Cipriano's father, for example, his mother kept in close contact with her former companions in captivity, some of whom had already been freed and among whom solidarity was visible in multiple forms.[8] This custom forged new forms of sociability between Africans from various regions of origin and allowed for the exchange and the discovery of shared cultural values. Through this proximity with Africans from different parts of the continent, Cipriano had shared in African values and customs, probably including language, complemented by what he would have seen on the streets of the village.

In these two Brazilian localities, the culture and customs carried over by massive numbers of recently arrived African slaves were vividly present, including their music, dances, rituals, drumming, ceremonies, and religions. Today it is estimated that 40 percent of all slaves to undergo the Middle Passage across the Atlantic Ocean through 1725—around four hundred thousand captives in all—were taken from Dahomey to Salvador da Bahia, an important port of arrival in the slave trade.[9] According to Voyages: The Trans-Atlantic Slave Trade Database, out of 1,736,308 slaves disembarked in Bahia between 1576 and 1875, a total of 809,840 embarked in the Bight of Benin, representing 46.61 percent.[10] In spite of the significant presence of traces of African culture in Brazil in places like the village of Tejuco and the city of Salvador, given that recently arrived Africans were a huge part of both the slave and freed populations in these communities, alterity and intolerance ultimately marked the relationship between the author of the *Viagem de África em o Reino de Dahomé* and the Africa of his forefathers.[11]

It should be said that one key reason for both priests having been chosen for the venture was quite likely their African heritage; it guaranteed some familiarity with both African languages and certain local customs, vestiges of which abided in daily life in Tejuco and Salvador. For example, when the Bahian doctor Luís Antônio de Oliveira Mendes, a white man born in Salvador, presented a memoir on Dahomey to the Royal Academy of Sciences of Lisbon in 1806, he described the text as partly "based on the memories of what he had been told in childhood [by] Fon slaves."[12]

It is almost certain that at least one of the two priests (most likely Cipriano) was able to communicate with the Africans in their own language. There are some clues of this skill in the manuscript *Viagem de África em o Reino de Dahomé*. First of all, they were not concerned with finding an interpreter in Brazil who might travel with them, although there were many Fon-speaking slaves in Salvador, their port of departure. Second, just after they arrived in Africa, the ambassador Dom João Carlos de Bragança (a cousin of the king of Dahomey, who had been representing him in Lisbon for almost a year), who had accompanied them on the ship, was separated from them; despite this, they were able to gather plenty of on-the-ground information during their trip through the kingdom. After being directly informed by a messenger that the king was waiting for them in his palace in Canamina they met the *meú*, a kind of a foreign minister, who directly spoke to them. In both occasions, and several others, they neither had nor even mentioned the need for a translator. Finally, in the report of the *Viagem de África em o Reino de Dahomé*, there are several references to the priests' "sp[eaking]" with people from that land," making no reference to the use of an interpreter.[13] This is clearly not a habitual elision, as on the one occasion they did use a translator, he is explicitly mentioned.

They used a translator only when they were received by King Agonglo, but in this case it appears to have been more of a security and protocol measure than a need in terms of communication. The king used one of his subjects, holding the office of *leguedé*, while the priests spoke through Dom João Carlos de Bragança, who was appointed to be their translator. The *leguedés* were trustworthy bilingual eunuch servants of the king, tasked with accompanying his ambassadors in their missions to ensure that envoys correctly represented the monarch's will. So Dahomeyan ambassadors representing the king and white people, as was their case, were always to speak in the presence of a *leguedé*, who would then report everything to the king. The priests also specifies in the account that they gathered most of their information from people from the land with whom they spoke directly.[14]

The prince regent of Portugal, Dom João; and the Royal Academy of Sciences of Lisbon had selected Father Cipriano for the task of conducting "scientific" observation during the trip and writing up a travel report. Written in the scientific style of the eighteenth century, the dominant tone of the narrative in the travel report to Dahomey is that of empirical observation—although, as the author warns at the start, what was observed may seem incredible to the reader. In spite of this dedication to simply describing what they saw, their remarks must be read and understood in the light of the cultural filters that separate representation from the object being represented. An understanding of the ways in which they described the ceremonies that they attended on African soil must be prefaced by a discussion of the extent to which they were familiar with certain of these customs and how they were reproduced, reconstructed, and reworked in Brazil.

THE FEASTS OF THE ROSARY BROTHERHOODS IN TEJUCO AND MINAS GERAIS

In Brazil as a whole, as well as in Tejuco and Salvador in particular, slave culture and the feasts celebrated by the enslaved black population were in flux, mixed through the cohabitation of people from different regions of Africa in the slave quarters, as well as molded and constrained by the imposition of Portuguese culture and its ingrained Catholicism. Even so, there are numerous accounts of the sharing of African traditions and customs in town life, though countless cultural assimilations meant they were no longer a simple reflection of original practices.

The rosary confraternity feasts are good examples in this sense. Religious sodalities in Brazil brought together people of similar origins and backgrounds, and the rosary brotherhoods were composed of blacks, whether enslaved or free, born in Africa or in Brazil—the latter known by the designation "Creole" (*crioulo*).[15] Every year the members of the brotherhoods chose a king of Congo and a Queen Ginga in many Brazilian cities, including Tejuco and Salvador, for the celebrations of Our Lady of the Rosary. This was a clear throwback to the political organization of African polities and kingdoms as understood by the Portuguese and patterned by the slave trade, albeit mixing Catholic symbols with African rituals. José Ramos Tinhorão calls attention to the fact that the title of king given by the Portuguese to the African chiefs had no real correspondence with their historical and political reality. The word referred to people invested with the power of command, especially those who benefited the Portuguese interests. "Being a black king meant for the Portuguese having a position of leadership in their land."[16] The Iberians also brought along Christianity. Around ten years after the arrival of the Portuguese on their shores, "in 1491, the Kongo monarch demanded to receive baptism and initiated the conversion of his realm."[17] Queen Njinga (1582–1663) of Angola, baptized as Ana de Sousa, embraced Catholicism during part of her life and also became a reference for this process in the Portuguese Empire. Since the seventeenth century there are references to the presence of representation of several African nations (*nação*) in the Corpus Christi festivals in Lisbon.[18] It was the Brotherhood of Rosario erected in the Saint Domingos parish of Lisbon who first accepted black slaves in the church as devotees to Our Lady of the Rosary. But a dispute with the white members of the confraternity lead to the creation in 1520 of the Brotherhood of the Rosary of the Black.[19] As pointed to in other chapters of this book, members of the rosary brotherhood incorporated monarchs into their celebrations.

These festivals also had an impact on religiosity in Brazil. On the one hand, among the enslaved population this recollection of African customs and political organization underscored their conversion to Christianity and their acceptance of Catholicism. But, on the other hand, the celebration could be a cause of disorder and unrest, as the queen and the king truly governed their subjects and could challenge white Portuguese power. With the latter in mind, the viceroy of Brazil formally forbade the rosary festivals between 1720 and 1735, but it appears that the ban was not strictly obeyed.[20]

The African crowning ceremonies were heavily imbued with significance for the monarchs' black slave subjects. In the Portuguese Empire the crowning of African kings could take on a variety of meanings, depending on the context of the coronation. Cécile Fromont recalls that "kings also emerged among rebel groups, the other significant context of African organization on the American continent."[21] For example, in the county of Rio das Mortes, in the south of the captaincy of Minas Gerais, April 1719 marked the discovery of a slave rebellion. The uprising was set to begin during Easter, on Holy Thursday, when the masters would be either distracted by religious observations or away from home—this being an ideal moment to attack their houses and steal weaponry. The local governor, the Count of Assumar, later revealed that the rebels had elected a "king, a prince, and a military officer" and had sent out emissaries to reach out to other regions of the captaincy in the process of negotiating their leadership and attempting to swell the ranks of the movement. A turning point came when differences emerged among African slaves of different nations. The most important point of contention were a set of disputes between slaves from Angola and Congo, on one side, and those hailing from West Africa (Costa da Mina), a region stretching from Guinea-Bissau down to Equatorial Guinea, on the other. The former refused to accept a king of any ethnicity other than their own, as did the latter. This dissension amplified rumblings of the imminent rebellion, and authorities soon discovered the plans. The governor immediately called for the imprisonment of "the so-called kings of the Mina and Angola nations and the officers and other military men elected by the movement."[22] This arrest of the leadership to break the movement, as well as the ethnic schism over the choice of a king, reveal the symbolic importance of the crowning of kings and queens for the African population in the Americas.

In 1771, in the city of Mariana, the seat of the bishopric of Minas Gerais, Father Leonardo de Azevedo Castro railed against the "abusive employment of the titles of 'king' and 'queen'" by Africans elected to those ranks in the rosary brotherhood. He exclaimed, "How indecent, abominable, and unfitting it was for such people to attire themselves with emblems of majesty" such as the "crown and scepter."[23] According to the priest, "all that spurious apparatus had no effect beyond convincing the blacks themselves and some of the people that the man bearing the title of king was indeed the true one." The priest's declaration reveals a number of important elements. First of all, these kings and queens bore the emblems that were the exclusive prerogative of the "true" monarchs back in Europe; this posed a threat to order at a local level, in a sense rivaling power with the real Portuguese royalty and their representatives in the colonial soil as the governors who were of noble origin.[24] Second, in dressing this way and in channeling this power, they inverted the organization of this hierarchical slave society: black African slaves, who made up the bottom of the social pyramid, made themselves equal to the European monarchs anointed by God. Third, as already mentioned, this act reveals the importance and the deference that Africans and their descendants bestowed on these kings, mirroring the political structures they had experienced in Africa. And there is a fourth and quite interesting aspect, namely, that the blacks were not alone in pledging their loyalty to these kings but were joined by "some of the people," or free whites.

The logic of slavery was thus inverted, with the slave conferring power on the free, potentially representing an even greater threat to the established order.

The scandalized priest forbade royal titles from being used locally, but he was met with resistance. According to him, blacks began to pay him visits "in pairs and in groups, secretly armed." The power of these visitors may be gauged by the fact that the local rosary brotherhood reached out to the bishop with a request for the ban to be lifted, which indeed came to pass—and about which Father Leonardo would complain to the governor of the captaincy, the Count of Valadares.[25] The overturning of the ban reveals that the authorities knew that this was not merely innocuous folklore mimicking European templates. Rather, beneath a veiled syncretism, aspects of African society, culture, and politics were being recreated on American soil, operating in large part to relieve the tensions arising from the enslavement to which blacks were subjected but also potentially to attempt subverting order. The enslaved could derive great power and fortitute from the elections even if they did not per se recreate African society in the Americas. Being recognized as Christians also could be a way of distinction from the other slaves, giving them a sense of prestige.

It is true that there were occasional abuses. In the city of São José, Father Leonardo reported how the two elected monarchs forced two white men serving on the municipal council to rise from the pew where they were sitting in the Igreja (Church) do Ó to make room for them. The black men said "that His Majesty was there, and that those seats were for royalty and officials of the king, and that they might go sit farther down."[26] Seating arrangements in a Catholic church, at that time, were neither random nor inconsequential; rather, they were meticulously studied and fought over, since each individual occupied the place his condition dictated. In this case, these two men, in addition to being white, "served the republic," a fact that conferred a certain prestige in and of itself. The two Africans' act represented an affront to the hierarchical order that governed the Luso-Brazilian Empire, as the priest clearly perceived.

Festivities put on by the rosary brotherhoods "always involved dances, music, processions, pageants, [and liberal] consumption of food and drink."[27] The celebration consisted of some religious ceremonies of Catholic origin, such as masses, and some of African origin, such as the congado (or *reinado*), which involved a reconstruction of the battle between the black and white monarchies and various dances, such as the *caboclos* and the *catopê*, as discussed in this volume by Dewulf and Dawson in their chapters.[28] The first "worked to some extent to reinforce the established order" and the second, in recalling African culture and society, "also lastingly challenged authorities."[29] Both priests, Cipriano and Vicente, were familiar with these festivals as well as with African dances, music, and instruments utilized and performed there. In Tejuco Cipriano was even a member of the rosary brotherhood, on whose board of directors (Mesa Diretora) he sat from 1787 to 1788.[30] These boards of directors were frequently occupied by people of higher social rank, mainly whites, to lend the brotherhood a measure of prestige.[31]

We have some documents that describe aspects of the rosary celebrations in Minas Gerais, allowing us to reconstruct how they were performed. The feast was celebrated on a variety of days, depending on the brotherhood. For example, the Rosary Brotherhood of Santa Rita in the village of Rio Acima, in the county of Sabará, stipulated that it be held on the Day of Our Lady of the Rosary, "on the first day of the eight days of the Christmas celebrations," while the brotherhood in Morro Vermelho, in the village of Caeté in the same county, celebrated it every February 2.[32]

In each rosary brotherhood, a queen and a king were chosen one year beforehand and were responsible for organizing the rehearsals and the ceremony, collecting funds and alms, and spreading the word about the festival.[33] Their importance might be measured by the amount they paid to the brotherhood. By the end of the nineteenth century, in the Rosary Brotherhood of Sabará in the county seat, while an ordinary member would pay 400 *réis*, those on the board of directors paid 2,000 *réis* and the queen disbursed an annual fee of 12,000 *réis*.[34] In the Rosary Brotherhood of Santa Rita, while the brothers paid 1 *oitava*, or octaves (1/8 oz.), of gold as an entrance fee and 1 *vintel* (1/5 octave) every year, members of the board of directors paid 4 octaves, the judges 16 octaves, and the king or the queen gave 20 octaves of gold per year. But while the board members and judges were "obligatorily white," the brothers and the king and queen were black people, most of them enslaved.[35]

Throughout the duration of the festival, the queen and the king exercised real power over their "subjects." In Tejuco they even went far as to free the village prisoners, which scandalized the imperial officials to no end. In 1771 the parish priest Mariana Leonardo de Azevedo Castro remarked that, in the village, "this is a custom and every year the king has free whomsoever he pleases, among a thousand other follies[;] they are venerated like real kings and even the white men must bow to them as they pass. They make them a throne bedecked with dossal, where they sit with crown and miter, dispatching petitions, giving audience to whites and blacks alike and send them all away when they want."[36]

For a two-year period around 1800, the queen of the Feast of the Rosary in the village of Sabará was one Ignacia Ferreira Codeço, a black freedwoman of unknown origin.[37] She rented a house, located behind the rosary church, which she renovated and had painted to serve as her "palace," where she held court and received her subjects, as was customary.[38] The luxury of the palace expressed the importance and power with which African queens and kings should be imbued. At the same time, the monarchs also mimicked European customs present in African kingdoms, even when the white Luso-Brazilian elite failed to pick up on this. On the voyage to Dahomey, the priests described the few palaces they saw, criticizing the constructions built from "rough clay mixed with pebbles and grit." Even the royal palace was met with unflattering adjectives. Its buildings were said to be "similar to those shacks ironmongers work in, except they were thatched, like all the other roofs in this empire. . . . Around them are innumerable holes like those they make in pigeon houses, but which here those savages call windows"; in short, the priests declared the constructions "just like the hovels of our homeland."[39]

By the late eighteenth century, after centuries of contact, African monarchs continued to use once European symbols of monarchic power such as vestments, crowns, mantles, and other ornaments, associating such finery with the symbols from which they derived their power. The tribal king who lived around the fort of Elmina, "old and blind in one eye," presented himself to both priests on their way to Dahomey "seated on a large high-backed chair, old and antique, covered in floral satin drapery of a similar age." He bore "a gilded silver crown atop his head, apparently given to him by a governor of the Portuguese castle when this was still under the control of Portugal," but the authors clearly pity him as a pale shadow of European royalty.[40]

It was not by chance, then, that Agonglo, king of Dahomey, asked the prince regent Dom João to send him silk fabric embroidered in gold and diamonds as well as "everything else that belongs to a king" in Europe.[41] His successor, Adandozan, asked for a fine chariot as well as silk, large and richly made umbrellas to protect him from the sun, small silver-plated swords, beautiful chairs, and fine hats.[42] Just as chariots, silk, and silver-plated swords were all signs of prestige within European culture, large umbrellas and chairs were prestige items within Africa; in Dahomey the latter were restricted to the king's family, high authorities, and whites.[43] It is notable in this light that the king and the queen in the *rosario* festivals also were protected by an umbrella, a sign in Benin of celestial protection as illustrated, for instance, in Carlos Julião's late eighteenth-century depictions of the event (plates 5, 6, 7 in the color insert).[44]

This attention to the trappings of royalty also was a great concern in Brazilian rosary festivals. As queen, Ignacia Ferreira Codeço bought fabric to make new dresses, one of pink cotton, another of satin—both European fabrics—and one of ordinary *xita*, a handmade cotton fabric produced in Minas Gerais according to African traditions.[45] She also bought a "fine hat with a high crown" (*chapéu de copa alta*).[46] When we look at the images that military officer Carlos Julião left us of the village of Tejuco and the city of Rio de Janeiro, some of them depicting the rosary queens and kings, we can observe that they are surrounded by the elements that represented royalty in both European and African contexts of the time: they are followed by a retinue of "princesses" or princes, and their sumptuous clothes are made from either the bright African fabrics of the Mina Coast or from fine European materials such as satin (plates 5, 6, 7 in color insert).[47] Their clothes are decorated with ribbons and with colorful kerchiefs worn around their necks, throats, or hips. Some wear capes, and most have feathers adorning their heads. Almost all are wearing shoes with silk stockings—a stark contrast from the simple clothing that slaves wore on an everyday basis, which would be a simple *pano-da-Costa* tied at the waist and bare feet.[48] The monarchs wear crowns; they carry fans and scepters; they wear mantles, with the trains carried by children so as not to drag or be dirtied on the ground; and on their outings they are shaded by fine colorful parasols, carried by members of their retinue. All inspires reverence, a sense of dignity and importance. Though they were often seen as "decorative" or "burlesque," these monarchs were in fact "imbued with profound dignity during the fleeting days of their domain; they were evocative images of a royal power on the African coast, which the slave trade had extinguished by reducing those who held it to the status of field slaves."[49]

In Carlos Julião's images, we can observe some musical instruments of African origin (drums, boxlike scrapers, wooden scrapers, marimbas, *reco-recos*, and a tambourine) as well as some of European provenance (guitars, flutes, trumpets, and castanets), evoking a mixture of sounds. The African sound also makes itself present through hand clapping and the hip-swaying dances, where dancers shuffle their feet and stamp them on the ground. In the village of Sabará, Ignacia Ferreira Codeço hired a Portuguese man to play guitar but also to organize the *congo* dance rehearsals where he would play his instrument. She also ordered that five painted round metal shields be made to be used in the *congo* dances, as well as another painting that was carried in the village to collect alms, revealing how European and African elements mingled in the feast.[50]

Alms gathering was essential in funding the festivities, and a part of what was brought in went directly to the brotherhood in support of its continued existence and sponsorship of worship activities. While this might outwardly point to Christian piety, it should be recalled that it was among the prerogatives of African monarchs to gather tributes from their subjects, a practice that often coincided with feasts. This was the reason for another complaint from Father Leonardo de Azevedo Castro, in Mariana, who reported that money was spent on "drink and abominable dances, which was taken from alms in the name of praising God and [Our] Lady."[51] The term "abominable," as well as Ignacia Codeço's hiring of a guitarist, is a sign of the syncretic, or mixed, character that these dances took on during the festivities of the rosary brotherhood, one not always accepted by the white elites. The memory of the African world, real or imagined, was there, for those—Africans and their descendants—able to make it out, recognizing its marks among the various syncretic elements incorporated into the feast. Nor was it completely invisible to those who, albeit unable to understand the full range of its meanings (as was the case with Father Leonardo), were perfectly able of grasping the degree of alterity that they represented in relation to European culture, which was a source of scandal and condemnation.

The German painter Johann Moritz Rugendas, who traveled through Brazil from 1822 to 1825, also depicted a Feast of the Rosary in the area around Tejuco. The image is more caricatural than Julião's, revealing the filters through which the painter observed and illustrated the Americas, but there are the king and queen in all their pomp, with their crowns, scepters, robes, insignias, and sashes (plate 4 in color insert). To their left one subject throws himself to his knees in utter reverence; nearby, another is going around with a hat, collecting donations. One of them shows his respect by prostrating himself and covering his head with dirt. The monarchs are better dressed and shod than most of those present, almost all of whom are black and barefoot. The exceptions are two white men, one of them a priest, in the foreground—mounted on their horses and elevated above the rest; they are impassive observers of the scene. And two soldiers are posted at the edges of the crowd, as if to reinforce that order must be maintained, albeit in a more flexible form than the white elites were traditionally accustomed to. Besides these four, all of the other black and *mestiço* (mixed blood) bodies are in movement: one plays a drum, some toss their hats in the air, others wave their hands or flags, and some dance, shake their hips, and clap their hands. Sounds, music, and the crackling of shots and fireworks radiates out from the scene, where bodies cluster together in immodest proximity. Other pictures by Rugendas, such as *Capoeira or the Dance of War, Batuque Dance in Minas Gerais,* and *Lundu Dance in Slave Quarters in Rio de Janeiro*, accentuate the spectacularly supple movements that characterize African dance, with the performers leaping, twisting, hopping, kicking, waving their hands in the air, and clapping.

The painter has portrayed a sociability worlds away from that of orderly, European-style religious processions, such as the 1733 transfer of the Blessed Sacrament from the rosary brotherhood church to the newly built main church (Nossa Senhora do Pilar) in Vila Rica, the capital of Minas Gerais captaincy, as described in Lisa Voigt's chapter in this book. A description of this feast that lasted one month and a half with various events, such as the procession performed to transfer the Blessed Sacrament, circulated in a printed pamphlet written by Simão Ferreira Machado.[52] The text was meant to have a pedagogical effect, teaching individuals about—or reminding them of—the role that each occupied in the various hierarchies of a society that strove to structure itself in accordance with ancien régime models.[53]

During his life in Tejuco, Cipriano Pires Sardinha came into contact with African customs, feasts, dances, and rituals at any number of points. These practices were spread throughout everyday life in the village, hardly restricted to the Feast of the Rosary. Traces of them emerge in a number of documents, most of which were produced precisely with the aim of stamping them out. In 1750, for example, the *mulatta* woman Arcângela was seen by several people late at night, hitting her back or rear on the door of the main church in Tejuco, saying, "Open up!" and other phrases reported by witnesses as superstitious. Some other individuals of mixed race (*pardos*) passing by were scandalized and began throwing rocks to shoo her away. At José Coelho Cardozo's big house (*sobrado*) on Rua do Contrato, the main thoroughfare in the village, the bush captain (*capitão do mato*) João Correa, who had a relationship with the black freedwoman Rosa Angola, frequently hosted feasts that began in the day and stretched into the night, where "black and mulatto" people played their African drums (*batuques*) and "committed several sins." These goings-on were both public and notorious, scandalizing the entire neighborhood.[54]

Elements of African culture also emerged at other feasts besides that of the rosary brotherhoods, at celebrations organized by whites where only Europeans and Catholics, in theory, ought to be present. In the capital of Minas Gerais, the city of Vila Rica, an important and erudite Catholic feast celebrating the creation of the local bishopric presented several dances and music described as being "in the manner of the black people."[55] Not only was the audience able to recognize the characteristics of African dances and its sounds but they were also capable to distinguish them from the European and the Carijó Indian traditions they had seen previously. It should be noted that those dancing in the ceremony were not blacks but seven white men wearing masks that "imitate the faces of blacks and their color." Whites were allowed to imitate African dances, then, but at the sole moment in the feast when black traditions were featured, African people were denied the dignity of representing themselves.

The use of instruments, particularly drums that conjured up the sounds of African musicality, was not confined to feast days. Africans performed their music, instruments, and dances in many settings and on many occasions. They sang their music as they worked and in their spare time, frequently accompanied by drums. It was said by a traveler that throughout the captaincy, "at night the blacks danced while clapping and stamping on the ground with their feet," accompanied by the "clatter of log-drums, tambourines, rattles, jars and castanets."[56] And some of the dances that were very popular in colonial Brazil, such as *lundu* and *fofa*, were clearly of African origin, mixed with European elements.[57] With all this in mind, it would be inconceivable that the two priests only heard African music and saw African dances for the first time in Africa; they would have been used to them both from Tejuco and Salvador, where a huge black population continued to practice customs linked to their African places of origin.[58]

As Fromont reveals, symbols of royalty from west-central African kingdoms were present at the feasts of the rosary.[59] But several of them were also visible in the ceremonies in Dahomey. It may be said, then, that the two priests were accustomed to these elements, as they were common to the slaves circulating through Tejuco and Salvador. But, despite this familiarity, alterity is the dominant tone of their descriptions of the ceremonies to which they were witness over the course of the journey. I call *alterity* the incapacity of sharing any identity with the other. In analyzing the meeting of European and indigenous culture, Tzvetan Todorov speaks of the almost impossibility of dialogue or the misunderstanding of the other and of the self-referential monologue of Europeans. About Colombo he says that he "does not understand the Indians better now: he never really comes out of himself."[60] In Cipriano's description this intolerance against the other puts the Africans as inferiors to both Portuguese and Brazilian subjects in a context of emerging racism.

DAHOMEYAN FEASTS

On their way to Abome, the capital of the kingdom, the priests are met with one ceremony after another as they travel through the interior. Despite their familiarity with such similar ceremonies they witnessed in Brazil and despite a professed "desire to understand all of these customs in depth," the rhetoric of the account of the voyage through Dahomey is marked by a sense of intolerance toward the African world that reveals itself over the course of the expedition. The priests write that they "began to observe [what they called] the extravagant difference there was between our customs and those of the barbarians, and the savage ways of that unhappy race."[61] The adjectives that the author uses to describe the people he encounters along the way reveal the same general vision. The litany of pejoratives includes heathens, darkies, knaves, barbarians, braves, savages, low and vile plebs, people of *that* color, kaffirs, idolaters, and people who "slake their hunger on human flesh." These lines, like most of the rest of the text, reveal a heavily negative vision of the continent: local habits and customs are always referred to in terms of a lack of civilization, and feasts and ceremonies, described in detail, are yet another sign of barbarism.

The descriptions of the local customs (which the narrator never tires of inquiring about, such is his curiosity—meaning thirst for knowledge) present the ritual feasts as absolute novelties to the author. But many of the forms of sociability with which the priests were received—the drinks, dances, drums, and music—were, as has already been shown, omnipresent during festivities among slaves in Portuguese America.[62] Nevertheless, they criticize their hosts for their excessive indulgence in liquor "of the most unpleasant taste" and the "screaming and fuss . . . with which they tripled the deafening disturbances and chatter surrounding the exhausted cortege," as well as the "out-of-tune crowing, which, together with the tones that issued from their ninny instruments, formed the most discordant notes."[63]

Upon their arrival at Elmina Castle, on their way to Dahomey, the priests were met with what they called a strange tribal dance. Although it entertained the locals, the dance struck the priests as a decidedly terrifying affair, in which the dancer, screaming and speaking quickly in his native tongue, threateningly waved a cutlass in the face of the very dignitaries who were ostensibly the guests of honor. Despite the fear instilled by the spectacle, the priests tried to use what they saw and experienced to grasp the meaning of the act according to its culture of origin: "The spirit of curiosity, which has always gripped me, did not wish to see me pass over the question or fail to inquire of such things that cannot be observed in general and of the meaning of that nonsensical entertainment in particular."[64]

The first dance ritual they saw was performed in the Portuguese fort of Ajudá, located on the coast, just after their arrival. A group of natives came to pay their respects to the fort commander. The priests simply note that the Africans performed their "usual greetings," as if they were familiar with the customary salutations in the country: first they performed several strange movements with their bodies—*acenos* (jumps) and *mocancos* (leaps)—and then served drinks. The spirit was not the usual *cachaça*, made of sugar cane, but a fine liqueur, perceived by the priests as indicative of some civilization, which they could explain only as a result of contact with Europeans along the coast. Later at night some young men performed some dances, resembling a coordinated fight. Another group approached the priests and struck up a dance in turn, with their hair and bodies smeared with dirt and their heads adorned with feather caps. Their leader danced up to the commander of the fort with an ax in his hands, gesturing ferociously as if threatening to slash his face. This last performance should not have been strange to them, as in one of Carlos Julião's images of the Feast of the Rosary in Tejuco, a little black boy is dancing in front of some black women selling food, holding an ax and a shield.[65]

The rest played local instruments such as tambourines (*tamborilicos*), drums (*tambor*), harmonicas (*gaitas*), rectangular tambourines (*adufes*), and conga drums (*atabaque*), which he named in a pejorative way as a "black orchestra"; the priests have no difficulty in identifying and naming every single one of them, although they go to lengths to make it seem as if all of this were a novelty. This group was followed by two dancing women dressed in what they called Moorish costumes and by others that danced around them, waving fans. The choreography is described in terms of monkey-like jumps, and the priests say that the music and chanting was dissonant and hurt their ears, complaining of an onslaught of "grimaces, braying, bawling, and scowls," as if everything were unfamiliar to them.[66] To the bewildered priests, the commander explained that this was meant to renew their friendship with the Europeans as a new *cabeceira*—the king's most important adviser—was named. But as for capoeira, which could easily be dubbed a sort of choreographed fighting, these sorts of African performances were common in Brazil among the slaves, and the priests would certainly have seen some of those being performed in the streets of Tejuco and Salvador.

Similarly, the author criticizes *cachaça*; it was a popular drink in Minas Gerais, although consumed mostly by slaves.[67] The use of sugar-cane drinks in Dahomey was a ceremonial ritual of welcome and good will. The priests described this as happening several times on the trip, whenever they were introduced to a new authority figure and invariably complained about being obliged to drink some rough spirit, generally *cachaça*. (In this they echoed the habits of Brazilian elites, where whites scorned *cachaça* for Portuguese brandy but also consumed a sugar-cane distilled drink of higher quality that they named as Brazilian brandy, or *aguardente*, to differentiate it from the former.) They said it tasted as unpleasant as a local beer made of fermented corn, a favorite of the local elite, and complained that "indeed, there can be no land more favorable for drunkenness, as all greetings, courtesies, politics, and signs of respect involve the downing of a cup." By the end of these sodden rituals, all present—priests included—were thoroughly drunk.[68] The priests also criticized the sounds of the African instruments (drums, whistles, bagpipes, and "marimbas," punctuated by the firing of guns) and the piping, shrill sounds of their songs. They described this cacophony as reminiscent of the suffering of the damned in hell, calling it worse than the din of battle; at one such event the noise was so loud they prayed not to be deafened. The exception to these critiques was a sort of pipe, which they described as a "delicate instrument" that a "guard of the roads" played to herald them as they marched through the countryside, comparing it to the Luso-Brazilian custom of playing trumpets to announce the arrival of authorities. In addition to countless references to *batuque* and the songs that slaves sang in Brazilian city streets as they worked (*jongos*), African instruments and songs were played also during the feasts of the rosary. In the village of Santo Amaro, near Salvador, in 1760, the festivities around the rosary were accompanied by the performance of several African dances (*talheiras* and *cucumbis*), scored by "the sound of the instruments proper to their use and rite."[69]

The priests also described three other elements present in the Dahomey ceremonies. First, as a sign of respect, the Africans greeted the Europeans by shaking their hands and snapping their fingers three times ("clasping the hand of each one and executing in the process three sets of snaps with their fingers: a form and sign by which one demonstrates the utmost respect").[70] By the end of the trip the priests were complaining that their fingers were sore and began balling up their hands in an attempt to avoid these greetings. Second, the locals carried flags. Religious flags were used in the feasts of the rosary as well, like the one that Queen Ignacia Codeço in Sabará ordered to be painted with images of saints. The priests refrain from describing the African flags, except that they were made of rags, but we can extrapolate from the flag that the Dahomeyan king sent to Dom João VI in 1810 as a present in the Dahomey ceremonies, currently in the Museu Nacional in Rio de Janeiro.[71] The flag portrays the battle of Agonsa in 1805, with a sword in the center, prisoners with their wrists tied, two knives covered in the enemy's blood, and a man carrying a basket full of decapitated heads, as chopping off heads was a common local custom. This kind of African flag served no religious aim but was clearly a way to demonstrate monarchs' power and ferocity—yet another source of scandal for the priests. Third, they used to be covered with earth that made their bodies reek, and, especially in the presence of the king, subjects would throw themselves to the ground in a show of respect and cover themselves with dirt ("they prostrate themselves on the ground and throw soil onto their heads and faces"), the same costume seen in Johann Moritz Rugendas' image of rosary feasts in Minas Gerais.[72]

Food was an important part of the festivities as well, besides drink. In the city of Aladá, where they met the *meú*, a kind of secretary to the king, the ordinary ceremonies were accompanied by a dish called a "chicken *caruru*." This African dish, which had been brought to Brazil, was served with okra and cooked with *dendê*, or red palm oil. The priests tasted the *caruru* and compared it to the Brazilian recipe, evidently displaying their familiarity with at least some local customs. As a rule, however, they generally criticized both food and drink. On this same occasion the priests received their visitors in the custom of the land, offering them something to drink—this time, a "superb" Luso-Brazilian *aguardente*.[73] The cornmeal-based dish, known as *angu*, however, "made with a number of herbs [and] large balls of [mashed] corn cooked in water and salt, and two small chickens" cooked in the local style—the rations they received twice a day—left them positively "sick of the continuous *angu* and the wretched mixtures with which they tend to season such stews, none of it befitting the European spirit or palate."[74]

The priests also described the two main local feasts, which were celebrated every year on June 24 and December 25. The people celebrated en masse with "drums, whistles, pipes, marimbas, tambourines, [and] rattles" and waved flags, "all scored by musket shots being fired and the rattling of old swords," with "the black instruments keeping up a constant, frenzied chorus." On days like these not only did the king collect a huge amount of gifts and tax, but in each ceremony a hundred prisoners and equal number of horses were also decapitated in front of the court, guests, and subjects.[75] The priests' manuscript was followed by a map of the site of the feast, which has unfortunately not survived; but we have other images of the ceremony, thanks to the British governor of the Gold Coast, Archibald Dalzel, who depicted it in a book published in 1793.[76] Food and drink were ample, but this time the Europeans were served by "a black cook taught in the European style, and the Ethiopes [were served] according to the customs of their country." There followed multiple toasts with "wines, liqueurs, and *aguardente*," revealing that the Dahomeyan king, for his part, had begun to incorporate ceremonial gestures from European courts into African routine. The priests were astonished by the violence of the ritual, symptomatic of what they called African barbarism, but the connection between celebrations and brutality shouldn't have surprised them; in the Portuguese Empire of the late eighteenth century, public displays of terrible violence inflicted on the bodies of the condemned, such as the whipping of slaves or the spectacle of hanging, drawing, and quartering traitors to the Crown, were organized and presented quite festively.

TAXONOMY OF BARBARISM

While the feasts of the rosary may allow us to see how African voices are present in Christian-derived practices in the Americas, particularly in Brazil, the two Brazilian priests' descriptions of the African ceremonies in Dahomey reveal that cultural filters prevented them from recognizing the origin of those voices. They described as unfamiliar the elements undeniably present in the mixed culture that characterized the places where they had been born—the village of Tejuco and the city of Salvador—but their descriptions also reveal that elements of European ceremony were also present at the court of the king of Dahomey.

One last question must be asked. If "point by point correspondences in the regalia, musical instruments, [clothes] and choreographies offer an evocative portrait of cultural continuity" between Africa and Brazil—or, more specifically, between Dahomey and Salvador/Tejuco—then why did the priests' writing mark such distance and alterity in relation to these customs?[77] An attempt to answer the question must be threefold: one aspect has to do with the priests' place of origin and the other two to the simultaneously scientific and Christian nature of their mission in Dahomey.

As for their origin—although they were mulattos, both (Cipriano in particular) saw themselves as part of the new Brazilian elite, which, with progress and science as their watchwords, gathered around Prince Regent Dom João, the future Dom João VI; and Dom Rodrigo de Sousa Coutinho, named overseas secretary in 1796. This Brazilian intellectual elite wanted to be taken as an active voice in the formulation of new state imperial policy, with their knowledge valued. They saw themselves as on par with their Portuguese-born colleagues, neither identifying with nor wishing to be defined by their African background.

As for the scientific tone of the report, the Royal Academy of Sciences of Lisbon, under the banner of progress, hoped to impose empirical standards on a rationally framed observation of reality out of the natural world, thus constructing a new body of knowledge. The priests' text reveals itself from the outset as the product of naturalists determined to carefully observe reality—nature, humans, and their customs. But in the end, their gaze tilts toward an imperialist frame for understanding civilizations around the world, placing black Africans on the lower side of the civilizational scale and white Luso-Brazilians at the upper end, constructing what I have called a "taxonomy of barbarism" and civilization.[78]

In terms of the religious tone of the report, it can also be said that the narrative is impregnated with the rhetoric one might find in a sermon, marked by the martyrdom of the trials undergone by the two missionaries. In embodying a narrative geared toward newly Christianized peoples, it served as an example of the Christian conversion of the infidels. After all, it was a religious tale of a moralizing and edifying sort, directed toward a Portuguese readership—of which the prince regent was the most illustrious member—with the aim of heralding the victory of Catholicism over pagan idolatry. In this battle between good and evil, what they understood as African idolatry could only be condemned as the geographic incarnation of hell on earth.

NOTES

My thanks to Conselho Nacional de Desenvolvimento Científico e Tecnológico (CNPq) and Fundação de Amparo à Pesquisa de Minas Gerais (Fapemig) for their support of my research for this chapter.

1. About the religious dimension of the mission, see Junia Ferreira Furtado, "Return as a Religious Mission: The Voyage to Dahomey Made by the Brazilian Mulatto Catholic Priests Cipriano Pires Sardinha and Vicente Ferreira Pires (1796–1798)," in *Religious Transformations in the Early Modern Americas*, ed. Stephanie Kirk and Sarah Rivett (Philadelphia: University of Pennsylvania Press, 2014), 180–204; and Junia F. Furtado, "The Journey Home: A Freed Mulatto Priest, Cipriano Pires Sardinha, and His Religious Mission," in *Slaves and Religions in Graeco-Roman Antiquity and the Modern Brazil*, ed. Dick Geary and Stephen Hodkinson (Cambridge: Cambridge Scholars, 2012), 149–73.

2. As for the scientific part of the mission, see Junia Ferreira Furtado, "The Eighteenth Century Luso-Brazilian Journey to Dahomey: West Africa Through a Scientific Lens," *Atlantic Studies: Global Currents* 11, no. 2 (2014): 256–76.

3. "Viagem de África em o Reino de Dahomé," Manuscript 54/V/10, Biblioteca da Ajuda, Lisbon. Published by Clado Ribeiro da Lessa, *Viagem de África em o Reino de Dahomé, escrita pelo padre Vicente Ferreira Pires no ano de 1800* (São Paulo: Companhia Editora Nacional, 1957).

4. Renato Pinto Venâncio, *Famílias abandonadas* (Campinas: Papirus, 1999). Despite the authorities' care to prevent children of color from being abandoned, when this practice was successful it could serve to whiten and

legitimize the descendants of blacks, especially those with mixed ancestry and light skin.

5. "Livro de batismos do Tejuco, 1752–1895," cx. 350, Arquivo Eclesiástico da Arquidiocese de Diamantina (hereafter cited as AEAD), Brazil, 27.

6. The heirs in his will include Cipriano, as well as two other former slave boys: "Three freed mulatto children born into my household and who, for the love I bear them, I raised as my own [três mulatinhos forros que me nasceram em casa, pelo amor que lhes tenho, e os criar como filhos]." All were born to slave women he had owned. The boys—Cipriano, Simão, and Plácido—always declared they were half brothers and used the surname Pires Sardinha. "Óbitos de irmãos da Irmandade de São Francisco," cx. 350, AEAD, 27.

7. Marina de Mello e Souza, *Reis negros no Brasil escravista: História da festa de coroação de Rei Congo* (Belo Horizonte, Brazil: Editora da Universidade Federal de Minas Gerais, 2002), 254.

8. For example, Cipriano's godfather was the companion of Maria Gomes, and his half brother was Simão Pires Sardinha, son of the famous Chica da Silva, who protected him throughout his life and played a role in helping him to attend the University of Coimbra. Both women were former slaves of Manoel Pires Sardinha. See Junia Ferreira Furtado, *Chica da Silva: A Brazilian Slave of the Eighteenth Century* (Cambridge: Cambridge University Press, 2009).

9. Alberto da Costa e Silva, *Francisco Félix de Souza, mercador de escravos* (Rio de Janeiro: Nova Fronteira/Editora Eduerj, 2004), 44. According to David Eltis, Stephen D. Behrendt, David Richardson, and Herbert S. Klein, this number is lower. Out of 3,278,919 slaves embarked in Africa between 1676 and 1750, 10.15 percent, or 332,809, were embarked in the Bight of Benin and disembarked in Bahia. See Voyages: The Trans-Atlantic Slave Trade Database, accessed January 20, 2018, www.slave voyages.org/assessment/estimates/.

10. Eltis et al., Voyages.

11. Salvador was an important entry point for slaves and had a significant African slave population; Tejuco also had a massive slave population of African origin as late as the mid-nineteenth century. See Laird W. Begard, *Slavery and the Demographic and Economic History of Minas Gerais, Brazil, 1720–1888* (Cambridge: Cambridge University Press, 1999). In 1774 Tejuco, of 501 heads of household, 276 were former slaves (55 percent of the total), 110 women, and 23 men of African origin (26.5 percent of the total and 48.2 percent of the freed population), forming what I have called a "Little Africa." See Junia F. Furtado, "Piccola Africa: Il mondo degli schiavi nel Distretto Diamantino e nel villaggio di Tejuco (Minas Gerais, Brasile)," *Terra d'Africa* 14 (2005): 143–59. The report was signed by Vicente Ferreira Pires and sent to Prince Dom João after his return to Brazil. Cipriano died in Africa. I believe that he was the true author of the text, but this is a theory I won't expand on here.

12. Mendes also interviewed "one Francisco Leite, a native of that country" in the city of Salvador. Pierre Verger, *Fluxo e refluxo do tráfico de escravos entre o Golfo do Benin e a Bahia de Todos os Santos dos Séculos XVII a XIX*, 4th ed. (Salvador, Brazil: Corrupio, 2002), 253.

13. Lessa, *Viagem de África*, 86.

14. Ibid., 60, 51, 86.

15. The term "Creole" (*crioulo*) referred then "to the slave born in the master's house," meaning in Minas Gerais that they were the descendents of two black African slaves born in Brazil. Raphael Bluteau, *Vocabulário português e latino* (Lisbon: Oficina de Thadeo Ferreira, 1739), 613. The African-born and mixed-blood slaves were referred to by their color. Black (*negro/a*) for the former and mulatto or pardo or *cabra*—mixed with Indian—for the latter.

16. José Ramos Tinhorão, *Rei do Congo: A mentira histórica que virou folclore* (São Paulo: Editora 34, 2016), 117–18.

17. Cécile Fromont, "Dancing for the King of Congo from Early Modern Central Africa to Slavery-Era Brazil," *Colonial Latin American Review* 22, no. 2 (2013): 186.

18. In the slave trade context the Portuguese used the term *nations* (*nações*) and not *kingdoms* to refer to different groups. It was a European reinterpretation of the African organization and generally refers to a port of shipment in Africa, a religious or ethnic group, or a geographic

African kingdom or area. It also has a local use in Brazil, varying among different regions.

19. Tinhorão, *Rei do Congo*, 182–85.

20. Carlos Drummond de Andrade, "Rosário dos homens pretos," in *Obra completa*, ed. Carlos Drummond de Andrade (Rio de Janeiro: Aguilar, 1967), 643.

21. Fromont, "Dancing for the King," 186.

22. "Motins do sertão e outras ocorrencias em Minas Geraes durante o governo interino de Martinho de Mendonça de Pina e de Proença conforme a correspondencia deste com o governo da metrópole," *Revista do Arquivo Público Mineiro* 1 (1896): 263–64.

23. Leonardo de Azevedo Castro, qtd. in Andrade, "Rosário dos homens pretos," in Andrade, *Obra completa*, 643.

24. In the Pernambuco captaincy in 1776 there were a "governor of the black people of the Sabarei nation [Governador dos pretos da costa da nação Sabarei]" and a "governor of the Ardas nation of the Mina Coast [Governador da nação dos Ardas da Costa da mina]" which also mimicked the Portuguese administrative organization. Tinhorão, *Rei do Congo*, 197.

25. Andrade, "Rosário dos homens pretos," in Andrade, *Obra completa*, 643.

26. Ibid.

27. Mello e Souza, *Reis negros no Brasil escravista*, 257.

28. For the Rosary Brotherhood of Santa Rita in Rio Acima, also in the county of Sabará, this part of the celebration consisted of a sung mass. "Livro de compromisso da Irmandade do Rosário de Santa Rita," Casa Borba Gato, Museu do Ouro (hereafter cited as CBG, MO), Sabará, Brazil; Affonso Ávila (org.), "Minas Gerais: Monumentos Históricos e Artísticos—Circuito dos Diamantes," *Revista Barroco* 16 (1994–95): 276. About the staged battles, see Dewulf's and Dawson's chapters, in this volume.

29. Fromont, "Dancing for the King," 184.

30. "Livro de inventário da Irmandade de Nossa Senhora do Rosário, 1733–1892," cx. 514, AEAD, 76v. His mother, Francisca Pires, had been a member of the board between 1754 and 1755, in homage of Saint Francis (43).

31. The reason the Rosary Brotherhood of Santa Rita gave was that "blacks lack the intelligence to occupy those places [os pretos não têm inteligência para ocupar esses postos]," since the posts required that their occupants be literate. In fact, the first nineteen founding brothers were illiterate and signed with a cross, as did the thirty-five brothers who signed the Book of Rules (Compromisso) in 1785. "Livro de compromisso," CBG, MO.

32. If the given date posed some problem, the board of directors would stipulate another one. "Compromisso da Irmandade da Virgem Senhora do Rosário dos Pretos do arraial do Morro Vermelho, da freguesia da Senhora do Bom Sucesso do Caeté, comarca do Sabará, 1790," Coleção Brasiliana, Universidade de São Paulo, accessed March 3, 2017, www.brasiliana.usp.br/bitstream/handle/1918/02441100/024411_COMPLETO.pdf.

33. At the Rosary Brotherhood of Santa Rita in the village of Rio Acima, the monarchs were chosen on the same day as the election for the board of directors, which was held on the Day of Our Lady of the Rosary, with their tenure beginning on the first of January of the following year. "Livro de compromisso," CBG, MO. About their responsabilities, see the same manuscript.

34. For 1881–93, see "Livro de contas da Irmandade do Rosário de Sabará, 1876/1923," CBG, MO, 6.

35. "Livro de compromisso," CBG, MO. In the Rosary Brotherhood of Morro Vermelho, in Caeté, brothers paid half an *oitava* to enter and another half every year; members of the board of directors paid one and a half *oitavas*, the treasurer and the notary two *oitavas*, and the judges three *oitavas*. "Compromisso da Irmandade."

36. Andrade, "Rosário dos homens pretos," in Andrade, *Obra completa*, 643–44.

37. The document is dated 1803 and indicates that "she was the queen in one of the past years" and elsewhere that "she was also the queen another year." The document also refers to another Queen Dorotéia without giving the date of her coronation. "Inventário de Ignácia Ferreira Condeço," OB/ABG–LIB (02) 32, 1803, CBG, MO, 3.

38. Ibid.

39. Lessa, *Viagem de África*, 40–42, 18.

40. Ibid., 18.

41. Verger, *Fluxo e refluxo*, 291.

42. Luis Nicolau Parés, "Cartas do Daomé: Uma Introdução," *Afro-Ásia* 47 (2003): 342.

43. Lessa, *Viagem de África*, 113.

44. Tinhorão, *Rei do Congo*, 202.

45. Through the late nineteenth century, this fabric was largely manufactured in homes in Minas Gerais. See Douglas Cole Libby, "A Produção Doméstica de Tecidos: A Indústria Mais Difundida em Minas Gerais no Século XIX," in *Transformação e trabalho em uma economia escravista: Minas Gerais no século XIX* (São Paulo: Brasiliense, 1988), 186–214.

46. "Inventário de Ignácia Ferreira Condeço," OB/ABG–LIB (02) 32, 1803, CBG, MO, 3.

47. Carlos Julião, *Riscos iluminados de figurinhas de brancos e negros dos uzos do Rio de Janeiro e Serro do Frio*, ed. Lygia da Fonseca Fernandes da Cunha (Rio de Janeiro: Biblioteca Nacional, 1960).

48. In one image they are barefoot but wear silver anklets.

49. Andrade, "Rosário dos homens pretos," in Andrade, *Obra completa*, 643.

50. "Inventário de Ignácia Ferreira Condeço," OB/ABG–LIB (02) 32, 1803, CBG, MO, 3.

51. Andrade, "Rosário dos homens pretos," in Andrade, *Obra completa*, 643.

52. Simão Ferreira Machado, "Triunfo eucharistico," *Revista do Arquivo Público Mineiro* 6 (1901): 985–1062.

53. See Junia F. Furtado, "Desfilar: A procissão barroca," *Revista Brasileira de História* 17, no. 33 (1997): 251–79.

54. "Livro de Devassas, 1750–1753," Arquivo Eclesiástico de Mariana, 40–41, 41v.

55. Furtado, "Desfilar," 270.

56. Auguste de Saint-Hilaire, *Viagem pelas províncias de Rio de Janeiro e Minas Gerais* (São Paulo: Companhia Editora Nacional, 1938); Nuno Marques Pereira, *Compêndio narrativo do peregrino da América* (Rio de Janeiro: Academia Brasileira de Letras, 1939), 1:123, 175, 138, 202, 254.

57. José Ramos Tinhorão, *Os sons dos negros no Brasil: Cantos, danças, folguedos; Origens* (São Paulo: Editora 34, 2008); Lessa, *Viagem de África*, 86.

58. Furtado, "Piccola Africa."

59. Fromont, "Dancing for the King." Fromont holds that Congo's *sangamento* ceremonies were very similar to the feasts of the rosary.

60. Tzvetan Todorov, *A conquista da América: A questão do outro* (São Paulo: Martins Fontes, 1983), 39.

61. Lessa, *Viagem de África*, 12, 53.

62. Mello e Souza, *Reis negros no Brasil escravista*.

63. Lessa, *Viagem de África*, 20, 37, 53.

64. Ibid., 21.

65. Carlos Julião, *Riscos illuminados de figurinhos de brancos e negros dos uzos do Rio de Janeiro e Serro do Frio*, ed. Lygia da Fonseca Fernandes da Cunha (Rio de Janeiro: Biblioteca Nacional, 1960), plate 35.

66. Lessa, *Viagem de África*, 20–21.

67. Valquíria Ferreira da Silva, *De cabeça de porco à bebida de negro um estudo sobre a produção e consumo de aguardente nas Minas Gerais no século XVIII* (Belo Horizonte, Brazil: Editora da Universidade Federal de Minas Gerais, 2015).

68. Lessa, *Viagem de África*, 30, 32.

69. Fromont, "Dancing for the King," 197.

70. Lessa, *Viagem de África*, 30.

71. Mariza de Carvalho Soares, "Trocando galanterias, a diplomacia do comércio de escravos, Brasil-Daomé, 1810–1812," *Afro-Ásia* 49 (2014): 253.

72. Lessa, *Viagem de África*, 57.

73. Ibid., 37, 36.

74. *Angu* made of corn flour was the usual meal gave to slaves in Brazil. Lessa, *Viagem de África*, 63–64.

75. Ibid., 46–47.

76. Archibald Dalzel, *History of Dahomy, an Inland Kingdom of Africa* (London: Spilsbury and Son, 1793).

77. Fromont, "Dancing for the King," 194.

78. Concerning this taxonomy of barbarism, "interestingly enough, in terms of civilization, the report does not simply seek to put the black Africans on one side and the

white Europeans on the other. The author sketches out an entire spectrum between barbarism and civilization [among African kingdoms], with each rung in the hierarchy evinced by cultural and material markets observed in the populations he encountered along the way. These distinctions also represent his own relative tolerance or intolerance of these customs and locals." Furtado, "Eighteenth Century Luso-Brazilian Journey," 269.

FURTHER READING

"Compromisso da Irmandade da Virgem Senhora do Rosário dos Pretos do arraial do Morro Vermelho, da freguesia da Senhora do Bom Sucesso do Caeté, comarca do Sabará, 1790." Coleção Brasiliana, Universidade de São Paulo. Accessed March 15, 2017. www.brasiliana.usp.br/bitstream /handle/1918/02441100/024411 _COMPLETO.pdf.

Eltis, David, Stephen D. Behrendt, David Richardson, and Herbert S. Klein, eds. Voyages: The Trans-Atlantic Slave Trade Database. Accessed January 20, 2018. www.slavevoyages.org/assess ment/estimates.

"Inventário de Ignácia Ferreira Condeço." Manuscript OB/ABG–LIB (02) 32. 1803. Casa Borba Gato. Museu do Ouro, Sabará, Brazil.

"Livro de batismos do Tejuco, 1752–1895." Caixa 350. Arquivo Eclesiástico da Arquidiocese de Diamantina, Brazil.

"Livro de compromisso da Irmandade do Rosário de Santa Rita." Casa Borba Gato. Museu do Ouro, Sabará, Brazil.

"Livro de contas da Irmandade do Rosário de Sabará, 1876/1923." Casa Borba Gato. Museu do Ouro, Sabará, Brazil.

"Livro de Devassas, 1750–1753." Arquivo Eclesiástico da Arquidiocese de Mariana, Brazil.

"Livro de inventário da Irmandade de Nossa Senhora do Rosário, 1733–1892." Caixa 514. Arquivo Eclesiástico da Arquidiocese de Diamantina, Brazil.

"Viagem de África em o Reino de Dahomé." Manuscript 54/V/10. Biblioteca da Ajuda, Lisbon.

◇◇◇

PART 3

Reconsidering
Primary Sources

CHAPTER 6

Envisioning Brazil's Afro-Christian *Congados*

The Black King and Queen Festival Lithograph of Johann Moritz Rugendas

CÉCILE FROMONT

Men and women of African origins and descent, leaving in freedom or enslaved first in Europe and later in the Americas, have chosen and celebrated leaders they hailed as their kings and queens since the fifteenth century. While groups claiming connections with a range of regions of the African continent have elected such figures and staged coronation festivals, kings and queens of Congo emerged as prominent characters in these ceremonies and the social organizations they enacted and supported. Today the best-known and most visible manifestations of these centuries-old practices are the celebrations organized by Brazilian socioreligious organizations called *congados* or *congadas*, whose very name draws an explicit connection between them and the west-central African region once home to the mighty Kingdom of Kongo. The realm, located on the Atlantic coast of Africa, south of the Congo River, participated heavily in the slave trade and owed its fame to the influential culture that its elite, who have self-identified as Christian since circa 1500, crafted and projected on neighboring regions as well as around the Atlantic world.[1]

Similarities between the kingdom's festive traditions and American black kings and queens' festivals are not limited to their name. On either side of the Atlantic, the celebrations of black rulers are staged in the orbit of the church and make creative use of a comparable mix of European and central African regalia. These nominal, institutional, and sartorial links between Kongo and congados should not, however, be read as a tightrope binding the two shores. Rather, they formed at times thin, yet enduring threads that withstood time and changing historical and social circumstances, as forcibly displaced Africans gradually found their footing on the new continent and drew on their overseas past to reinvent themselves as Afro-Brazilians. Beyond Brazil, similar coronation festivals, also often linked demographically or symbolically with west-central Africa, have been recorded, if not yet systematically studied, in a range of locales and eras throughout the Americas. Examples include the Pinkster celebration in Dutch North America, Election Day festivals in eighteenth-century New England, and the contemporary feast of San Juan Congo in Venezuela. Similar celebrations also emerged in the British or French Caribbean.[2] Several chapters in this book explore closely or loosely related manifestations from Mexico (Miguel A. Valerio's), Trinidad (Dianne M. Stewart's), and the United States (Jeroen Dewulf's).

The congado's contemporary visibility has led scholars to probe the history of the festival, making the Brazilian coronations the best-known examples of what, by all indications, was a widespread hemispheric phenomenon.[3] This chapter aims at providing a clearer understanding of the historical black king and queen celebrations in Brazil by analyzing the creation, contents, and composition of one of the best-known and most frequently used image of Afro-Christian festivals in Brazil, the lithograph in figure 6.1 and plate 4. It combines insights gathered from written and visual historical documents and secondary literature, along with a careful formal analysis, to form a rigorous examination of an image that is as emblematic as it is seldom critically approached as a complex source. Afro-Brazilian men and women performed in their festivals sophisticated manipulations of social norms, religious codes, and visual discourses to exercise and advance their political and social agendas. To what extent, this chapter interrogates, did the print attempt and variously succeed and fail to make visible these social, religious, and political stakes of the performance?

The lithograph is one of only a handful of images documenting black kings and queens' festivals before the twentieth century. The black and white vignette, also known in hand-colored versions, depicts, according to its caption, the "Feast of Saint Rosalia, Patron of the Blacks" and advertises in small print its origins in sketches "from nature" by Johann Moritz Rugendas. It belongs to a large editorial venture lead by Franco-German editor and lithographer Godefroy Engelmann. The project turned the sketches of young Bavarian artist and traveler Rugendas, produced during his journey to Brazil between 1821 and 1825, into a commercially successful publication, titled in its simultaneous French and German editions *Voyage pittoresque au Brésil*

FÊTE DE Sᵗᵉ ROSALIE, PATRONE DES NÈGRES.

FIGURE 6.1 Johann Moritz Rugendas, *Feast of Saint Rosaly, Patroness of the Blacks*, in *Voyage pittoresque dans le Brésil* (Paris: Engelmann et Cie, 1835), division 4, book 16, plate 19. Photo courtesy of Oliveira Lima Library, Catholic University of America.

or *Malerische Reise in Brasilien*. It appeared in Paris between 1827 and 1835 in twenty installments, or cahiers, of nine folio sheets, organized in four divisions: "Landscapes," "Costumes and Portraits of Blacks and Indians," "Mores and Customs of Indians and Europeans," and "Mores and Customs of Blacks."[4] Together the four parts include around one hundred lithographs presenting natural and urban landscapes as well as mores and customs vignettes. Each fascicle includes five plates, glossed "sketched from nature by Rugendas" to the exception of two, attributed to designs by Jean-Baptiste Debret, a contemporary of Rugendas's and member of a French artistic mission to Brazil.[5] Rugendas was a prolific artist but not a wordsmith. To compose the *Voyage pittoresque*'s text, he relied on the assistance of Victor Aimé Huber, an intellectual from southern Germany, whom he met through Alexander von Humbolt, their common acquaintance.[6] Rugendas also liberally used text from previously published accounts, with or without explicit citations.

Quoting a long passage written by Henry Koster, an earlier British chronicler of Brazil, Rugendas identified the event pictured in the *Sainte Rosalie* lithograph as "the yearly festival of our Lady of the Rosary," under the direction of a "black [Catholic] fraternity," during which "is chosen the King of the Congo nation."[7] Indeed, since the fifteenth century, free and enslaved Africans living in Spain and Portugal and in the overseas territories under direct or indirect Iberian influence had organized in lay sodalities in the orbit of the Catholic Church. Confraternities with African membership existed in Portugal but also in the African kingdom of Kongo as early as the sixteenth century and in Angola and Brazil since at least the seventeenth.[8] These black confraternities have feted their elected queens and kings in Minas Gerais, the region of Rugendas's sketch, since the first decades of the eighteenth century.

The Portuguese ruling class, in turn, regarded this practice with ambivalence. Lay and ecclesiastical authorities wavered between dismissively mocking the coronation festivals as grotesque, low-class distractions; encouraging them as proof of their success at converting the enslaved to Catholicism; or fighting them for fear of the potential of such events to foster the kind of social cohesion and leadership among Africans and their descendants that could bring about rebellion. The oral history of the Morro Alto rosary confraternity—whose festival Rugendas likely pictures in the lithograph—gives center place to precisely such a figure of slave resistance, its founding hero a man known as Chico Rei, that is, King Chico. According to oral tradition, which archival documents neither convincingly prove nor disprove, the enslaved Francisco (the long form of Chico) was once a king in Africa. He lost most of his family during the Middle Passage, which brought him to Vila Rica (now Ouro Preto), a boomtown of the Brazilian mining region of Minas Gerais. Bound to the mines, he smuggled gold flakes hidden in his hair and little by little gathered enough wealth to buy his freedom and that of an entire nation of followers who acclaimed him as their king.[9] Together, the members of the newly formed nation acquired and worked their own mine, which allowed them, the story continues, to construct the church of Santa Efigênia on the Alto da Cruz hill as the home for their confraternity, dedicated to Our Lady of the Rosary. Chico's coronation, the story further explains, was the first festival that the brotherhood staged in honor of a black king.[10]

The Morro Alto Rosary Confraternity of the Antônio Dias neighborhood of Ouro Preto dates back to 1718. Its membership was at first racially mixed, but it became de facto, if not de jure, a black confraternity in 1733, after an internal dispute led its white members to create a sodality of their own in the neighboring vicinity of Padre Faria.[11] On the occasion of the split, the brothers and sisters of the Morro Alto brotherhood signed a new *compromisso*, or statutes, in which they were eager to underline their independence. They insisted in particular that the chapel they outfitted in the Matriz, or Mother Church, of Nossa Senhora da Conceição de Antônio Dias before the split had been "built at the expense of the devotion and [its] faithful [feita a expensas da devoção e fiéis]" without any outside help. The confraternity thus owed nothing to the parish or its priest.[12]

The same year of the schism, the brothers and sisters broke ground on a church of their own, Santa Efigênia, designed by the same architect as the church hosting their old chapel, Nossa Senhora da Conceição, which had been under works of expansion since 1727. Notably, that builder was Antônio Francisco Lisboa, none other than the father, along with a unnamed black woman, of arguably the most famous artist of Minas Gerais's baroque era, Aleijadinho. The construction of the two churches, the Conceição and Santa Efigênia, advanced simultaneously, and the two structures unsurprisingly share common design features, such as a similar facade and square bell towers topped with bulbous domes. Located in clear view of each other, in the hilly landscape of Ouro Preto, the two temples still face off today, with Santa Efigênia clearly having the upper hand, perched on its hilltop (plate 8 in color insert). The white rosary confraternity would later sponsor the construction of a modest free-standing structure of its own in the Padre Faria neighborhood, the chapel of Nossa Senhora do Rosário do Padre Faria.[13]

In Morro Alto, as elsewhere in colonial Brazil, confraternities of the Rosary of the Blacks were, and still are, famous for their election and festive celebration of kings and queens. The events took place either on the feast day of Our Lady of the Rosary in October or around Christmastime and Epiphany, and the members considered them a central feature of their devotional practices, a point voiced in many of the associations' statutes.[14] Today the black kings and queens' festivals and the broad musical, performative, religious, and philosophical realms surrounding them are known as *congados* or *congadas*, a term that appeared only in the nineteenth century, with a first recorded mention dated to the 1810s in travel literature.[15] Eighteenth-century rosary confraternity records from Minas Gerais, however, did note in their bookkeeping the functions of elected royalty. Some held positions labeled as kings and queens of Congo, which, historian Elizabeth Kiddy suggests, may have been distinct from that of the royal couple at large. In at least one case, the documents identified the king of Congo as a slave named José Congo, an appellation that likely described his birth in central Africa in contradistinction to the other king and queen of the group labeled in the same record as *crioulos*, that is, born in Brazil.[16]

VISUALIZING THE CORONATION FESTIVAL IN SLAVERY-ERA BRAZIL

Carlos Julião, or Carlo Giuliani, a Turin-born draftsman serving in the Portuguese army, created the oldest known depictions of black queens and kings festivals in Brazil in a set of watercolors dated to the last quarter of the eighteenth century and now in the Biblioteca Nacional of Rio de Janeiro (plates 5, 6, 7 in color insert).[17] Rugendas's lithograph is, to my knowledge, the second-oldest depiction of this type of event. Although fifty years separate the two sets of images, they concord on many aspects that also prove consistent with textual descriptions. All documents present a royal couple dressed in European clothes enhanced with accessories associated with regal status such as crowns and scepters. The chosen monarchs also wear items foreign to European fashion such as loincloths for men or elaborate headscarves for women. Central African and European instruments chime in concert to create the soundtrack of the scene. In Julião's paintings African instruments such as scratchers and a marimba—a percussion piece made of wooden planks attached over gourds—surround the king, alongside a seven-string guitar and castanets of European origins. Rugendas pictures a thumb piano in the hand of the fourth man from the right of the image, along with European drums, flutes, bagpipe, and trumpets. Flags and feathers also appear prominently in both sets of images, a significant detail, also spelling links to central Africa, as discussed in this volume by Jeroen Dewulf.

A notable difference between visual and written documents about the festivals, however, existed in the tone of descriptions. Negative qualifiers abounded in the texts. Koster, for instance, described the royal couple as wearing an "old fashioned suit of divers tints" and a "blue silk gown, also of ancient make." Rugendas's or Julião's images, in contrast, do not convey such nuances, or at least not as explicitly, in particular to viewers distant in time from the period and its prevailing fashions.[18] Bringing together written and visual documents creates an array of information that helps establish that Rugendas's view of the coronation festival provides much valid information. The type of evidence contained in different media, however, differs, which can either help or hinder analysis. It is crucial to approach and confront different categories of documents with a rigorous consideration of the advantages and limitations of each of their genres.

About forty years after the creation of the lithograph, photography became available to artistically inclined travelers eager to capture for personal or commercial use Brazil's spectacular landscapes and exotic mores and customs. Augusto Riedel, the Brazil-born son of a member of the Russian-sponsored Langsdorff Scientific Expedition, which had first brought Rugendas to South America, followed in the footsteps of the earlier generation and produced photographic views of the country. In what seems a continuation of the traveling artist tradition, he used the new technology in 1868 to capture a *Congado dos pretos em Morro Velho, Provincia de Minas, Brazil* (plate 9 in color insert). It was likely a reenactment of the festival staged for the entertainment of the Duke of Saxe-Coburg and Gotha and his aristocratic entourage, who toured what was then the Empire of Brazil in the company of Riedel.[19] Far from the lively celebration conveyed in Rugendas's print, the photograph offers but a tamed, oddly static, and lifeless scene. Technical limitations of early photography, which required relatively long exposure time certainly played a role in the images' stiffness, along with the artificial staging of the performance for the foreigners' visit rather than on an occasion of the performers' choosing. Another group of photographs of contrived *congadeiros* from around 1865 emerged in the orbit of Christiano Jr.'s studio in Rio de Janeiro, although at least one of the prints bears the signature of another image maker or image broker, Arsênio da Silva (fig. 6.2).

Striking similarities in the festivities depicted from Julião to Christiano Jr. lends further credibility to the iconographic sources used in the making of the *Voyage pittoresque* lithograph and to the keen eye of Rugendas in sketching the festival.[20] The common traits observable over the span of almost a century are particularly valuable because they bring to the fore some characteristics of the coronation festivals that texts did not record. For example, in all images the royal court wears European clothing of its own era. The empire-waisted, puffed-sleeved dress of the black queen in Rugendas's print may have been last year's fashion, as Koster vocally opined, but nonetheless belonged to its decade's sartorial style. And so did the crinolines of the female posers of the 1865 photographs and the chintz and brocade of Julião's 1770s black courtiers. This observation indicates the intent of the festival participants to present themselves in the performances as personas whose outfits encoded social prestige in the terms dictated by their current social and cultural environment.

FIGURE 6.2 Arsênio da Silva, *Congada*, 1860. Photograph, 17.5 × 23.5 cm on ca. 32 × 45 cm sheet, in the collections of the Fundação Biblioteca Nacional, Rio de Janeiro. Photo: Acervo Fundação Biblioteca Nacional do Brasil.

Written accounts of the coronation festivals often dismissively and derisively noted emulation of European luxuries in vague terms that did not convey the connections between coronation outfits and changing fashions. The images bring into focus the actual use of European clothing by black performers as current in its style, resourceful in its implementation, and meaningful to the festivals' participants. They also allow us to identify what parts of the festivals' visual and material makeup changed (for instance, the queens' dresses) and what parts remained consistent over the centuries, such as the use of feathers and flags. These observations, in turn, make possible analyses of the role that continuity and change played in the construction of *congada* traditions over-time, challenging ahistorical accounts of Afro-Brazilian culture.

Similarly, some objects, at first easily dismissed as tokens of festive fancy or exoticizing exaggerations that European image makers would have ran-domly inserted, emerge from one picture to the next as central, characteristic insignia of the groups. Feathers are among the most prominent ones but so are the loincloths worn by male participants and the use of capes and scarves

FIGURE 6.3   Paolo da Lorena (attributed) after Giovanni Antonio Cavazzi, *Wars and Way to Proceed Therein*, engraving in Giovanni Antonio Cavazzi and Fortunato Alamandini, *Istorica descrizione de' tre' regni Congo, Matamba, et Angola sitvati nell' Etiopia inferiore occidentale e delle missioni apostoliche esercitateui da religiosi capuccini* (Bologna: Giacomo Monti, 1687), 157. Photo courtesy of the James Ford Bell Library, University of Minnesota.

as badges of status. Notable in these details is the consistency with which they are used, even as the rest of the outfits change overtime. Noting these features is key to an accurate analysis of the festival's symbolism and its visual and material expressions. Thus, for instance, the chintz in Julião's images or the lace at the collar of Rugendas's queen in the middle of the lithograph can be confidently read as expressions intended to encode luxury and pomp in the events' contemporary environment. They likely did not hold further, even obfuscated, symbolic meaning other than the weight pageantry and refined paraphernalia carried as means to express social and political prestige ostentatiously.

The constant presence of the feathers point, on the contrary, to their role as essential insignia of the ceremonies that carried specific significance. Emblems par excellence of the exotic other in general and the American savage in particular in a European reading, feathers also certainly encompassed in the coronation festivals a different dimension specific to their wearers' worldview.[21] Jeroen Dewulf discusses at length in this volume the particular significance of feathers in the Kongo as well as in Kongo-derived festivals in the Americas.

The prominent role they played in the visual vocabulary of spiritual interme-
diation and power among the religious and political elite of the Kingdoms of
Kongo and its neighbor Ndongo in central Africa offers but one example of
their possible significance within the coronation rites.[22] The war band in figure
6.3 depicted in Capuchin missionary and author Giovanni Antonio Cavazzi's
description of central Africa published in 1687 provides a visual pendant for
the musical instruments, loincloths, and feathered headdresses of Brazilian
festival performers. Such an image is only one example among a robust corpus
of written descriptions and visual representations of feathers in central African
regalia during the early modern period.

AFRICAN ROOTS, OR WHAT IS KONGO ABOUT CONGADO?

Such a comparison between Cavazzi's image of seventeenth-century central
African warriors and Brazilian coronation festivals of later centuries draws its
relevance from the broad and deep connections between the two regions. Men
and women claiming origins or descent from central Africa played a key role in
the coronation festivals of slavery-era Brazil. Specifically, the American festivals' instruments, choreography, and insignia paralleled in many regards those
used in performances from the central African Kongo Kingdom called *sangamentos*.[23] Central Africans forcibly taken through the slave trade away from
their homeland, and later their descendants, transposed the danced martial
encounters and pageantry of the kingdom's central political ritual to Europe
and the Americas. In their new environment of life in enslavement and disen-
franchisement, they staged the sangamento-inspired black kings and queens'
festivals as a means to create limited but concrete spaces of social empowerment and cultural expression. The celebrations took place in the orbit of the
church not only because of the relative freedom the institution afforded them
in the conduct of their devotion and associated social endeavors but also in
keeping with the central place Christianity held in Kongo symbolism of power
and prestige since the conversion of the realm circa 1500.[24]

This central African genealogy, however, was not the single root of the
American festivals; rather, it mixed and merged in the celebrations with other
inputs such as the Portuguese *Moros e Christianos* staged battles, which, in
fact, had already participated in the cross-cultural construction of the Kongo
Christian sangamento.[25] By the nineteenth century and Rugendas's lithograph,
the performances derived or inspired by sangamentos had become a deeply
Brazilian phenomenon. Yet the office of kings and queens was still often

bestowed to men and women born in Africa, a gesture that was at a minimum ripe with symbolism, if not performed out of ritual imperative. Historian Kiddy, we recall, found evidence in the nineteenth century of the existence of the separate positions of king and queen at large versus king and queen of Congo in the confraternities' archives.[26]

In this regard, the black kings and queens' festival presents an important opportunity to think about the process through which, generation after generation, Africans newly arrived or born in the Americas forged social, ritual, and devotional traditions of their own on the new continent. That queens and kings of Congo took part in the organization and festivities of Catholic confraternities in colonial Brazil is a crucial hint about this often elusive process of cumulative creation and transformation at the core of the African collective experience in the Americas. The presence of royalty bearing the label of Congo, and the preference that they be born in Africa, demonstrates a certain level of mutual recognition and collaboration between newly arrived and already established members of the central African diaspora in Brazil.[27] It also points to the lasting coexistence and overlap between different personal experiences, knowledge, and imaginaries about central Africa based on a diversity of individual itineraries.

In slavery-era Brazil central Africa could encompass for members of the black confraternities a specific place of birth, a former home, a distant place of family origins, or a more broadly defined abode of ancestral spirits. It also became, for others, a wholly abstract, mythical place linked with shared social and religious conceptions at the core of their group identity in Brazil as part of a Congo or Angola nation. Over time, the notions encoded under the term "Congo" changed from ideas and practices partly linked to specific aspects of the Kongo region in Africa to a set of conceptions rooted in an Afro-Brazilian lore with strong yet mythologized connections to central African precedents. In the case Kiddy discusses, the demographic shift resulting from the end of the slave trade likely played a role in the transition. The disappearance within congados of the two separate royal titles of king and queen at large and king and queen of Congo logically reflects the end of an era in which the slave trade continuously brought to Brazil newcomers from Africa.

SITUATING SOCIAL RELATIONS IN RUGENDAS'S PRINT

The coronation festival formed a prominent space within which Africans and Afro-descendants reflected on, honed, and exercised social, religious, and political claims through performances whose significance easily eluded outside observers. A useful aspect of Rugendas's lithograph is precisely its encoding of a variety of personal and collective positioning, which helps shed light on the social relations at play between participants in the coronation festivals as well as between actors and bystanders. While Julião's images isolate the festival figures on a blank background, Rugendas's print includes them within a complex composition. The lithograph after the German man's observations does not merely depict participants in the festival but places them within a social, natural, and urban environment. The towering araucaria trees on the left of the image, or the banana plants framing the middle ground of the scene on the print's two vertical edges, draw from his repertoire of naturalist sketches. The buildings in the distance identifiable as the hilltop church of Santa Efigênia and surrounding structures of the Antônio Dias locality firmly place the scene in a defined space. Socially, even if unruliness seems to dominate this scene of reveling, a range of defined characters and relationships actually structure the image and the event it depicts. Whether or not the artist made any sense of his observations about social relations is unclear. Understanding was not, in any case, central to his artistic process in a project that aimed primarily at capturing Brazil's natural and social landscape in dramatic, picturesque compositions.[28]

Let's take a closer look at the lithograph. A procession of black men and women progresses slowly and with great fanfare on a wide dirt road. Dozens of figures in heteroclite dress and many different poses form the busy core of the image. A tall and large black man in a stringy white wig and tricorn hat is at the geometric center of the page. His distinctive garments suggest that he may serve as an officer of the group, a majordomo, of the confraternity, perhaps. The protagonists of the scene, however, direct their gazes and gestures to his right, toward two figures one step in front of him that emerge as the main characters. They are a man and a woman wearing crowns and fancy European dress, holding hands and stepping forward confidently to greet the people around them. Although the viewer has a clear line of sight on their whole bodies and distinctive outfits, the pageantry surrounding them is not as easily readable. What makes the scene appear particularly chaotic is the treatment of the main compositional feature of the print, the division of the crowd in two groups: the processing performers on the one hand and bystanders greeting them on the other hand. The two sets are best distinguished to the right of the image, where musicians open the path for the royal cortege walking toward the right, while onlookers stand still, faces turned the opposite direction, toward the royal couple. The collapse of the two types of characters—revelers and bystanders—may be a compositional infelicity or the result of a purposeful decision on the part of the printmaker to convey the black ceremony as disorderly and confused. On the one hand, the procession walks down a hilly, curving road, demanding a composition that made a perspectival rendering of the group a challenge that the lithographer may not have fully met.[29] On the other hand, a purposefully negative take on the subject matter at hand would not come as a surprise and in fact would aptly echo the disparaging tone of Koster's written description. In any case, instead of a readable divide between the two groups, faces and bodies meld in a jumble of limbs, heads, and gestures; the gunpowder smoke in the background, pebbly road, and dense vegetation surrounding the crowd further add to the graphic confusion.

In spite of the overall mayhem, significant elements clearly emerge from the image. One of them is the range of bodily attitudes recorded in the scene. In addition to an eye for detail, honed from drafting painstakingly thorough natural landscapes, Rugendas has demonstrated elsewhere in his work an interest in the representation of bodies in movement. This inclination derived in part from an aesthetic interest in the allegorical potential of gestures, in particular in service of his abolitionist sensibilities.[30] But he also aimed in images such as *Danse batuca* (Batuca dance), *Danse landu* (Landu dance), and *Jogar capoëra—ou danse de la guerre* (Capoeira play—or war dance) to capture specific choreographed movements and gestures.[31] In keeping with this trend, he sketched the figures of the coronation festival in a range of attitudes, which he must have perceived as notable, specific, and meaningful. Raising their arms high, throwing their hats off, or shooting pistols in the air, revelers in the background extend joyous salutations to the royal cortege. Others kneel and prostrate on the ground in deep salutation of the crowned couple, whose "chief power and superiority over their countrymen," Koster's words remind us, "is shown on the day of the festival."[32] These gestures of greeting and respect resonant across a broad range of cultures, including that of west-central Africa, appear side by side with more specific attitudes. One woman to the proper left of the couple, for instance, has crossed her arms on her chest and bowed her head in a pose readable through the lens of both Christian and central African iconography. The gesture has long featured in Catholic liturgy and iconography as a posture of humility, for example, in Annunciation scenes, where it connotes the Virgin's *humilatio* or humble acceptance of God's plan for her to birth his child. It also recalls Kongo poses as seen in nineteenth- and twentieth-century *ntadi* (steatite stone markers) or, earlier, in an enigmatic ivory object now in the Detroit Museum of Art.[33]

To the left of the print, a man extends his right hand toward the right arm of the king. Other black spectators have climbed up to better see and excitedly greet the royal cortege with wide arms gestures linked, perhaps, to central African acrobatic moves and poses central to ritual martial dances such as the African sangamento and its Brazilian kin, capoeira.[34] Broadly resonant, and hailing from a range of cultures, these meaningful gestures of respect mixing European and African body language express particularly well the real allegiance that the black king and queens mustered among their Brazilian subjects and demonstrate the power they exercised over them. The festivities that European travelers saw as comical were in fact affairs of utmost gravity for their participants, a seriousness the authorities—who at different times tolerated, feared, and attempted to control them—also keenly perceived.[35]

Considered from another angle, the chaotic rendering of the scene may in fact function as further evidence about the unfolding of the event. The European observer may have attempted to represent in visual form some key aesthetic features of central African and congado performances alike: asymmetric pairings, material accumulation, and rhythmic variations.[36] Many of the figures are in fact acting in pairs, such as the king and queen or the thumb piano and bagpipe players. A profusion of emblems and regalia accumulate signs of prestige around the main figures. The king has a crown, a scepter, feathers, galloons, a military uniform, and a sash; the confraternity's flags fly on high poles alongside wreaths and ribbons. Revelers simultaneously skip in rapid jumps, march, and slowly bow to their kings, in a range of choreographed and spontaneous moves, each following different rhythms. The print's busy composition may in fact ably visualize the complex aural and performative dimension of the event. This is a form of visual and aural synesthesia in keeping with the adage, "see the music, hear the dance," derived from ancient Greek writer Lucian; revived by twentieth-century choreographer George Balanchine; and, closer to the point, ably reused by African art historian Frederick Lamp in "rethinking African art," in particular, danced masquerade traditions.[37]

A step away from the main fray, on either side of the crowd, European men watch the procession in a reminder of the power structure within which the event takes place, tolerated but firmly framed by imperial Brazil's elite of predominantly Portuguese descent. Two travelers on horseback, to the left, wait for the road to clear as they look down at the scene. Humorously, their horses turn their heads toward the print's viewers, with knowing looks, weary of the commotion. A garbed friar to the right looks at the procession with a neutral expression, in keeping with the church's ambiguous position toward the coronation festivals, neither clearly condemning nor fully supporting them. Finally, two military men of color enclose the scene, embodying the control the ruling elite exerted even in events carving spaces of relative freedom for the black population.

In addition to these interpretable figures, another significant but enigmatic presence is that of the black man in a top hat to the far right of the image. He stands remarkably still, waiting, perhaps, for his turn to greet the royal couple. But his outfit approximates him more to the participants than to the bystanders. In addition to his remarkable top hat, his large loincloth, festooned at the bottom with a zigzag line, and the cloak and scarf wrapped over his right shoulder lends him a ceremonious air. Black male figures from Brazil depicted in Julião's and Rugendas's images as well as in other traveling artists' vignettes only occasionally wear wrappers around the legs outside of festive occasions.[38] The man standing proudly is thus likely dressed up for the feast day, whether or not he belongs to the confraternity. A possible reading of his outfit and dignified stand would see them as sartorial and gestural statements of identity, yet ones not associated with the coronation festival. It is possible, for instance, to approximate him to the photograph of a man portrayed in Christiano Jr.'s studio circa 1865, wearing the full regalia of Kongo nobility, which he had ostensibly reinvented with the modest means his low social standing in Brazil afforded him (fig. 6.4).[39] We could also conjecture that he and the short-haired female figure next to him could be the Congo king and queen who served in some sodalities, as mentioned earlier, as pendants to the Creole royal couple, pictured in the center. Another parallel to the outfit the man wears for the holiday is the use of the particular headgear on the African continents as a statement of both modernity and tradition in a variety of contexts, which art historian Monica Visonà discusses in her essay, "Warriors in Top Hats."[40]

If a definitive reading of the figure remains elusive, considering the many possibilities embedded in the man's outfit and its contrast with the festival, performers brings to the fore once more the multiplicity of individual points of views and actions that made up the African and Afro-descendant experience in slavery-era Brazil. Prominent men and women figured in the print used European clothing and regalia to craft a variety of visual statements of identity, group belonging, and social status. The diversity of reconfiguration of European finery among the festival goers and onlookers illustrates particularly well the nimble, creative, and sophisticated manner in which Africans and Afro-descendants reckoned with the possibilities that the American visual, material, and social environment afforded them.

FIGURE 6.4 Christiano Jr., *African Man in Rio de Janeiro*, ca. 1865. Photograph, 9 × 6 cm. Central Archive of the Instituto do Patrimônio Histórico e Artístico Nacional–Section Rio de Janeiro: Collection Christiano Jr. Photo: IPHAN.

FACT OR FICTION?

The product of a long and not entirely amicable publication process, the *Fête de Sainte Rosalie* lithograph is not directly by Rugendas's hand. Although trained in printmaking, he did not participate in the creation of the later part of the *Voyage pittoresque* that appeared after his departure from Paris and the beginning of his second, fifteen-year-long Latin American journey in 1831. Rather, two French artists working for Godefroy Engelmann, Jules Villeneuve and Victor Adam, produced the print after one or several of the German traveler's sketches. This complex creation history contributed to the image's ambivalent fate, considered at times as an irreplaceable early document of a black king and queen coronation festival and on other occasions as an unreliable product of European exotic fantasies replete of artistic clichés.[41] Yet, in spite of the unresolved—and warranted—doubts about its documentary value, the *Sainte Rosalie* lithograph has been used time and again to illustrate black festive life, lending it an "over familiarity" that has, in the words of historian

Marcus Wood, "turned [European traveling artists' images of Brazil] into visual cliché."[42] The composition appears, for instance, as an illustration or cover design, sometimes without being discussed, in a range of publications about slavery or Afro-Brazilian experiences.[43] Images featuring African ritual or everyday life by other nineteenth-century traveling artists such as Frenchman Jean-Baptiste Debret followed a similar trajectory.[44] Used as illustrations presented without critical framing, they have not been given the opportunity to fulfill their potential as historical documents.

Historian Mary Karasch wrote already in 1987 about the ability of these images to serve as a corrective to the blindness of what she calls "elite sources" to the presence of Africans in nineteenth-century Brazil.[45] The country's administrative and commercial upper class, who produced the bulk of the written and visual archive, did not concern themselves much with the lower echelons of society. In contrast, the European artists that arrived in the country as part of naturalist or artistic expeditions, in search of picturesque and local color, did not fail to notice and record the enslaved population in their writings and sketches. Often steeped in abolitionist thought prevalent in Europe at the time but also eager to seize exotic sights and register mores and customs in a mode they deemed scientific, Rugendas and his colleagues left us an immense visual corpus envisioning the African presence in Portuguese America. Hundreds of Africans of various origins and status, involved in a range of activities, appear in the artists' sketchbooks, as well as some of their more ambitious compositions in a vibrant archive making visible slavery, the enslaved, and the freed in nineteenth-century Brazil.

Yet the pitfalls of these images are immediately evident. "Few" of the foreigners who had recently arrived in Brazil, Karasch pointedly writes, "were able to avoid ethnocentric criticisms or color prejudices, while most were unable to penetrate the true meaning of what they described and painted."[46] Their visual productions, as any observations of an ethnographic nature, wove together multiple points of view: that of the artists but also that of the people they pictured, as well as that of the authorities who controlled their itineraries and access to particular locales. That is to say, traveling artists created images shaped all at once by the self-representation of the characters they supposedly transparently pictured, by the powerful, controlling gaze of the local elite, and by their own artistic subjectivities.[47] These pictures, which have become the paradigmatic representations of the black presence in urban Brazil in the nineteenth century, are eminently complex, layered images. They are irreplaceable documents of nineteenth-century Brazil, all the richer if approached with the critical attention they require.

I have attempted in this chapter to take a new look at the lithograph that neither dismisses its documentary potential nor understates the deep inter-pretative challenges its composition and edition process pose. A historically grounded visual analysis of the print paired cautiously with relevant written documentary sources brings about a reading that lends itself to rigorous his-torical inquiry. I regard Rugendas's image as interesting in two interrelated ways. On one level its busy composition captures a density of information that, indeed, makes it an irreplaceable, if not unquestionable, source of information on black coronation festivals. On another level the artistic circumstances of its production and composition are also key documents, shedding light on the staging, reception, and social role of Afro-Christian festivals in slavery-era Brazil. Being part fact and part fiction makes Rugendas's image, I argue, all the richer a historical artifact.

In this regard, the print actually gives us more information than just doc-umenting the coronation festivals. It tells us about conflicted attitudes and the ambivalent reception of Europeans toward the feast, from clergy to for-eigners. It also points to the multiplicity of status, perspectives, and social positions of members of the African diaspora and to the diversity of their forms of devotions in Brazil. Further, it sketches out the contours of the visible and the invisible in history and historiography. Visible is the racial bias and ethnocentric limitations of the European gaze and ear in seeing and depicting the event as chaotic. Less visible is the social organization of the African pop-ulation in Brazil. Even more faded are the many ways in which the memory of Africa lingered while also being reframed and reinvented in a push and pull between memory and innovation perhaps best embodied by the coexistence and eventual fading of Congo kings alongside Creole kings in confraternities such as that of the Rosario of Morro Alto.

This visual approach of the festival avoids the pitfall Rugendas and Koster did not dodge in their commentary of the *rosario* feast, that of considering African Christianity as a sign of acculturation. They insisted, "One may be surprised to find among the blacks so little traces of the religious ideas and customs from their land [i.e., Africa], but this . . . is proof that for the blacks the crossing that led them to the Americas is a true death" and "In Brazil, the blacks quickly become zealous Christians, and . . . all memories of paganism fade in them or become odious to them."[48] Yet it is abundantly clear, as illustrated by the coronation festivals and their multivalent links to Kongo Catholicism and its sangamentos, that Africans and their descendants used the concrete and intangible ritual spaces Christianity offered to nurture, celebrate, and eventually reinvent practices, thoughts, and memories from Africa into Afro-Brazilian gestures, worldviews, and myths.

NOTES

I extend my gratitude to Genevieve Dempsey and the anonymous readers for their thoughtful comments on previous versions of this chapter. I also thank Yale's Institute for Sacred Music for its financial and logistical support of the conference that led to this project and the American Academy in Rome for time and space to finish this chapter.

1. Cécile Fromont, *The Art of Conversion: Christian Visual Culture in the Kingdom of Kongo* (Chapel Hill: University of North Carolina Press, 2014).

2. William Dillon Piersen, *Black Yankees: The Development of an Afro-American Subculture in Eighteenth-Century New England* (Amherst: University of Massachusetts Press, 1988), 117–42; Jeffrey R. Kerr-Ritchie, *Rites of August First: Emancipation Day in the Black Atlantic World* (Baton Rouge: Louisiana State University Press, 2007); Eileen Southern, *The Music of Black Americans: A History* (New York: Norton, 1997); Bridget Brereton, *Social Life in the Caribbean* (Oxford: Heinemann Educational, 1985), 57; Jeroen Dewulf, "Pinkster: An Atlantic Creole Festival in a Dutch-American Context," *Journal of American Folklore* 126, no. 501 (2013): 245–71; Dewulf, *From the Kingdom of Kongo to Congo Square: Kongo Dances and the Origins of the Mardi Gras Indians* (Lafayette: University of Louisiana at Lafayette Press, 2017); Sue Peabody, "'A Dangerous Zeal': Catholic Missions to Slaves in the French Antilles, 1635–1800," *French Historical Studies* 25, no. 1 (2002): 79–80; David M. Guss, "The Selling of San Juan: The Performance of History in an Afro-Venezuelan Community," *American Ethnologist* 20, no. 3 (1993): 451–73.

3. For historical studies of the Brazilian case, see Marina de Mello e Souza, *Reis negros no Brasil escravista: História da festa de coroação de Rei Congo* (Belo Horizonte, Brazil: Editora

da Universidade Federal de Minas Gerais, 2002); Patricia Ann Mulvey, "The Black Lay Brotherhoods of Colonial Brazil: A History" (PhD diss., City University of New York, 1976); Luís da Câmara Cascudo, *Dicionário do folclore brasileiro* (Rio de Janeiro: Instituto Nacional do Livro, Ministério da Educação e Cultura, 1962); Silvia Hunold Lara, "Significados cruzados: As embaixadas de congos na Bahia setecentista," in *Carnavais e outras f(r)estas*, ed. Maria Clementina Pereira Cunha (Campinas: Editora Unicamp, 2001); Julita Scarano, *Devoção e escravidão: A irmandade de Nossa Senhora do Rosario dos pretos no distrito diamantino no século XVIII*, 2nd ed., vol. 357, Coleção Brasiliana (São Paulo: Companhia Editora Nacional, 1976); and Mary C. Karasch, *Slave Life in Rio de Janeiro, 1808–1850* (Princeton: Princeton University Press, 1987).

4. For Rugendas and the voyage, see Pablo Diener, *Rugendas e o Brasil*, ed. Maria de Fátima G. Costa and Johann Moritz Rugendas (São Paulo: Capivara, 2012), 134. For a broader contextualization of the works of traveling artists to Brazil, see Ana Lucia Araujo, *Brazil Through French Eyes: A Nineteenth-Century Artist in the Tropics* (Albuquerque: University of New Mexico Press, 2015).

5. The two lithographs labeled as designed after Debret rather than Rugendas are *Vue d'Olinda* in the first division, cahier 6, plate 30, and *Colonie Européenne près d'Ilheos* in the third division, cahier 5, plate 24, in Johann Moritz Rugendas, *Voyage pittoresque dans le Brésil* (Paris: Engelmann, 1835). For a catalogue raisonné of Debret, see Júlio Bandeira, *Debret e o Brasil: Obra completa, 1816–1831*, ed. Pedro Corrêa do Lago (Rio de Janeiro: Capivara, 2007).

6. About Huber, see Charles E. McClelland, *The German Historians and England: A Study*

in *Nineteenth-Century Views* (Cambridge: Cambridge University Press, 1971), 245–46.

7. Henry Koster, *Travels in Brazil* (London: Longman, Hurst, Rees, Orme, and Brown, 1816), 273–75. See the longer discussion of Koster's writings in Dawson's chapter, in this volume.

8. For black confraternities in Portugal, see Didier Lahon, "Esclavage et confréries noires au Portugal durant l'Ancien Régime (1441–1830)" (PhD diss., École des Hautes Études en Sciences Sociales, 2001). For Brazil, see Mulvey, "Black Lay Brotherhoods." For the Kongo, see Fromont, *Art of Conversion*, 202–6. For Angola, see Linda M. Heywood, "The Angolan-Afro-Brazilian Cultural Connections," *Slavery and Abolition* 20, no. 1 (1999): 13–14.

9. Traders and slave owners, as well as the enslaved themselves, used *nações*, or nations, as markers of collective or individual identity, sometimes in lieu of patronyms. The nation names referred to regions on the African coast from where enslaved individuals or groups presumably originated but also encompassed a Brazil-honed significance. See Camilla Agostini, "Africanos e a formação de identidades no além-mar: Um estudo de etnicidade na experiência africana no Rio de Janeiro do século XIX," *Revista História e Perspectivas* 1, no. 39 (2009).

10. Elizabeth W. Kiddy, *Blacks of the Rosary: Memory and History in Minas Gerais, Brazil* (University Park: Pennsylvania State University Press, 2005), 78–79.

11. The Morro Alto Rosary Confraternity is known under a variety of names, referring to its location on the Morro Alto or Alto da Cruz or Morro do Alto da Cruz; its situation in the locality known as Antônio Dias, which later became part of the modern city of Ouro Preto; or the name of its church, Santa Iphigênia, also written Ifigênia or Efigênia. Another black rosary confraternity in what is now Ouro Preto was seated in another parish, in its own Church of Our Lady of the Rosary, known for its role in the Triunfo Eucharistico festival in 1733 on the occasion of the translation of the Holy Sacrament from the temple of Our Lady of the Rosary to the Church of Pilar. For their self-celebratory publication of the *Triunfo eucharistico* of 1733, see Lisa Voigt, *Spectacular Wealth:*

Festivals in Colonial South American Mining Towns (Austin: University of Texas Press, 2016). About the schism, see "Compromisso da Irmandade de Nossa Senhora do Rosário dos Pretos, denominada do Alto da Cruz," 1733, códice 1733–1788, Casa dos Contos, Arquivo Eclesiástico da Paróquia de Nossa Senhora da Conceição/Antônio Dias, cited in Kiddy, *Blacks of the Rosary*, 81.

12. "Compromisso da Irmandade de Nossa Senhora," cited in Marcos Magalhães de Aguiar, "Tensões e conflitos entre párocos e irmandades na Capitania de Minas Gerais," *Textos de História: Revista do Programa de Pós-graduação em História da UnB* 5, no. 2 (1997): 85. Note that most black confraternities in colonial Brazil relied on their own resources, as did the one in Morro Alto; their funding and struggles for autonomy are not exceptional but rather typical.

13. See the online records about the two churches abstracted from the register of Brazilian national patrimony: "Igreja Matriz de Nossa Senhora da Conceição de Antônio Dias (Ouro Preto, MG)," Instituto do Patrimônio Histórico e Artístico Nacional, accessed October 2, 2018, http://portal.iphan.gov.br /ans.net/tema_consulta.asp?Linha=tc_belas .gif&Cod=1381; and "Igreja de Santa Efigênia (Ouro Preto, MG)," Instituto do Patrimônio Histórico e Artístico Nacional, accessed October 2, 2018, http://portal.iphan.gov.br/ans .net/tema_consulta.asp?Linha=tc_belas.gif &Cod=1376. See also Percival Tirapeli, *Igrejas barrocas do Brasil* (São Paulo: Metalivros, 2008), 248–49, 254–57, 246–47.

14. Kiddy, *Blacks of the Rosary*, 125. About the rosary confraternity in Brazil, see, in addition to the works cited elsewhere in this chapter, Mulvey, "Black Lay Brotherhoods"; João José Reis, "Identidade e diversidade nas irmandades no tempo da escravidão," *Tempo: Revista do Departamento de História da Universidade Federal Fluminense* 2, no. 3 (1996): 7–33; Scarano, *Devoção e escravidão*.

15. Cécile Fromont, "Dancing for the King of Congo from Early Modern Central Africa to Slavery-Era Brazil," *Colonial Latin American Review* 22, no. 2 (2013): 184–208. Early mentions of the king of Congo in Brazil appear in Koster,

Travels in Brazil, 273–74. Johann Emanuel Pohl describes a celebration of Saint Ifigeny with Congo instruments. *Reise im innern von Brasilien: Auf allerhöchsten befehl Seiner Majestät des Kaisers von Österreich, Franz des Ersten, in den jahren, 1817–1821, unternommen und heraus-gegeben* (Wien, 1832), 82–83. Johann Baptist von Spix and Karl Friedrich Philipp von Martius mention a "king of Congo," a "queen Xinga," and the term "congada"; see *Reise in Brasilien auf befehl Sr. Majestät Maximilian Joseph I., königs von Baiern: In den jahren 1817 bis 1820 gemacht und beschrieben*, 3 vols. (München: Lindauer, 1823), 3:468–69.

16. Kiddy, *Blacks of the Rosary*, 127.

17. See Carlos Julião, *Riscos illuminados de figurinhos de brancos e negros dos uzos do Rio de Janeiro e Serro do Frio*, ed. Lygia da Fonseca and Fernandes da Cunha (Rio de Janeiro: Biblioteca Nacional, 1960); and Fromont, "Dancing for the King."

18. See Koster, *Travels in Brazil*, 274.

19. About Riedel, see George Ermakoff, *O negro na fotografia brasileira do século XIX* (Rio de Janeiro: Ermakoff Casa Editorial, 2004), 226–29.

20. Of course, one of the reasons for the similarities between the European representations resides in the biases they shared.

21. About the iconography of feathers as a marker of savagery and of the exotic in early modern art, see Stephanie Leitch, "Burgkmair's Peoples of Africa and India (1508) and the Origins of Ethnography in Print," *Art Bulletin* 91, no. 2 (2009): 134–59; and William C. Sturtevant, "La tupinambisation des Indiens d'Amérique du Nord," *Les Cahiers du Department d'Études Littéraires* 9 (1988): 293–303.

22. See, for example, depictions of feathers in the ritual and ceremonial outfits of central Africans in the seventeenth-century images published in Ezio Bassani and Giovanni Antonio Cavazzi, *Un Cappuccino nell'Africa nera del Seicento: I disegni dei Manoscritti Araldi del Padre Giovanni Antonio Cavazzi da Montecuccolo*, Quaderni Poro 4 (Milano: Associazione "Poro," 1987); Paolo Collo and Silvia Benso, *Sogno: Bamba, Pemba, Ovando e altre contrade dei regni di Congo, Angola e*

adiacenti, Guide impossibili (Milano: Ricci, 1986).

23. See Souza, *Reis negros no Brasil escravista*; Fromont, "Dancing for the King."

24. Fromont, *Art of Conversion*.

25. About the *Moros e Christianos*, see Voigt's, Dawson's, Valerio's, and Dewulf's chapters, in this volume.

26. Kiddy, *Blacks of the Rosary*, 127.

27. For the preference for kings born in Africa, see, for Portugal, Maria do Rosário Pimentel and Instituto de Cultura Ibero-Atlântica, *Portugal e Brasil no advento do mundo moderno: Sextas jornadas de história Ibero-Americana* (Lisbon: Edições Colibri, 2001), 385. See also Kiddy, *Blacks of the Rosary*.

28. Daniela Bleichmar, *Visual Voyages: Images of Latin American Nature from Columbus to Darwin* (New Haven: Yale University Press, 2017), 165–69.

29. Rugendas's original design or designs did not survive; it is difficult to judge from whose hands the composition and its infelicities originated.

30. See Robert Slenes, "African Abrahams, Lucretias, and Men of Sorrows: Allegory and Allusion in the Brazilian Anti-Slavery Lithographs (1827–1835) of Johann Moritz Rugendas," in *Representing the Body of the Slave*, ed. Thomas Wiedemann and Jane Gardner (London: Cass, 2002).

31. *Danse batuca, Danse landu*, and *Jogar capoëra* appear respectively in Rugendas, *Voyage pittoresque dans le Brésil*, 4e div., cahier 16, plates 16, 17, 18.

32. Koster, *Travels in Brazil*, 273.

33. For the Virgin's *humilatio*, see, for example, Michael Baxandall, *Painting and Experience in Fifteenth-Century Italy* (Oxford: Oxford University Press, 1971), 51, 55; for a *ntadi* example, see the one from the Royal Museum for Central Africa published in Christiane Falgayrettes-Leveau and Musée Dapper (Paris, France), *Le geste kôngo* (Paris: Musée Dapper, 2002), 103. The ivory box from the Detroit Institute of Arts, inv. 25.183, is published in Ezio Bassani et al., *Africa and the Renaissance: Art in Ivory* (New York: Center for African Art, 1988), fig. 190, 248. See also Jay A. Levenson, *Encompassing the Globe: Portugal and the World*

in the Sixteenth and Seventeenth Centuries, 3 vols. With Diogo Ramada Curto and Jack Turner (Washington, D.C.: Sackler Gallery, Smithsonian Institution, 2007), 2:84. Of course, the two sets of readings of the gestures in the west-central African context may in fact be connected through the Kongo's centuries-long engagement with Christian visual culture.

34. About the martial practice of capoeira, see also Dawson's chapter, in this volume.

35. See Furtado's chapter, in this volume.

36. About the aesthetic of accumulation in African art, see, for example, Arnold Rubin, "Accumulation: Power and Display in African Sculpture," *Artforum* 13, no. 9 (1975): 35–47.

37. In the words of the Greek poet: "No, in the words of the Delphic oracle, whosoever beholds dancing must be able 'to understand the mute and hear the silent' dancer." See Lucian, "The Dance," in *The Passing of Peregrinus; The Runaways; Toxaris or Friendship; The Dance; Lexiphanes; The Eunuch; Astrology; The Mistaken Critic; The Parliament of the Gods; The Tyrannicide; Disowned,* Loeb Classical Library 302 (Cambridge, Mass.: Harvard University Press, 1936), 5:264–65; Frederick Lamp, *See the Music, Hear the Dance: Rethinking African Art at the Baltimore Museum of Art* (Munich: Prestel, 2004).

38. One example of a male figure pictured with a loincloth outside of a ceremonial or ritual context is the milk seller in Julião, *Riscos illuminados de figurinhos,* plate 18. Top hats appear a little more frequently, often as part of the livery of men in domestic service, most memorably in the circa 1860 photograph of two sedan chair carriers, on the head of a black servant, whose nonchalant attitude in the face of the camera and his arduous task has made an icon of Afro-Brazil's indomitable spirit. See the photograph in Ermakoff, *O negro na fotografia brasileira,* 73.

39. Fromont, "Dancing for the King," 201–4.

40. Monica Blackmun Visonà, "Warriors in Top Hats: Images of Modernity and Military Power on West African Coasts," in *A Companion to Modern African Art,* ed. Gitti Salami and Monica Blackmun Visonà (Chichester, West Sussex: Wiley Blackwell, 2013).

41. Elizabeth W. Kiddy talks about the documentary value of the image, in "Who Is the King of Congo? A New Look at African and Afro-Brazilian Kings in Brazil," in *Central Africans and Cultural Transformations in the American Diaspora,* ed. Linda M. Heywood (Cambridge: Cambridge University Press 2002), 173.

42. Marcus Wood, *Black Milk: Imagining Slavery in the Visual Cultures of Brazil and America* (Oxford: Oxford University Press, 2013), 37.

43. Among other examples, the composition appears in such important publications as the cover of the English edition of the important volume by Mariza de Carvalho Soares, *People of Faith: Slavery and African Catholics in Eighteenth-Century Rio de Janeiro,* Latin America in Translation/En Traducción/Em Tradução (Durham: Duke University Press, 2011). It features also in the excellent João José Reis, *Death Is a Festival: Funeral Rites and Rebellion in Nineteenth-Century Brazil,* Latin America in Translation/En Traducción/Em Tradução (Chapel Hill: University of North Carolina Press, 2003), 59. It is also in Kiddy, *Blacks of the Rosary,* 134.

44. Other nineteenth-century visual projects are still less known, such as those by Thomas Ender or attributed to Mary Graham. See Andrea C. Valente, "Black Slaves *in Farbe*: Representations of the Subaltern in Thomas Ender's Landscape Paintings from Old Rio," *Austrian Studies* 20 (2012): 24–42.

45. Karasch, *Slave Life in Rio de Janeiro,* xvi. The African population in nineteenth-century Brazil was a diverse group composed of men and women of various ethnicities, born in different locales of the African continents, as well as their Brazil-born *crioulo* descendants, including those of mixed ethnicity or race. Legal status also ranged from enslaved to *forros,* or free-born.

46. Ibid., xvii.

47. See Araujo, *Brazil Through French Eyes.*

48. Rugendas, *Voyage pittoresque dans le Brésil,* part 4, fasc. 10, p. 28.

FURTHER READING

Primary Sources

Julião, Carlos. *Riscos illuminados de figurinhos de brancos e negros dos uzos do Rio de Janeiro e Serro do Frio*, edited by Lygia da Fonseca and Fernandes da Cunha. Rio de Janeiro: Biblioteca Nacional, 1960.

Rugendas, Johann Moritz. *Voyage pittoresque dans le Brésil*. Paris: Engelmann, 1835.

Secondary Sources

Karasch, Mary C. *Slave Life in Rio de Janeiro, 1808–1850*. Princeton: Princeton University Press, 1987.

Kiddy, Elizabeth W. *Blacks of the Rosary: Memory and History in Minas Gerais, Brazil*. University Park: Pennsylvania State University Press, 2005.

Mello e Souza, Marina de. *Reis negros no Brasil escravista: História da festa de coroação de Rei Congo*. Belo Horizonte, Brazil: Editora da Universidade Federal de Minas Gerais, 2002.

Slenes, Robert. "African Abrahams, Lucretias, and Men of Sorrows: Allegory and Allusion in the Brazilian Anti-slavery Lithographs (1827–1835) of Johann Moritz Rugendas." In *Representing the Body of the Slave*, edited by Thomas Wiedemann and Jane Gardner, 147–68. London: Cass, 2002.

CHAPTER 7

The Orisa House That Afro-Catholics Built

Africana Antecedents to Yoruba Religious Formation in Trinidad

DIANNE M. STEWART

Across the centuries Orisa devotees in the Americas and the Caribbean have incorporated Catholic elements into their ritual and ceremonial lives.[1] Adherents in Trinidad are no exception. Scholars note that close to twenty of the more than sixty powers they worship are from the Catholic tradition, and devotees typically assign these Catholic personalities Yoruba counterparts. For example, saints such as Peter, Catherine, and Michael are associated respectively with the Orisa powers Ebeje (Ibeji), Oya, and Ogun. Inspired in part by this panoply of apparent interreligious theistic entities, scholars have argued for decades that Afro-Euro syncretism is a definitive feature of the Orisa religion in Trinidad. In fact, in most studies, similar to other African heritage religions of the Caribbean and the Americas, Trinidadian Orisa finds a cozy position under the "syncretism" taxon categorizing the marriage between African indigenous spirituality and Euro-Catholicism during the slave and indentured labor periods.

At first notice the logic of opting for the classificatory possibilities the syncretic construct evokes seems quite reasonable. Syncretism is a seductive trope with a *veneer* of truth concerning endless situations of human encounters across the globe. But far too many scholars apply this preferred trope so indiscriminately in African diaspora religious studies with no reflection on the term's alien status vis-à-vis the inner logics of traditions such as Orisa, Candomblé, Vodou, and Lucumí. The operative assumption is that African diasporic religions are essentially syncretic, while recognized "world" religions such as Christianity and Judaism are not. All too often this clichéd category becomes a dead signifier gesturing toward taxonomic and typological preoccupations in scholarly agendas. Imposed on complex emic religious orientations, it obscures the internal dynamics of an engaged religious consciousness and forecloses grounded theoretical interpretations of African heritage religious cultures in the Americas and the Caribbean. This chapter argues for a different approach to theorizing Orisa religious formation in Trinidad as a process not determined by syncretic fusions of African spirituality and Euro-Western Christianity. Rather, interpreting ellipses within and reading between the lines of archival records, it locates an institutional genesis for the tradition within a ritual dialogue involving ex-enslaved Afro-Catholic communities during the latter half of the nineteenth century.

Although not much is known about the conditions in which the Orisa religion took root in Trinidad, we do know that it was not a slave religion.[2] Established by liberated Yoruba indentured laborers in the aftermath of emancipation (1840s–60s), the Orisa religious culture, with its elaborate veneration of a family of powers—also called Orisa—was known by the name of one of its most prominent deities, "Shango," for most of the twentieth century, if not before.[3] Nearly all studies of the tradition, however, are anthropological and fall short of providing any substantive historical framing of Orisa beginnings. Even cursory historical inquiries into antecedent African cultural patterns and cross-cultural exchanges that might provide additional resources for understanding the perceived syncretic identities of Orisa and other African diaspora heritage religions are lacking. The dearth of nuanced historical studies leads most scholars to presume, as does Steven Glazier, that "Caribbean slaves had more than a passing interest in the religion of their masters." They weren't simply resourceful or hospitable when they adopted Catholic saints into their ritual practices. Rather, "they had an urgent need," Glazier insists, "to incorporate European gods (and the powers of those gods) into their own lives. This urgent need, too," he conjectures, "is perhaps at the root of perceived correspondences between Sango, Saint John, Saint Jerome, Saint Peter, and Saint Barbara."[4]

Unable to dodge the ghost of the Herskovits-Frazier debate, Glazier's perspective typifies widespread uninterrogated accounts of "syncretic" Afro-diasporic religions that have left little room for alternative starting points in studies of African religious cultures in the Caribbean and Americas. Rooted in the dilemmas of respectability politics, beginning in the early twentieth century, Melville Herskovits and E. Franklin Frazier launched scholarly agendas that negated established theories of black deviance. Their efforts to address reigning stereotypes about black "difference" (read: "black pathology") led Herskovits to locate the source of that "difference" within a respectable African heritage whose influence could be documented across the Americas and the Caribbean. Frazier, however, refuted Herskovits's theory of African "retentions" in the U.S. context and instead argued that Euro-American traditions and institutions, reshaped through the African American cultural prism and imagination, rapidly replaced African ones. He furthermore disputed any hint of social Darwinism in contemporary scholarly assessments of "the Negro problem" by identifying the institutions of slave trading and slavery as the source of black "difference."[5]

As research on African diaspora religions intensified during the mid-twentieth century, the ideologies that shaped the Herskovits-Frasier debate about African heritage and African diaspora religious formation seemed inescapable. Scholars were compelled to enter the polemic from some angle, even as they endeavored to advance the field of African diaspora religious studies from their varied disciplinary locations. The question of how "African" or how "European" particular African diaspora religious cultures were influenced the parameters of scholarly inquiry and imagination when approaching and analyzing data. For example, in the case of Trinidad, few scholars have examined how Yoruba custodians of the Orisa tradition responded to existing African religious institutions and customs. David Trotman's position is that "the heterogeneous and numerically small slave population [20,656] for the short-lived slave society [1783–1838] did not bequeath a sufficiently cohesive religious culture to which subaltern newcomers were forced to assimilate."[6] Missionary documents that comment on postemancipation Afro-Creole ceremonies, however, beg the question of whether Trotman may have drawn this conclusion prematurely.

I argue that something else accounts for the "perceived correspondences" between Catholic saints and the Orisa in Trinidad. Additionally, the oft-framed inquiries into Catholic (read: white) and indigenous African dimensions of Yoruba-Orisa ritual life can converge differently to produce new knowledge if scholars denaturalize the association of Catholicism with a monolithic Euro-Western religious heritage. Placing historical ethnography and missionary records in conversation, the ensuing analysis moves in exactly this direction, challenging unexamined assumptions about syncretism and African heritage religions in the African diaspora generally and particularly within the Yoruba Trinidadian diaspora. Yoruba-Orisa custodians were not enslaved, but they *were* captives. And to address their condition of captivity, they, with the support of their emancipated African-descended neighbors, mobilized ritual, political, and cultural memories of sovereignty and social belonging that privileged fusions of Africana religious cultures over direct appropriations of Euro-colonial gods.

Archival records pertaining to postemancipation Afro-Catholic festivals offer a fertile starting point to investigate connections that likely emerged among formerly enslaved African descendants and liberated Yorubas between the 1840s and the 1890s. It appears that, when forging a religious culture in Trinidad, liberated Yorubas began to take cues and direction not primarily from Euro-colonial institutional patterns but from their ex-enslaved Afro-Creole neighbors. To explore such cues and connections in more detail, we might ask, "Why was the Yoruba ritual system called Shango in Trinidad? And why were its shrines and rituals housed in a palace?" In "Whither Sango? An Inquiry into Sango's 'Authenticity' and Prominence in the Caribbean," Glazier attempts an answer to this first question, explaining that "the term 'Sango was . . . introduced . . . by four prominent American anthropologists: Melville J. Herskovits, Frances Henry, William Bascom, and George Eaton Simpson," since each of them "dealt with informants who saw themselves primarily as followers of Sango. While many of their informants' public rituals were open to other members of the *orisa* pantheon, their personal (house) altars were dedicated solely to Sango."[7] Glazier's explanation is less than satisfying, however, for it fails to account for the term's popular designation of Orisa devotion in Trinidad before Melville Herskovits—the first of this scholarly quartet to travel to Trinidad—conducted and published his research between 1939 and 1947.

By the mid-1930s Trinidadian calypsonians began recording songs about the Yoruba religion, including Gerald Clark and the Keskidee Trio's "Shango" (1935), Tiger's "Yaraba Shango" (1936), Cobra's "Shango Song" (1937), and Lord Caresser's "Shango" (1938). Roaring Lion's "Shango Dance" (1940), released the year following Herskovits's research trip to Trinidad, only expanded this repertoire, and other calypsos addressing Trinidad's Yoruba-based religious complex as "Shango" would appear in ensuing decades.[8] Herskovits himself became interested in studying Trinidadian "Shango" in 1929 because his ship docked briefly at Port of Spain on a return trip from Dutch Guiana (Suriname). This timely layover allowed his serendipitous discovery of a citizen's complaint about local "Shangoo" ceremonies.[9] Herskovits's field diaries offer even further indication that when he finally returned to Trinidad ten years later, residents from the community he studied in Toco, far from the center of Shango activities in Port of Spain, regularly referenced the Yoruba-Orisa religion by the term "Shango."[10]

Regarding the second question, Glazier does not address directly why Yoruba shrines and rituals were housed in a palace, but he expresses curiosity about why "words for buildings, [*palais, tapia,* and *chapelle*] continue to be referred to in the French, while leadership titles [*iyá* and *mọgbà*] are expressed in African terms."[11] Glazier pauses at this apparent conundrum because the discussion of Orisa beginnings in Trinidad remains ensnared within an ossified narrative that situates a merger of African deities and Euro-Catholic saints at the center of the tradition. I maintain that fundamental yet largely overlooked aspects of Afro-Creole Catholic ceremonies arguably explain the reason particular French terms became salient within the Orisa ritual vocabulary. My theory is that Yoruba settlers in Trinidad were *not* the original architects of the Orisa *palais,* as commonly assumed today; the palais structure was initially a borrowed space.

At least since 1838, and before Yoruba-identified people groups came in droves to Trinidad, the palais had an institutional legacy in the ceremonial life of Afro-Catholic communities, housing their spiritual, cultural, and political expressions of sovereignty. Despite the British conquest of Trinidad in 1802, the colony's unique multicultural composition during the eighteenth and nineteenth centuries meant that these Afro-Catholic communities were composed of French-Creole speakers whose linguistic culture had not even begun to feel the intrusion of Anglicization and the English tongue before the last decade of the nineteenth century.[12] During the period of massive transportation of liberated Yorubas to Trinidad (1840s–60s), the Afro-Creole term for any royal residence would not have been "palace"; it would have been *palais*—and Afro-Creoles apparently were the only Trinidadians at the time who held special palais ceremonies.

In his 1893 diary, chronicling two and a half years of missionary work in Trinidad (October 1882–January 1885), Dominican priest Marie-Bertrand Cothonay describes an annual emancipation-celebration ritual performed in 1882 by ex-enslaved persons in Carenage that involved the erection of a palais. Hardly matched in English sources, this French account offers rare insight into the lesser-known religiocultural world of a people whose traditions typically were buried beneath the generic indictment of the colonial signifier "obeah":

I have told you that our blacks of Trinidad and those of Carénage in particular, are former slaves or sons of slaves. Upon emancipation, which took place the 1st of August (1838), they resolved to celebrate every year, that very day, a solemn holiday, *in perpetual remembrance*. That holiday would begin in the morning with a high mass, with heavy musical participation, blessed bread, procession, etc., which prolonged itself over the course of three days, during which there was feasting, dances and orgies without name, all souvenirs of African life. The incumbent parish priest, initially well liked by his parishioners, had finally obtained, after much patience and many struggles, the suppression of this holiday of the devil. Since six years prior, it was no longer celebrated in Carénage. . . . Last year [1882], unbeknownst to him, the former slaves gathered in concert, brashly to take up the old traditions. They raised up therefore a bamboo hut, covered in *feuilles de carates* [palm leaves]; and bestowed upon it the pompous name of *palais*. A negro was named *king*. The alimentary provisions, drink, etc., accumulated around the palace. The 1st of August arrived, and the parishioners of P. Poujade piously attended the customary mass. At night, the good priest heard again the beating of the horrible African drum. Without a doubt; it was the holiday of the Negroes. During three days and three nights, Carénage was sullied by bachanalias the like of which it had never seen, doubtless to compensate for those that had been suppressed in the preceding years. The following Sunday, the priest railed, but . . . impassive parishioners! . . . In these sorts of holidays, the king, usually elected by popular acclaim, is the one who gathers the necessary funds, makes invitations, presents the blessed bread, etc. . . , and opens the dance. The king of this year was called Peter, Pierre. He is approaching fifty and has not yet received confirmation; he has attended preparatory instruction, and is counting on being admitted to the sacrament. Doubtless, he believes that the priest is ignorant of his participation in the holiday of the devil, or that he would not dare to reject a great character such as himself. But he is mistaken. One evening, at my request, the priest had him come to the parsonage, in the company of an accomplice, himself a former king. I hoped to be able to manage the affair amicably with the two principal parties, to obtain from them the abandonment of projects, which were impermissible to me. But, the conversation had but begun, when the priest interjected himself, with impertinent reproaches that compromised all of the success of my designs. Our poor Negro kings retired, irritated, and absolutely refused to promise that which we asked of them, *viz.*, to demolish the *palais*, if they wished to take part in the confirmation.[13]

Cothonay's identification of these African parishioners with a slave past is credible, seeing how his larger 470-page *Trinidad* journal offers evidence that he was well aware of the distinctions between ex-enslaved and liberated Africans. On one occasion he describes having just met an Angolan nobleman who "still spoke his language."[14] Cothonay explains how the young prince was captured by slave traders, sold to the Portuguese, and eventually rescued by the British naval squadron while at sea and indicates having knowledge of "a good number of blacks who were brought to Trinidad under the same conditions as the Angolan prince."[15]

His account lends credence to my contention that the palais structure originally surfaced in tandem with Emancipation Day ceremonies among ex-enslaved African descendants in Trinidad. Every king or queen needs a "palace"—an arena to hold court and a theater of royal operations where political, cultural, and religious customs are tightly braided, symbolized, and reinforced in sacrosanct monarchic rituals. Studies of African diaspora societies, including several in this collection, document analogous regal productions unveiled at pageants and festive occasions in regions as disparate as Brazil, Jamaica, the northeastern United States and Saint Lucia.[16] The movement of African descendants across slave territories in the Western Hemisphere might have influenced the wide appeal these kinds of sovereignty rituals had among disparate Africana communities. But the unbearable weight of chattel enslavement could make sovereignty a principal preoccupation of social life among any population of bondpersons. It is reasonable then to consider sovereignty rituals as parallel developments among enslaved Africans and their descendants across diverse regions of the Western Hemisphere that also benefited from cross-fertilization through the intradiasporic movement of African people and the new elements they introduced to the cultures and communities they encountered.[17]

In the events described earlier, we can plausibly imagine that participants attached spiritual significance to the symbolic assertion and dramatic enactment of some if not all sovereignty rituals in a designated space—the palais—where a communally endorsed "king" oversaw the sharing of "blessed bread" and other provisions during a ceremony marked by intense drumming and dancing. Without additional sources we cannot know with certainty whether ancestors or African deities were invoked during sovereignty ceremonies. We can infer, however, that the palais edifice that liberated

Yorubas encountered in the postemancipation period actually did provide a "sufficiently cohesive" Africana religiocultural space conducive to welcoming the "subaltern newcomers'" Òrìṣà into Trinidad, especially the royal deity, Kábíyèsí Ṣàngó.[18]

Although definitive sources indicating exactly when Yoruba-Orisa devotees began associating their worship spaces with the Creole term *palais* are unavailable, Trotman's point that internal migration caused the dissolution of many Yoruba-Orisa palais during the cocoa and oil booms implies an active palais structure among Yoruba-Orisa devotees as early as the 1870s.[19] Additionally, oral data pertaining to liberated African groups in Trinidad describe how Yoruba newcomers "roofed" their living quarters and ritual palais "with thrash, usually leaves of the carat palm," the same *Sabal mauritiiformis* or *Sabal glaucescens* palm species Cothonay identifies in his description of the nineteenth-century Afro-Creole palais.[20] Most compelling, however, are accounts of nineteenth-century liberated Africans' ritual practices and built environment. They not only indicate conformity to patterns Cothonay attributes to Afro-Creole residents; they also confirm that liberated Africans participated in annual celebrations, including Afro-Creole Emancipation Day festivities:

> Animal sacrifice and possession were the spiritual cores of . . . [religious] ceremonies, which lasted from three days to a week. Such ceremonies involved much communal organization as regards fundraising, provision of food; accommodation of guests, and building of bamboo-framed, palm-covered tents, *chapelles* for housing sacred insignia such as flags, swords, food, and sacrificial vessels and consecrated musical instruments. These rites were held at particular times of the year, for instance to celebrate Emancipation and the New Year. And with the eventual syncretism of orisha with Catholic saints, the rites were increasingly held to synchronize with special dates in the Catholic Church calendar: an ebo would often be preceded by a mass which the Africans attended as a fraternity.[21]

Gathered from elders—a number of them having reached adolescence in the final decade of the nineteenth century—these details seem to corroborate an account of the "half religious, half civil" celebration our same Dominican missionary, Marie-Bertrand Cothonay, attended in San Fernando in 1885. Hosted by the society of Saint Dominique, participants (presumably Afro-Creole) displayed banners and flags for their patron saint. Cothonay goes on to describe elements of the moving panorama with attention to the palais. In his estimation there was nothing palatial about its rudimentary nineteenth-century architectural design. Rather, the palais captured the irony underlining such subaltern demonstrations of sovereignty in a colony "divided into castes as strongly marked as those of Hindustan," with African descendants stationed at the bottom:[22]

> Their procession was deployed with much order on the flanks of the Papuré hill; the women would recite the rosary, the men sang the litanies of the saints, the children, English canticles. I closed out the ceremony with a panegyric of saint Dominique in English. After the mass the civil holiday took place; the *King* of the Society appeared with his diadem in gilded paper and his vestments festooned in faux gold. One also saw the *Queen* present herself in her most magnificent ensemble; her function is to distribute the blessed bread; she presides with the king at the feast given by the Society. . . . Each one contributes, one with the chicken, one with the rice, one with the cassava, etc. This common meal takes place in the house one calls the *Palais*. To give you an idea, imagine twenty or so posts three meters high approximately on which a roof of palm leaves rests; no doors, no windows, for flooring, the earth. Such is the *Palais* of Their Majesties. The king and the queen are elected each year. They have the right to choose a vice-king and a vice-queen. There is also a governor whose vestments and attributes are determined.[23]

Cothonay's and Warner-Lewis's narratives suggest that Afro-Creole communities actually did establish palais sovereignty customs that Yoruba indentured laborers came to adopt in their confraternal activities and adapt to address their devotional obligations to the Orisa. In keeping with the antecedent Afro-Creole emancipation custom of electing a *roi* of the palais to represent a sovereign *nation*'s release from the tyranny of slavery, whom but Ṣàngó would a *nation* exiled from home elect to hold the title *king of the palace*?[24] Of all the Orisa worshipped in Trinidad, Ṣàngó was distinguished as the patron deity of the Ọ̀yọ́ Empire who repeatedly manifested in Ọ̀yọ́'s long lineage of kings and rulers. The fact that male Orisa leaders traditionally assumed the title of *mogba* in Trinidad is only additional evidence of the Yoruba community's preoccupation with Ọ̀yọ́ sovereignty rituals grounded in the cult of Ṣàngó, since the *mọ́gbà* were senior priests of Ṣàngó who served the royal shrine at Kòso, a capital city of the Ọ̀yọ́ Empire.[25]

Ṣàngó worship had spread across Yorùbá and neighboring Dahomean territories by the time Yorùbás were entering the slave trade in high numbers.

In addition, many Ọyọ́ Yorùbás became captives within the trade after the empire collapsed in the 1830s. Thus, some scholars have been satisfied with the conclusion that the high percentage of Sango worshippers among liberated Yorubas who settled in Trinidad after 1840 accounts for the eponymous relationship between their patron deity and the wider religious system.[26] This perspective is more than tenable, especially since twentieth-century scholarship provides a window into the Ṣàngó-based heritage symbols Yoruba-Orisa devotees invested with new significations under the roof of the Trinidadian palais. A 1977 exchange between the late Dr. James Adeyinka Olawaiye and Father Isaac, a Shango leader from the San Fernando area in southern Trinidad, indicates the significance of divine rulership personified through Shango aka Obakoso:

> Then Father Isaac invited me and the friends accompanying me to break bread with him in his house. During this social time together we discussed religious practices. He was eager to know more of Yoruba religious customs and concepts. For example, he asked me whether Obakoso was a town. I said, "No, but that Oyo is Sango's town and there is a gate there called Koso where several people, mostly women went to meet Sango and plead with him not to hang himself. That place where Sango returned home to heaven is called "Obakoso" or "Koso" which means, "The Chief or King does not hang himself."[27]

Maureen Warner-Lewis found references to Shango as "Obakoso" among the 160 Yoruba songs and chants she recorded from elder Yoruba-Trinidadians in 1968 and 1970. Additionally, one of her chief informants, Titi, described Shango as "Obakuso (king of Koso)." Melville Herskovits also encountered Orisa devotees in Port of Spain (Laventille) whose theistic community included the deity Aba Koso, a member of the "Thunder group," with his brothers "Shango" and "Dada." Frances Henry's extensive contact with Orisa leaders since the 1950s allowed her access to a collection of practices and customs spanning a good deal of the twentieth century, and she too confirms that Aba Koso had been a standard member of Trinidad's Yoruba-Orisa divine community during her "earlier period of fieldwork."[28]

The prominence of Sango in Trinidadian Orisa religion notwithstanding, it is curious that, with the exception of neighboring Grenada, Yorubas who settled in other regions of the African diaspora during the nineteenth century did not come to identify the name of Sango with their collective religious practice. What accounts for this discrepancy? It could only be the ritual dialogue that took place between communities of ex-enslaved Catholic African descendants and communities of liberated Yoruba settlers in Trinidad.

RETHINKING AFRICAN RETENTIONS AND SYNCRETISM IN YORUBA-ORISA DIASPORA STUDIES

Yoruba exiles did not enter Trinidad in shackles, but their displacement from their homelands was the final stage of an involuntary journey that commenced with the same trauma of captivity, branding, and commodification that the formerly enslaved Afro-Creole population collectively endured.[29] Oral narratives further indicate that many such immigrants experienced the indentured labor program as a deceptive scheme concocted by colonial officials and landowning classes that subjected them to conditions of bondage.[30] By the time Yoruba exiles began pouring into Trinidad in the 1840s, both groups (the Yoruba and the Afro-Creole) knew something about enslavement and sovereignty, which in part might explain why many Yoruba exiles "lived in close relationships with Creole blacks."[31]

Holidays presented ideal circumstances for exchanging customs and cementing bonds across diverse communities of African descent, and the Afro-Creole emancipation holiday conceivably provided a space for some Yorubas to ritualize their yearning for home. To take one example, Trinidad's repertoire of Yoruba songs includes "Yé! Ekún ara wa la mí sun," a dirge reportedly performed as a melody on August 1, the anniversary of emancipation. Its appearance in Melville and Frances Herskovits's 1939 field recordings suggests that, at some point in their exchanges with Afro-Creole residents, perhaps owning the resonances between African exile and African enslavement in Trinidad, Yoruba newcomers composed commemorative rituals for this monumental Afro-Creole holiday.[32] The very fact that the phrase "Yé! Ekún ara wa la mí sun" is a refrain from the Odù *Ogbè Atẹ̀* of the Ifá sacred corpus (see appendix A) is evidence enough that first-generation Yoruba laborers with intimate knowledge of West African Yorùbá landscapes and literatures composed such commemorative danced songs from adapted Yoruba sacred literature.[33]

For "liberated" Yorubas who remarked on and danced through their suffering on a day intended for celebrating African freedom, commemoration amounted to mourning their exilic status in a distant land, as indicated by the verse "oku yoku rele o," which, Funso Aiyejina, Rawle Gibbons, and Baba Sam Phills translate as "the other dead have gone home."[34] Considering the oral-cultural data suggesting first-generation Yoruba participation in Emancipation

Day rituals and the wider orbit of Yoruba communal traditions, "the prominence of Shango not only in the annual *ebo* [feast], but also as the popular name of the religion in Trinidad may have been an attempt to" join, expand, or converse with an existing Afro-Creole institution—the sovereign palais—and replenish its African religious and political inheritance with the rituals and protocols of their Yorùbá homelands in West Africa.[35]

The material addressed here also introduces the probability that some Yorubas' involvement with Catholicism might well have been motivated by a desire for respectability and acceptance among their Afro-Creole Catholic neighbors and associates as opposed to a preoccupation with impressing or concealing their religion from white Catholics.[36] Yoruba newcomers to Trinidad in the mid- to late nineteenth century met Afro-Creole populations with established Catholic identities and distinct religious customs. As a result, some arriving Yorubas were likely empowered to conceive of their participation in Catholicism beyond the confines of colonial white constructions of Catholic piety. They witnessed and experienced firsthand African Catholic traditions unfolding around them and could locate familiar niches of cultural negotiation and imprints on a religious structure that was not immune to Africana cultural penetration.

Marie-Bertrand Cothonay's description of the 1882 Afro-Creole emancipation palais ceremony in Carenage, for example, removes from the realm of speculation theories of Afro-Creole autonomy and self-authorization in the face of oppositional white clerical power. He in fact presents a historical instance where he and the parish priest unsuccessfully attempted to disrupt this indigenous Afro-Creole custom by threatening to exclude Pierre, the "king" of the palais, and the preceding monarch, from the special rite of confirmation in the Catholic Church. Cothonay candidly confesses that clerical coercion failed because "our poor Negro kings retired, irritated, and absolutely refused to promise that which we asked of them, [namely] to demolish the *palais*, if they wished to take part in the confirmation."[37] Moreover, the "poor Negro kings" and queens arguably go as far as to restage the central liturgical event of the Catholic mass; thus, appropriating to themselves the authority to perform the church's most sacred rite of communion. In both of Cothonay's journal entries pertaining to two different palais ceremonies, he mentions repeatedly the "blessed bread" that the king "presents" and the queen "distribute[s]."

It goes without saying that Africana strategies of social belonging at times deliberately and at other times inadvertently accommodated societal coercion to adopt Euro-colonial norms at the expense of Africana norms. In this instance, however, a white Catholic missionary offers evidence to the contrary during the latter decades of the nineteenth century, when African traditions were increasingly censured and imagined as disruptions of cultural respectability. The very fact that the Orisa palais remains an operative institution in Trinidad today is evidence enough that nineteenth-century Yorubas and their descendants actually associated their inherited ritual norms with autonomous traditions of other African descendants in the colony and therefore chose their own norms over Euro-colonial norms in many arenas, even as they formed attachments to Catholic and other colonial structures.

Yoruba-Trinidadians' strategies of belonging disabuse us of reductionist frameworks (e.g., academic theories of Afro- and Euro-syncretism) that simplify the factors underlying human social behavior. Nothing less than a concatenation of complex motivations drives individual and collective human agency in any cultural context, and we cannot always adjudicate what those are by assessing the degree of intimacy or distance exploited groups permit between themselves and imposing regulatory structures. Moreover, postcolonial studies research suggests that colonized and oppressed subjects have always entered into complicated negotiations with imperial structures that both capitalize on and compromise the extent of their power and agency. As some sociologists have argued, rigid theories juxtaposing culture and agency with structure and constraint overlook the fact that these terms are "slippery" and "contested." Sharon Hays writes about the manner in which social scientists have deployed these categories, often talking past one another through unidimensional and static definitions that belie how culture is structured and how structures make room for the creative capacity of human actors within arenas of social behavior. "Social life is fundamentally structured," she maintains: "But social structures do make possible a whole range of choices in everyday life. Certain structural configurations of resources and constraints make it more or less possible for people to make larger or smaller 'creative' moves. Some portions of culture are easier to change than others (more open to reflective monitoring, less embedded in everyday practices), just as some elements of relational location are easier to change than others."[38]

Though not guided by a sustained focus on the agency debate in religious and sociological studies, this discussion takes Hays's conclusions seriously. By analyzing the role of sovereignty and social belonging in Yoruba-Orisa religious formation and their resonances with analogous antecedent Afro-Creole traditions, it attempts to "turn our attention" away from the explanatory impotency of Afro-and Euro-syncretism arguments. Instead, as Hays suggests, it seeks to address "the question of under what cultural and relational conditions, and *through what cultural and relational processes*, structurally transformative agency occurs" for custodians of Orisa and perhaps other African heritage religious traditions (my emphasis).[39] The argument levied here concerning Yoruba-Trinidadian ritual behavior, however, debunks any assumption that "human agency primarily consists in acts that challenge social norms and not those that uphold them."[40] Historian Ras Michael Brown is correct when he reminds scholars researching African diaspora religious cultures in the shadow of the Herskovits-Frazier debate that "both continuity and creativity entail cultural agency and represent normal interdependent processes."[41]

The historical display of Yoruba religious culture in Trinidad lends much to wider analyses of Africana continuity and creativity in the African diaspora, as it troubles the stereotypic boundary between African religion and European Catholicism and exposes instances of religiocultural collaboration and cooperation that prevailed among diverse African-descended populations during the postemancipation period. The racial politics informing the research agendas of African diaspora religious studies over the past century steered far too many scholars away from exhaustively engaging the dynamics of religious formation within and across African-descended communities during and after the era of slavery. Since the period of Melville Herskovits and E. Franklin Frazier's scholarly dominance, emphasis instead was placed on master-slave or white-black relations and negotiations at the expense of documenting and theorizing intra-African relations and negotiations. In many respects, such long-standing studies of religious syncretism among African diaspora populations obscure our current perception of African heritage religions and their legacies in the Americas and the Caribbean. They hinder our ability to access the remarkable role that Afro-Christian communities have played in nourishing and sustaining indigenous African heritage religions under diverse circumstances of encounter and interaction.[42] The case of Trinidadian Orisa seems to be one irrefutable example of this phenomenon, where nineteenth-century Afro-Catholics provided the ritual architecture that allowed Yoruba sacred traditions the necessary institutional space to manifest and blossom into a nationally recognized religion in the twenty-first century. From Carenage to San Fernando and beyond, the Orisa palaces that Afro-Catholics built are everywhere evident across Trinidad today.

Odù—Ogbè Atẹ̀

Ká dijú ká wí pá a kú,	Let us close our eyes and pretend to be dead,
Ká wẹnì tọ́ fẹ́ràn ẹni.	Then we will truly know those who love us.
Ká bùrìn bùrìn bùrìn,	Let us walk on a long and tiresome journey,
Ká fẹsẹ̀ kọ gbàrà gbàrà gbàrà;	Until we hit something with our foot, stumble and lose our balance;
Ká wẹni tí ó ṣeni pẹ̀lẹ́.	Let us observe those who sympathize with us.
Èèyàn yòówù tọ́ bá ṣeni pẹ̀lẹ́,	Whoever it is that sympathizes with us,
Eléyuunì lọ́ fẹ́ràn.	Is the person who truly loves us.
Ẹkún Aríra là ń sun,	We are weeping for Aríra,
Àaaa!	Àaaa!
Ẹkún ara wa là ń sun.	We are weeping for our own selves.
Ẹdú ọ́ mọ́ mọ́ kú mọ́,	Ẹdú is no longer dead,
Ṣe bí lajà lọ́ wà o?	Don't you know that he is just in the attic?
Ẹkún ara wa là ń sun.	We are weeping for our own benefit.

According to Kọ́lá Abímbọ́lá the refrain in lines 8, 10, and 13 exactly matches the title and refrain of the Yoruba-Trinidadian song, "Yé! Ekún ara wa la mí sun."[43] Abímbọ́lá goes on to explain his interpretation as follows:

> To an English speaker, the words from the two sources may not look the same, but actually they are. First, "Àaaa!" is an onomatopoeic synonym for "crying." Just as crying can sound like "aaaa," so can it sound like "ye." Hence, "Àaaa!"—an onomatopoeic word for crying—is conveyed by "Yé!" in the Yoruba-Trinidadian song. Therefore: Àaaa! = Yé![44]
>
> Second, Ọ̀yọ́ Yoruba is notorious for what are called "vowel assimilation" and "consonant elision" in linguistics. Basically, Ọ̀yọ́ Yoruba cuts out unnecessary consonants and contrasts or changes two, three or four sequential vowels to form shorter or different words. This is because Ọ̀yọ́ Yoruba functions in Yoruba language the same way Queen's English functions in English language. That is, anyone who speaks any dialect of English (be it Cockney English, Black County English, or Texan English) will understand the Queen's English. In the same way, anyone who speaks any dialect of Yoruba will understand Ọ̀yọ́ Yoruba. Hence the rendition of lines 8, 10, and 13 as "Ẹkún ara wa là ń sun" is exactly the same as "Ẹkún ara wa là mí sun." The consonant "m" in the word "mí" has been removed, and vowel elision has been applied to "i" to turn it into a new vowel "n."

Although the stand-alone word "n" in lines 8, 10, and 13 may look like a consonant to an English speaker, in this case, it is actually a vowel—and that is why it has the accent mark above it. In Yoruba language, only vowels take accent marks (upper or lower). The one and only exception to this accent mark rule is the "s" that sometimes has a dot underneath. Therefore, *Ekun ara wa la mi sun* = *Ekun ara wa la n sun*."

APPENDIX B

Pour cette fois, je me contenterai de vous parler d'une cérémonie qui certainement ne se trouve pas dans le rituel romain. Je vous ai dit que nos noirs de Trinidad, et ceux du Carénage en particulier, sont d'anciens esclaves ou fils d'esclaves. Lors de l'émancipation, qui tomba le 1ᵉʳ août (1838), ils résolurent de célébrer chaque année, ce jour-là, une fête solennelle, *pour perpétuelle mémoire*. Cette fête commençait le matin par une grand'messe, avec force musique, pain bénit, procession, etc., et se prolongeait trois jours durant au milieu de festins, de danses et d'orgies sans nom, souvenirs de la vie africaine.

Le curé actuel, très aimé d'abord de ses paroissiens, avait enfin obtenu, après beaucoup de patience et de luttes, la suppression de cette fête du diable. Depuis six ans, elle ne se célébrait plus au Carénage. . . .

L'année dernière, à son insu, les anciens esclaves se concertèrent tous ensemble, pour reprendre bruyamment les anciennes traditions. Ils élevèrent donc une case en bambous, couverte en feuilles de carates; et la décorèrent du nom pompeux de *palais*. Un nègre fut nommé *roi*. Les provisions de bouche, les boissons, etc., s'accumulèrent autour du palais. Le 1ᵉʳ août arriva, et les paroissiens du P. Poujade assistèrent pieusement à la messe d'usage. Le soir, le bon curé entendit battre de nouveau l'horrible tambour africain. Plus de doute; c'était la fête des nègres. Pendant trois jours et trois nuits, le Carénage fut souillé par des bacchanales comme jamais il n'en avait vu, sans doute pour compenser celles qu'on avait supprimées les années précédentes. Le dimanche suivant, le curé tempêta, mais . . . paroissiens impassibles! . . .

Dans ces sortes de fêtes, le roi, ordinairement élu par acclamation, est celui qui réunit les fonds nécessaires, fait les invitations, présente le pain bénit, etc. . . , et ouvre la danse. Le roi de cette année s'appelait Peter, Pierre. Il est sur la cinquantaine et n'a pas encore reçu la confirmation; il a assisté aux instructions préparatoires, et compte bien être admis au sacrement. Sans doute, il croit que le curé ignore sa participation à la fête du diable, ou qu'il n'osera pas renvoyer un gros personnage comme lui. Mais il se trompe.

Un soir, sur ma demande, le curé le fait venir au presbytère, ainsi qu'un autre compère, ancien roi, lui aussi. J'espérais pouvoir régler l'affaire à l'amiable avec les deux principaux chefs, et obtenir l'abandon de projets qui ne m'allaient pas du tout. Mais à peine la conversation était-elle commencée, que le curé s'y mêla, et par des reproches intempestifs compromit tout le succès de ma démarche. Nos pauvres rois nègres se retirèrent irrités, et refusèrent absolument de promettre ce que nous leur demandions, à savoir, de démolir *le palais*, s'ils voulaient prendre part à la confirmation.

NOTES

1. Unless quoting a source that does not include them, I apply diacritical marks to Yoruba terms when specifically referencing the Yorùbá-Òrìṣà religion and other phenomena on the African continent. Diacritical marks are not employed for generic references or for references to the Yoruba-Orisa religion in Trinidad and the larger African diaspora, unless directly cited from another source. I often conform to the Anglicization convention for pluralizing nouns such as Yoruba and Orisa (pl. Yorubas, Orisas). No such terms appear in the Yorùbá language, and I use them for semantic ease and convenience, since I am working in the English language. Orisa is pronounced "Oreesha" in the English language.

2. Between 1779 and 1833 roughly 25,300 captives disembarked in Trinidad. Of that number approximately 12.5 percent were purchased or embarked in west-central Africa; 46 percent in the Bight of Biafra and Gulf of Guinea islands; 26 percent in unspecified regions of Africa; 6 percent in the Gold Coast; 3.5 percent in Sierra Leone; 2.5 percent in the Bight of Benin, Senegambia, and offshore Atlantic, and 1 percent in the Windward Coast. Among this group of 25,300 captives, roughly 19,700 captives' ports of purchase are known, and fewer than 500 of these captives were purchased at ports in and around Yorùbá-speaking areas. These and other relevant data concerning the 101 individual voyages that brought more than 25,000 African captives to Trinidad can be viewed at David

Eltis, Stephen D. Behrendt, David Richardson, and Herbert S. Klein, eds., Voyages: The Transatlantic Slave Trade Database, accessed March 18, 2018, www.slavevoyages.org/assess ment/estimates/. Beginning in 1783 Trinidad also received a large percentage of its African population from neighboring Caribbean islands, after planters were given incentives to relocate and develop the colony's plantation economy.

3. The African groups identified as "Yoruba" in Trinidad (or "Yaraba," as they were called in the nineteenth century) had been "liberated" from slave vessels by Britain's Royal Navy West Africa Squadron. Most were transported to Sierra Leone for immediate residency and later resettled in Trinidad and other British colonies under Britain's indentured labor program, primarily between the 1830s and 1860s. During these decades no fewer than thirty-two thousand "liberated" or "recaptive" Africans, as they came to be known, entered the British Caribbean and Guyana through what I have labeled elsewhere an "extended Middle Passage." According to Daniel Domingues da Silva, David Eltis, Philip Misevich, and Olatunji Ojo, 180,969 liberated Africans were settled in new homelands across the Atlantic world. They add, "The very first of the group came ashore in Philadelphia in 1800 and the last in St. Helena in 1863." See "The Diaspora of Africans Liberated from Slave Ships in the Nineteenth Century," *Journal of African History* 55 (2014): 347–48. For

my concept of the "extended Middle Passage," see Dianne Stewart, "Indigenous Wisdom at Work in Jamaica: The Power of Kumina," in *Indigenous Peoples' Wisdom and Power: Affirming Our Knowledge Through Narratives*, ed. Ivy Goduka and Julian Kunnie (London: Ashgate, 2006), 127–42. Additional spellings of "Shango" include "Sango" and "Ṣango." Shango is associated with thunder, lightning, and justice in Yoruba theology.

4. Stephen D. Glazier, "Whither Sango? An Inquiry into Sango's 'Authenticity' and Prominence in the Caribbean," in *Ṣàngó in Africa and the African Diaspora*, ed. Joel Tishken, Toyin Falola, and Akintunde Akinyemi (Bloomington: Indiana University Press, 2009), 239.

5. For the two scholars' central arguments on the subject, see Melville J. Herskovits, *The Myth of the Negro Past* (New York: Harper, 1941); and E. Franklin Frazier, *The Negro Church in America* (1964; repr., New York: Schocken Books, 1974), 1–102. For additional analysis of the Herskovits-Frazier debate and its impact on the field of Africana religious studies, see Dianne Stewart Diakité and Tracey Hucks, "Africana Religious Studies: Toward a Transdisciplinary Agenda in an Emerging Field," *Journal of Africana Religions* 1, no. 1 (2013): 28–77. See also Curtis Evans, *The Burden of Black Religion* (New York: Oxford University Press, 2008), 105–76.

6. David Trotman, "Reflections on the Children of Shango: An Essay on a History of Orisa Worship in Trinidad," *Slavery and Abolition* 28, no. 2 (2007): 216–17. For figures concerning the 20,656 slaves turned apprentices who were fully emancipated on August 1, 1838, see *Reports from Committees, 1847–8: Supplement No. 1 to the Eighth Report from the Select Committee on Sugar and Coffee Planting* (ordered by the House of Commons to be printed May 29, 1848), 66.

7. Glazier, "Whither Sango," in Tishken, Falola, and Akinyemi, *Ṣàngó in Africa*, 234.

8. Most of the early calypsos about "Shango" were recorded first by RCA/Rounder records between 1934 and 1940. For more on this subject, see Gordon Rohlehr, *Calypso and Society in Pre-independence Trinidad* (Port of

Spain, Trinidad: Rohlehr, 1990); and Donald R. Hill. *Calypso Calaloo: Early Carnival Music in Trinidad* (Gainesville: University Press of Florida, 1993), 252–55. See also Trotman, "Reflections on the Children, 226–27, for a critical analysis of the "self-denigrating agenda" many early calypsonians promoted in Trinidadian popular culture through demeaning lyrics about Yoruba-Orisa religion.

9. See "Interested," *Trinidad Guardian*, September 11, 1929.

10. "Trinidad Field Trip-Diary," folder 83A, box 15, Melville and Frances Herskovits Papers, Schomburg Center for Research in Black Culture, New York Public Library.

11. Ibid., 242. *Mọgbà* is often spelled *mongba or mogba* in the literature on Trinidadian Orisa.

12. French Creole remained Trinidad's predominant language throughout most of the late nineteenth century, especially among commoners. See Maureen Warner-Lewis, *Trinidad Yoruba: From Mother Tongue to Memory* (Kingston: University of the West Indies Press, 1997), 51; Donald Wood, *Trinidad in Transition: The Years After Slavery* (New York: Oxford University Press, 1986); and Bridget Brereton, *Race Relations in Colonial Trinidad, 1870–1900* (1979; repr., Cambridge: Cambridge University Press, 2002), 165–66.

13. Marie Bertrand Cothonay, *Trinidad: Journal d'un missionnaire dominicain des Antilles anglaises* (Paris: Retaux et Fils, 1893), 62–66. Original translation with the assistance of Dali Cintras Bathares (see appendix B for the original French version). Subsequent to locating Cothonay's journal, I discovered that Bridget Brereton had also commented on the same passage examined here. Brereton, however, mistranslates the final section of the wider narrative (which I do not include in this chapter discussion) as a "triumph over primitivism" in the mind of the *curé*, for she claims that, a year later (1883) the *curé* cursed the palais before a large group of witnesses, and "when the news spread in the district, the festival was cancelled." In fact, the passage offers no such indication. While the original French suggests that the *curé* attributed to his own cunning the power to coerce the Afro-Creole population

into abandoning plans to hold the festival, the passage offers no confirmation that the "festival was cancelled." Rather, it conveys the arrogant prediction on the part of the *curé* that his ritual "cursing" of the palais was enough to instill doubt and fear in the minds and hearts of the ex-enslaved community and effect the death of the tradition. See Brereton, *Race Relations in Colonial Trinidad*, 157.

14. "Il parle couramment sa langue"; Cothonay, *Trinidad*, 291.

15. "Je connais à la Trinidad bon nombre de nègres amenés ici dans les mêmes conditions"; ibid. (see pages 290–91 for the complete narrative). See also Bridget Brereton's remarks on the question of the relationship between the Afro-Creole and African populations: "To some extent, the African immigrants were beginning, in the later nineteenth century, to merge with the rest of the black population. One Governor thought that by 1871 the Africans 'had been merged among the general population as natives of Trinidad.' But he certainly overstated the case. The Africans formed a distinct and separate group at least until the end of the century." Brereton, *Race Relations in Colonial Trinidad*, 135.

16. William Dillon Piersen, *Black Yankees: The Development of an Afro-American Subculture in Eighteenth-Century New England* (Amherst: University of Massachusetts Press, 1988), 117–42; Jeffrey R. Kerr-Ritchie, *Rites of August First: Emancipation Day in the Black Atlantic World* (Baton Rouge: Louisiana State University Press, 2007); Eileen Southern, *The Music of Black Americans: A History* (New York: Norton, 1997); Jeroen Dewulf, *The Pinkster King and the King of Kongo: The Forgotten History of America's Dutch-Owned Slaves* (Jackson: University Press of Mississippi, 2017).

17. For documentation of parallel traditions among African descendants in Spain, Portugal, and Latin America, see Sue Peabody, "'A Dangerous Zeal': Catholic Missions to Slaves in the French Antilles, 1635–1800," *French Historical Studies* 25, no. 1 (2002): 79–80. Peabody also notes that similar celebrations among French natives were occasions for the "reversal of social roles, with apprentices acting as kings and wives ruling their husbands," 80.

18. Trotman, "Reflections on the Children," 217. "Kábíyèsí" translated means "No-one-dare-challenge-or-question-your-authority"; see Akíntúndé Akínyẹmí, "The Place of Ṣàngó in the Yorùbá Pantheon," in Tishken, Falola, and Akinyemi, *Ṣàngó in Africa*, 26.

19. Cocoa production and trade exploded during the late 1870s and lasted until 1920, when oil production went on the rise. See Trotman, "Reflections on the Children, 222–23.

20. Maureen Warner-Lewis, *Guinea's Other Suns* (Dover, Mass.: Majority Press, 1991); Warner-Lewis, *Trinidad Yoruba*; Warner-Lewis, *Central Africa in the Caribbean: Transcending Time, Transforming Cultures* (Kingston: University of West Indies Press, 2003), 42, 117, 123n10. The earliest written reference to an Orisa palais of which I am aware is from an apparently unpublished paper by Charles S. Espinet, who worked in different capacities, including editor in chief at the *Trinidad Guardian*. Espinet sent the paper, "Manifestation of Wêrê in Trinidad Shango," to Melville Herskovits with a cover letter dated November 29, 1945. Within the first page he writes about how "Wêrê mediums become mischievous" and "break 'palais' conventions." He follows this statement with a footnote, explaining that "Palais" is "the name given to the bamboo and thatched roof 'tent' in which the dancing takes place." In two of the earliest scholarly studies of African heritage religious cultures in Trinidad, Melville Herskovits (who studied the Shango/Yoruba-Orisa tradition) and Andrew Carr (who studied the Dahomean Rada tradition) both identify the ritual spaces reserved for worship as inclusive of a "tent" and *chapelle*. Their descriptions of the tent are consistent with Espinet's definition of the palais as well as later anthropological studies of Yoruba-Orisa palais. See Melville Herskovits, *Trinidad Village* (New York: Knopf, 1947), 326–27; and Andrew Carr, "A Rada Community in Trinidad," *Caribbean Quarterly* 3, no. 1 (1953): 39, 41, 53–54. For more on the carat palm *Sabal mauritiiformis* species in Trinidad, see Lise Winer, ed., *Dictionary of the English/Creole of Trinidad and Tobago: On Historical Principles* (Montreal: McGill-Queen's University Press, 2008), 169–70.

Other early studies that document the palais structure among Shango/Yoruba-Orisa worshippers include Frances Mischel (aka Henry), "African 'Powers' in Trinidad: The Shango Cult," *Anthropological Quarterly* 30, no. 2 (1957): 45; and George Eaton Simpson, "The Acculturative Process in Trinidadian Shango," *Anthropological Quarterly* 37, no. 1 (1964): 18. Mischel conducted her research in 1956 but does not indicate exactly where and among which shrines in Trinidad. Her notation that "there are, according to rough estimates, 100 Shango 'palais' in rural and urban Trinidad" suggests the term's standard usage at least by 1956. In his article Simpson also described the palais as the established Shango/Yoruba-Orisa worship space without reference to any specific shrines or regions. Collectively, these early to mid-twentieth-century sources suggest that both terms, *palais* and *tent*, were probably in use simultaneously for a wide array of shrines. Carr's research makes clear that the term *tent* was employed at the Rada shrine in the early 1950s. Although it is possible that the palais structure was adopted as a Yoruba-Orisa worship space during the early 1940s, Warner-Lewis's ethnographic research among second-generation Yoruba-Trinidadians leads me to think that it was adopted much earlier. Her data also confirm what Espinet's statement suggests—that the terms *palais* and *tent* were used interchangeably, but perhaps not without some shades of difference. Following the conceptual distinction many geographers and social theorists make between space and place, it appears to me that the palais designates a specific ritual place reserved for particular kinds of religious ceremonies and behaviors. The tent, however, is the structure that affords the palais an operative spatial arena. Certainly, more extensive studies and oral data would be required for a diachronic assessment of any widespread patterns in the naming of Orisa devotional spaces or ritual places. For a solid synthesis of how space and place have been theorized in critical geography, see Sandra Schmidt, "Theorizing Place: Students' Navigation of Place Outside the Classroom," *Journal of Curriculum Theorizing* 27, no. 1 (2011): 20–35.

21. Warner-Lewis, *Guinea's Other Suns*, 49–50.

22. Wood, *Trinidad in Transition*, 45.

23. Cothonay, *Trinidad*, 303–5.

24. *Nation, nationhood*, and other related word compounds are italicized to signify Africana constructions of sociocultural networks and institutions that often included governing offices and micropolitical activities but were not political state structures. Africana assertions of *nation* identities and productions of *nation* mechanisms constituted a widespread phenomenon among enslaved and indentured laborers in every corner of the European slaveholding and colonial world. For more information on these institutions and their religious frameworks, see Olabiyi Yai, "African Diasporan Concepts and Practice of the Nation and Their Implications in the Modern World," in *African Roots/American Cultures: Africa in the Creation of the Americas*, ed. Sheila S. Walker (Lanham, Md.: Rowman and Littlefield, 2001); Beatriz Góis Dantas, *Vovó Nagô e Papai Branco, Usos e abusos da África no Brasil* (Rio de Janeiro: Edições Graal, 1988); Beatriz Góis Dantas, *Nagô Grandma and White Papa: Candomblé and the Creation of Afro-Brazilian Identity*, trans. Stephen Berg (Chapel Hill: University of North Carolina Press, 2009); Edison Carneiro, *Candomblés da Bahia* (Bahia: Secretaria de Edicação e Saúde, 1948); John Thornton, *Africa and Africans in the Making of the Atlantic World: 1400–1800*, 2nd ed. (Cambridge: Cambridge University Press, 1998); J. Lorand Matory, *Black Atlantic Religion: Tradition, Transnationalism, and Matriarchy in the Afro-Brazilian Candomblé* (Princeton: Princeton University Press, 2005); Yvonne Daniel, *Dancing Wisdom: Embodied Knowledge in Haitian Vodou, Cuban Yoruba, and Bahian Candomblé* (Champaign: University of Illinois Press, 2005); Patrick Taylor, *Nation Dance: Religion, Identity, and Cultural Difference in the Caribbean* (Bloomington: Indiana University Press, 2001); and Rachel Harding, *A Refuge in Thunder: Candomblé and Alternative Spaces of Blackness* (Bloomington: Indiana University Press, 2000).

25. John Pemberton and Fúnṣọ Afọláyan, *Yorùbá Sacred Kinship: "A Power Like That of the Gods"* (Washington, D.C.: Smithsonian Institute Press, 1996), 152.

26. See Warner-Lewis, *Guinea's Other Suns*; Henry B. Lovejoy, "Drums of Ṣàngó: Bàtá Drum and the Symbolic Reestablishment of Ọ̀yọ́ in Colonial Cuba, 1817–1867," in Tishken, Falola, and Akinyemi, *Ṣàngó in Africa*, 285; and Toyin Falola and Matt Childs, eds., *The Yoruba Diaspora in the Atlantic World* (Bloomington: Indiana University Press, 2004).

27. James Adeyinka Olawaiye, "Yoruba Religious and Social Traditions in Ekiti, Nigeria, and Three Caribbean Countries: Trinidad-Tobago, Guyana, and Belize" (PhD diss., University of Missouri–Kansas City, 1980), 125. If not the first, Olawaiye was one of the earliest researchers to conduct a comparative study of varied Yoruba-based Nigerian and diasporic religious cultures. His insider-outsider location as a native Yorùbá-Nigerian is also worth noting, since scholars of West African Yorùbá heritage are still underrepresented among those studying Yoruba-Orisa religious traditions in the African diaspora. Still, his explanation of "Obakoso" is contested by other Yorùbá scholars and, in the end, also by the wider legacy of Yoruba-Trinidadian historical memory. Space limitations do not allow me to address this issue more substantively in this chapter. I address it at length, however, in chapter 5 of my and Tracey Hucks's book, *Obeah, Orisa, and Religious Identity in Trinidad* (Durham: Duke University Press, forthcoming).

28. Warner-Lewis, *Guinea's Other Suns*, 79, 83, 133; Herskovits, *Trinidad Village*, 330–31; Frances Henry, *Reclaiming African Religions in Trinidad: The Socio-political Legitimation of the Orisha and Spiritual Baptist Faiths* (Kingston: University of the West Indies Press, 2003), 22, 25. Lilith Dorsey also confirms this point in *Voodoo and Afro-Caribbean Paganism* (New York: Citadel Press, 2005), 102.

29. Branding is invoked here as both a psychological and physical ritual process. It is not clear how widespread was the physical practice of branding captive Africans with hot irons, but, according to Sharon Roger Hepburn, "many of the European governments, slave traders and trading companies, and African monarchs branded the Africans to ensure that others were aware to whom the slaves belonged." Other sources suggest that the Portuguese, Dutch, French, and British all engaged in the practice as well as individual slave owners. See Toyin Falola and Amanda Warnock, *Encyclopedia of the Middle Passage* (Westport, Conn.: Greenwood, 2007); see especially pages 67–68 for Hepburn's chapter on "Branding"; also consult chapters on "Enslavement and Procurement," "Torture," and "Violence." Additional insights can be gleaned from Rosanne Marion Adderley, *"New Negroes from Africa": Slave Trade Abolition and Free African Settlement in the Nineteenth-Century Caribbean* (Bloomington: Indiana University Press, 2006), 95. In the nineteenth century Alison C. Carmichael claimed never to have seen any Africans who had endured the brutal experience of hot-coal branding during her five years of residence in Trinidad and Saint Vincent. See *Domestic Manners and Social Condition of the White, Coloured, and Negro Population of the West Indies* (London: Whittaker, Treacher, 1833), 297–98.

30. Warner-Lewis, *Guinea's Other Suns*, 7–15, 28–29, 52.

31. Brereton, *Race Relations in Colonial Trinidad*, 135.

32. "Yé! Ekún ara wa la mí sun ," in *Peter Was a Fisherman: The 1939 Trinidad Field Recordings of Melville and Frances Herskovits*, vol. 1, Rounder Records, CD 1114, 1939.

33. *Ifá dídá* is the most commanding sacred text of the Yoruba religion. The Ifá literary corpus is composed of 16 major and 240 minor Odù (chapters), each containing six hundred to eight hundred poems or narratives. Although Ifá (the sacred corpus and the deity that rules this system) was widely known across the vast cultural landscapes where Yorùbá people groups maintained local and distinct traditions, a continental Yorùbá meta-identity had not yet unfolded during the period of massive resettlement of liberated "Yorubas" in Trinidad. Diverse peoples claiming Ẹgba, Iẹsha, Ìjẹbu, Ondo, Ikoyi, Ọ̀yọ́ and other pre-Yorùbá identities were caught up in the dynamics of the transatlantic slave trade just as the unifying concept of a Yorùbá *nation*—the concept of Yorùbáland—was emerging in West Africa. Furthermore, Yorùbá identity was not forged independently of the emergence of dispersed

Yoruba populations. Historians of Nigeria indicate that Yorùbáland as we conceive of it today did not exist during the eighteenth and much of the nineteenth centuries. A wide range of factors related to rise of capitalism, European colonial and missionary intrusion in Africa, the formation of modern nation-states, and other outcomes of globalization over several centuries led to the formation of the Yorùbá people as a distinct and unified group. See Robin Law, *The Oyo Empire, c. 1600–c. 1836: A West African Imperialism in the Era of the Atlantic Slave Trade* (New York: Oxford University Press, 1977); and John D. Y. Peel, *Religious Encounter and the Making of the Yoruba* (Bloomington: Indiana University Press, 2003). See also Alfred Ellis, *The Yoruba-Speaking Peoples of the Slave Coast of West Africa* (London: Chapman and Hall, 1894); Toyin Falola, *The Political Economy of a Pre-colonial West African State: Ibadan, 1830–1900* (Ilé-Ifè, Nigeria: University of Ifè Press, 1984); J. Lorand Matory, "The English Professors of Brazil: On the Diasporic Roots of the Yorùbá Nation," *Comparatives Studies in Society and History* 41, no. 1 (1999): 72–103; Matory, *Black Atlantic Religion*; and Olatunji Ojo, "'Heepa' (Hail) Òrìṣà: The Òrìṣà Factor in the Birth of Yoruba Identity," *Journal of Religion in Africa* 39, no. 1 (2009): 30–59. For more information on "Yé! Ekún ara wa la mí sun," see *Peter Was a Fisherman*.

34. Funso Aiyejina, Rawle Gibbons, and Baba Sam Phills, "Context and Meaning in Trinidad Yoruba Songs: *Peter Was a Fisherman* and *Songs of the Orisha Palais*," *Research in African Literatures* 40, no. 1 (2009): 129. Readers are referred to tracks 15, "Yé! Ekún ara wa la mí sun," and 16, "Explanation of Yé! Ekún ara wa la mí sun," in *Peter Was a Fisherman*.

35. Trotman completes this thought with two compelling suggestions about why "Shango" became so emblematic of Yoruba-Orisa religion in Trinidad. First, Shango "provide[d] the kind of unifying symbol for the original heterogeneous Yoruba imperial rule and serve[d] as a mechanism of cultural integration in the empire. In a strange land and a new environment, the various sub-ethnic Yoruba groups may have sought to transcend intra-regional animosities and rivalries by emphasising the common symbol of Shango." Second, "the preeminence of Shango may have also been the result of the numerical dominance of arrivals from Oyo or people from those areas where Shango was already the preeminent deity in the pantheon." See Trotman, "Reflections on the Children," 218–19.

36. Philip Scher raises this very point in his discussion of "syncretism" in the Orisa religion of Trinidad during the nineteenth century; see "Unveiling the Orisha," in *Africa's Ogun: Old World and New*, ed. Sandra T. Barnes (Bloomington: Indiana University Press, 1997), 320.

37. Cothonay, *Trinidad*, 66.

38. Sharon Hays, "Structure and Agency and the Sticky Problem of Culture," *Sociological Theory* 12, no. 1 (1994): 57–59, 70.

39. In my wider book project from which this chapter is adapted, I argue that the *nation* (as emically defined), kinship and familial customs, and the palais constitute salient "cultural and relational conditions" and "processes" for operationalizing "structurally transformative agency" among Yoruba-Trinidadians. See Sharon Hays, "Structure and Agency," 57–59, 70–71. See also Hays, "Constructing the Centrality of Culture—and Deconstructing Sociology?," *Contemporary Sociology* 29, no. 4 (July 2000): 594–602; and Yong Wang, "Agency: The Internal Split of Structure," *Sociological Forum* 23, no. 3 (2008): 481–502. For a complementary discussion that focuses on gender and religion, see Saba Mahmood, *Politics of Piety: The Islamic Revival and the Feminist Subject* (Princeton: Princeton University Press, 2004).

40. Mahmood, *Politics of Piety*, 5.

41. Ras Michael Brown, *African-Atlantic Cultures and the South Carolina Lowcountry* (Cambridge: Cambridge University Press, 2012), 17.

42. For example, I explore this pattern among nineteenth-century African Jamaicans in the religious exchanges between Myal and native Baptist practitioners. See Dianne Stewart, *Three Eyes for the Journey: African Dimensions of the Jamaican Religious Experience* (New York: Oxford University Press, 2005), 91–137.

43. See "Yé! Ekún ara wa la mí sun," in *Peter Was a Fisherman*, track 15.

44. The transcription and translation of these verses from *Ogbè Atè* are cited from Kọ́lá Abímbọ́lá, "Ifa Poems for Daily Encouragement" (unpublished manuscript, 2013). Abímbọ́lá's linguistic analysis of the two sources was provided in an electronic correspondence to the author, June 8, 2013.

FURTHER READING

Adderley, Rosanne Marion. *"New Negroes from Africa": Slave Trade Abolition and Free African Settlement in the Nineteenth-Century Caribbean*. Bloomington: Indiana University Press, 2006.

Brereton, Bridget. *Race Relations in Colonial Trinidad, 1870–1900*. 1979. Reprint, Cambridge: Cambridge University Press, 2002.

Castor, N. Fadeke. *Spiritual Citizenship: Transnational Pathways from Black Power to Ifa in Trinidad*. Durham: Duke University Press, 2017.

Houk, James. *Spirits, Blood, and Drums: The Orisha Religion in Trinidad*. Philadelphia: Temple University Press, 1995.

Simpson, George Eaton. "The Shango Cult in Nigeria and in Trinidad." *American Anthropologist* 64, no. 6 (1962): 1204–19.

Warner-Lewis, Maureen. *Guinea's Other Suns: The African Dynamic in Trinidad Culture*. Dover, Mass.: Majority Press, 1991.

◇◇◇

PART 4

Aurality and
Diasporic Traditions

CHAPTER 8

On Hearing Africas
in the Americas

Domestic Celebrations for Catholic Saints
as Afro-Diasporic Religious Tradition

MICHAEL IYANAGA

This chapter questions the sound of Africa in the Americas. More precisely, it questions the a priori assumptions that lead analysts to hear (or taste, or see, or smell, or feel) certain things instead of others as "African" in a hemisphere explicitly and profoundly reshaped—in human, geographic, cultural, architectural, and economical terms—by enslaved Africans and their descendants. To broach such a lofty topic, however, I pursue a much less ambitious goal, which is to offer a comparative overview of the musical, structural, social, and cosmological dimensions of domestic patron saint venerations as they are celebrated today (that is, in the "ethnographic present" of the twentieth and twentieth-first centuries) in Venezuela, Brazil, Colombia, parts of Ecuador, and the Dominican Republic.

Although some of the information included here comes from my own fieldwork in Brazil, the bulk of the data that fills the following pages relies on ethnographic reports that other scholars—mostly anthropologists, folklorists, and ethnomusicologists—have written over the past several decades. As such, this chapter aggregates the relatively isolated observations researchers have made about residential patron saint festivities in these American locations. When cross-referenced, these observations about residential celebrations—not unlike the more well-known public black kings' festivals—reveal broad hemispheric similarities in saint veneration, whether the celebrations themselves are called *velorios, velaciones, belenes, arrullos,* or *rezas.* Whether on Colombia's Pacific coast or along the Caribbean shoreline of Venezuela, in the

Dominican countryside or the maritime areas of northeast Brazil, the house parties people hold in honor of their saints look and sound remarkably alike: devotees gather in front of home altars to intone hymns, recite prayers, ring dance, and responsorially sing to the accompaniment of drums, hand claps, marimbas, guitars, or other instruments whose construction, timbres, and rhythmic patterns are largely traceable to central Africa.

In this chapter I insist that such domestic patron saint celebrations in Venezuela, Brazil, Colombia, parts of Ecuador, and the Dominican Republic share a strong genealogical link to the Catholicism that developed in central Africa from as early as the fifteenth century. This is a comparative Atlantic perspective insinuating that what scholars have often implicitly treated as the idiosyncrasies of "local," "popular," or "folk" Catholicism are actually ethnographic hints of a shared Catholic history. Or perhaps such a history might instead be conceived of as a shared set of Catholic *histories*, comprising not only the Iberian Catholicism that Portuguese and Spanish colonizers imported to the Americas but also the African Catholicism that enslaved central Africans surely brought with them across the Atlantic. By looking at the aesthetic and cosmological dynamics of contemporary domestic patron saint rituals in conjunction with both the demographics of the transatlantic slave trade and early modern central African Catholicism, this chapter draws attention to geographically broad transnational connections and suggests an Atlantic explanation for the hemispheric similarities apparent in residential saint veneration practices today.

With this argument I am not seeking to articulate a totalizing narrative about the history of these domestic prayer rituals. In fact, I am at too early a stage in this research project to risk what might be an instructive, but ultimately far too speculative, undertaking. Rather, my aim is to emphasize the important questions this comparative Atlantic—though at times perhaps more Africa-centric—study of domestic devotion raises, particularly about what "Africa in the Americas" might sound like. After all, if in fact the origins of a significant portion of Catholic beliefs and practices can be traced more or less directly to central Africa, then Catholicism, as a broad socioreligious institution and practice, might be as much a site of American black agency, innovation, resistance, and negotiation as are those religions typically celebrated as such, that is, the so-called Afro-Atlantic religions: Candomblé, Regla-de-Ocha (or Santería), Vodou, Orisha, and so on.

My suggested reframing seeks to revise the discursive treatment of Catholicism as the backdrop *against* which Afro-Atlantic religions have historically distinguished themselves. Specifically, it revises the historical binary and a priori interpretive position that nothing Catholic can also be African or Afro-American.[1] Instead, I argue, many Catholic traditions of the Americas are themselves "African," or at least Afro-diasporic in the same sense that orisha/*orichá*/*orixá* veneration is believed (and understood) to be. After all, Catholicism was already a relatively widespread "African religion," primarily in central Africa, generations before the transatlantic slave trade evolved into the insatiable funnel for human chattel that would eventually allow the Atlantic system to dominate global trade routes and transform the world. And indeed, it was mostly—at some moments almost exclusively—enslaved central Africans who were used to keep the ravenous machine running.

RESIDENTIAL PATRON SAINT FESTIVALS AS AFRO-DIASPORIC PRACTICE

As mentioned in the introduction to this volume, a larger number of enslaved Africans were taken from west-central Africa than from anywhere else in Africa, beginning fairly early on in the transatlantic slave trade. This suggests a foundational and substantive presence of Bantu-speaking Africans and their traditions in the Americas at the formative stages of the establishment of new colonies in the Western Hemisphere. Given the importance of Catholicism in central Africa preceding the transatlantic slave trade, it seems not insignificant that if we look at various Catholic traditions all over the Americas, we can find traces—sometimes bold, sometimes less so—of central African ideas, aesthetics, technologies, and practices. In particular, the study of residential patron saint festivities in a transnational perspective offers a means of connecting the dots and thus perceiving the ethnographic hints of this marginalized history. The vestiges of central African Christianity seem to be quite vibrant, in other words, in households throughout the Americas, and simply recognizing this may move us to rethink Catholic saints, human devotees, and the face (and sound) of religion in the African diaspora.

Venezuela and the Velorio

Let's begin in Venezuela, with the festivals held for Saint John (and other saints) in any number of different Afro-Venezuelan communities along the country's Caribbean coast.[2] These festivities have been viewed as part of the African diaspora at least since Viennese anthropologist Angelina Pollak-Eltz first theorized in the early 1970s that they harbored "old African deities" of

West African Yoruba traditions.[3] Since that time, however, scholars have begun suggesting that the Afro-Venezuelan penchant for Saint John's Day celebrations is in fact linked to central Africa. Ethnomusicologist Max Brandt, for example, explains that in Barlovento, Saint John (in Spanish, San Juan) is "sometimes called San Juan Congo, San Juan Congolé, and San Juan Guaricongo, revealing a connection to the Congo basin of central Africa."[4] These names, which suggest a link between Saint John and the Kongo, seem to intimate that the saint is imagined as Kongolese, reflecting the central African tradition of refiguring saints as Kongolese ancestors that we see, for instance, in King Afonso I's recasting of Saint James as part of the Kongo foundation myth (see the introduction and Dewulf's and Valerio's chapters, in this volume), as well as in the well-known case of the elite Kongolese woman Kimpa Vita (baptized as Dona Beatriz) who, serving as a human avatar for Saint Anthony in the early eighteenth century, preached that Jesus, Mary, and Saint Francis were all Kongolese.[5] Finally, the drums used in these Saint John's Day festivities (as well as in festivities for other saints) may offer other hints. Scholars have suggested, for example, that the prototypes for some of these drums (such as the *redondo* or the *culo e' puya*) probably come from central Africa.[6]

Even in parts of Venezuela outside of Barlovento, central Africa serves as a geohistorical reference point. According to scholar Jesús García, for instance, the state of Yaracuy is "one of the regions where music of African origin is best preserved, the music in this case being that of the Loango, an ethnic group in the Republic of the Congo."[7] While García's emphasis on "preservation" may infelicitously resound as somewhat reductionist, it is worth taking seriously the scholar's singling out of Loango as a source for this Afro-Catholic practice. After all, by the sixteenth century the Kingdom of Loango had already developed a close relationship with its southern (Christian) neighbor, the Kingdom of Kongo, and Loango also practiced its own variant of the martial arts dance known as a sangamento (discussed in the introduction and Dewulf's chapter, in this volume).[8] Furthermore, García notes, "in the Afro-Venezuelan community of Palmarejo and of Farriar, Yaracuy state, a musical genre known as Loango is used to accompany the San Juan [festivities] of these communities."[9]

We can also hear aural hints of central African provenance in musical performance. One illustrative example is a recording of a song in the processional *sangueo* genre, "Viene saliendo la luna [The moon is coming out]."[10] This particular example comes from a procession of Saint John and features short, repeated melodic phrases responsorially sung to the accompaniment of

FIGURE 8.1 Loose transcription of an excerpt of "Viene saliendo la luna" (at 0:45). Represented here is the verse and a broad outline of the accompanying rhythms (membrane drums and shaken idiophones). The verse itself emphasizes the rhythmic accents of the drums; note the *tresillo* rhythm accented in the drums (i.e., the first, fourth, and seventh sixteenth note of the bar). Transcription of Spanish-language text from recording by Iria Gómez-García. Photo © Michael Iyanaga.

shakers and membrane drums (fig. 8.1). While an in-depth musical analysis might be revelatory, I want to call attention only to the rhythmic accents in the membrane drums, which emphasize a repeated asymmetrical pattern, referred to in much of the Hispanophone Latin American ethnomusicological literature as a *tresillo*, or 3-3-2, pattern.[11] This pattern comprises eight pulses (/x. .x. .x./) that, when put into the context of the vocal phrases they accompany, constitute a cyclical rhythmic phrase of sixteen pulses. If in fact, as scholars such as Gerhard Kubik and Kazadi wa Mukuna assert, sixteen-pulse patterns (typically organized in asymmetrical patterns called "timelines") in the African Americas come primary from central Africa, then "Viene saliendo la luna" might very well give us aural clues of a Bantu musical pedigree.[12] Furthermore, the specific *tresillo* rhythm itself seems to suggest a central African connection. After all, although the rhythmic pattern is found in traditions the world over, its presence in innumerable Afro-diasporic musical traditions that are said to be linked to Bantu speakers does indeed seem to reinforce a possible central African lineage.[13]

Saint John is commemorated differently in different regions of Venezuela. In some communities the celebrations take place primarily in the streets rather than in homes, while in other communities the opposite seems true. Yet even the public processions associated with Saint John's Day festivities are largely linked to a widely disseminated residential tradition known as the *velorio de santo*. According to Brandt, the *velorio de santo* "is a family celebration that is conducted in the sponsor's home. . . . A velorio usually starts at sunset and begins with prayers dedicated to the saint. . . . On one occasion during [my] fieldwork [in Barlovento] the songs and tambura beats began while the host of the velorio was reciting his orations in front of the altar."[14] The singing and drumming is interspersed with the declamation of *décimas* (ten-line poetic verse structures) until dawn.

But this is not how velorios occur in all parts of Venezuela, at least not all of those held for Saint John. Scholars have noted that in the state of Aragua, for instance, people begin Saint John's velorio in front of the home altar by singing unaccompanied *sirenas* (akin to sung prayers) prior to dancing to drums in front of the house. The celebrants then repeat this at subsequent houses until eventually deciding to stop at a location called La Sabana, where "the men and women make a circle and sing and dance[,] taking each other by the hand."[15] In Curiepe (in the state of Miranda), too, the velorios for Saint John appear to be different. According to anthropologist David Guss, "During the velorio, which lasts the entire night, the image of San Juan, dressed in red and covered with flowers, is installed in a place of honor. Immediately in front of it, the culo e' puya drums are played, while outside in the street another group dances and sings to the mina and curbata [drums]. These velorios continue from house to house until the conclusion of the festival."[16] Although data on these residential velorios appear to be somewhat sparse, they all suggest that the diverse devotional events share a similar structure: singing, drumming, dancing, and a Catholic saint. More specifically, the linguistic (names, terminology), musical (rhythms, instruments), and cosmological (reimagining the saint as Kongolese) cues all tend to point toward central Africa. In some ways, this seems unsurprising, given that central Africans did indeed disembark in large numbers on the shores of Venezuela, even if the enslaved arrived in demographic waves.

Although more captives arrived to Venezuela from Upper Guinea (though never in exclusivity) than from west-central Africa (by way of Santo Domingo) until 1592, between 1595 and 1640, over half of all enslaved Africans to Venezuela had originally embarked from Angola.[17] As such, the central African presence was never marginal, nor was it dominating. And this ethnic diversity might in fact figure into some of the musical diversity we see in the saint devotions. For instance, devotees perform in drum ensembles comprising drums that appear to come from many different regions of Africa.[18] Venezuela's history of slavery stands in contrast to Brazil's, the context to which we turn next, where nearly one million Africans had already disembarked by the turn of the eighteenth century, with central Africans constituting, according to James Sweet, "more than 90 percent of slave imports to Brazil until the last decades of the seventeenth century."[19] And one of the most important musical legacies left by the arrival of so many Bantu speakers has been what people often recognize as Brazil's national music: samba.

Brazil and the Reza

Samba may be Brazil's storied carnival genre par excellence, but it also acts as an important mode of Catholic devotion in the northeastern Brazilian state of Bahia. Indeed, in Bahia the local form of samba (often called *samba de roda*) is a staple at feast days for Catholic saints. Perhaps the most famous example is the large three-day Festival of Our Lady of Good Death, held annually in the city of Cachoeira, which culminates in hours of celebratory samba dancing.[20] But the importance of dance as a medium for saint veneration is most pronounced in private patron saint house parties known as *rezas* (also referred to as *devoções* or *sambas*; plate 10, in color insert). The reza (literally, "prayer") is a participatory musical event that people sponsor annually in their homes to honor their personal Catholic patron saints. These events are typically seen as offerings to fulfill vows made to saints in exchange for their graces and continued protection but are also nearly always bound up in hereditary and family obligations that can extend back several generations.[21]

The event begins in front of the home altar, as participants intone prayers and sing hymns (in both Latin and Portuguese) with no instrumental accompaniment. This hour-long prayer cycle concludes with rollicking samba, which is responsorially sung and danced (in a ring) by all present and may include any number of instruments, such as tambourines, hand drums, scrapers, and a variety of guitars.[22] Importantly, the samba lyrics often laud the patron saint and his or her miracles, even though the lyrics can also deal with more quotidian affairs.[23] Participants generally accompany their collective singing with ostinato hand claps that emphasize a *tresillo* rhythm, as we heard emphasized in the Venezuelan *sangueó* rhythm from figure 8.1. Also like the *sangueó*, the ostinato pattern in Bahian samba not only is emphasized in the percussive accompaniment but also can be identified in the rhythmic accents of the sung melodies (fig. 8.2).[24]

FIGURE 8.2 Example of a samba song for Saint Cosmas and Saint Damian, showing the melody sung by participants and the rhythm they clap to accompany themselves. Sung on September 27, 2011, at a private residence in Cachoeira, Bahia, Brazil. Photo © Michael Iyanaga.

The etymological, rhythmic, and choreographic evidence all suggest that samba is traceable primarily to Bantu-speaking central Africa. Take, for instance, the word *samba*. Although there is much debate regarding the term's origins, scholars typically agree that it derives from a Bantu-language lexical.[25] Moreover, a Bantu origin is suggested in the rhythm's sixteen-pulse cycle as well as the integrated dance movements, two of the most important being the belly bounce (*umbigada*) and the *miudinho*, the latter being a dance step in which both feet shuffle back and forth in an even, sixteenth-note pattern. Both the belly bounce and the *miudinho* seem to have originated in central Africa.[26]

On certain occasions—when deemed both socially appropriate and rhythmically "hot" (*quente*) enough—the samba can prompt possession trance dancing.[27] While this dancing often resembles (in form) the possession dancing of *orixás* common in the Afro-Brazilian Candomblé religion, the cosmologies surrounding the deities that manifest themselves at rezas are somewhat distinct from those of the better-known Candomblé religious practices. At rezas the deities—generically called *caboclos*, *encantados* (charms), or *anjos de guarda* (guardian angels)—can be Catholic saints, West African *orixás*, or Brazilian archetypal figures such as sailors, cowboys, or Indians. The people who serve as mediums for *these* caboclo deities (which are categorically different from caboclos in Candomblé contexts[28]) are said to do so because they have inherited these deities from their ancestors, a cosmological reasoning that underscores a subtle link to the precolonial Bantu belief in the centrality of ancestors, or "first-comers."[29] Similarly, as I have elsewhere detailed, the caboclos' healing and oracular qualities in the reza context seem to connect them in significant ways to central African *ngoma* drum rituals and what Victor Turner called, for the Ndembu, a group of the broader Bantu realm, "cults of affliction."[30]

Despite the secular frame through which samba has historically been studied, in the reza context the samba is anything but a profane annex to a religious celebration. Rather, the samba is explicitly linked to the saints for whom the Afro-Brazilian dance is performed. This religious ethos manifests itself in a number of important ways. In some cases the explicit link is in what is sung by the participants. That is, samba texts regularly laud the patron saint of the night, sing about the saint's exploits, or simply communicate directly with the saint. Even when samba texts are not specifically about the saint or religious matters, appearing thus to be "profane," their performance at rezas highlight their sacredness, as they are a vital part of celebrating the patron saint. Moreover, dance movements and choreographies often indicate the samba's Catholic nature: the samba ring is generally slightly open where the saint's altar stands, as if to include the saint in the ring itself, and participants typically bow and make the Sign of the Cross while dancing before the altar.

Finally, of utmost importance are the cosmological motives that move people to perform samba for saints' feasts. Although it is true that people themselves generally enjoy the samba dancing, they perform the Afro-Brazilian dance in large part because they believe these holy figures also enjoy it.[31] In other words, this central African–derived art form is as intrinsically a part of saint veneration as intoned, church-inspired (and church-derived) prayers and hymns. It therefore seems hardly happenstance that it is central African–derived samba, rather than some other musical style, that moves both people and caboclos—deities traceable to Bantu-speaking central Africa—to sing and dance at rezas.

Colombia and the Arrullo

Private patron saint celebrations are also common along the Pacific coast of Colombia, particularly in the departments of Nariño and Chocó, as well as in parts of northwestern Ecuador, such as in Esmeraldas.[32] Here they are called *arrullos* or *belenes de santo*. Anthropologist Thomas Price, describing the patron saint rituals in Tumaco (in the Nariño Department), explains that the *belén de santo* "consists of a group of men and women who gather in a private home for a night of singing and drumming in honor of a saint."[33] A *belén* can either be a yearly obligation or be offered only once or twice in a lifetime as repayment for a specific blessing received by what anthropologist Anne-Marie Losonczy calls a "saint of special devotion" (*santo de devoción especial*).[34] According to Juan Sebastián Ochoa, Leonor Convers, and Oscar Hernández, the most commonly venerated saints in Colombia's southern Pacific region are Saint Joseph, Saint Peter, and Saint Anthony, as well as the Virgin Mary and Baby Jesus.[35]

On the night of the *belén*, Price tells us, the participants march from the church to the home of the event's host. The anthropologist further explains that "the service does not officially begin until the recitation of the rosary by a specially invited *rezandera*, when the gathering is as nearly silent as possible. When the prayer has ended, there is an outburst of shouting and laughter, intended to inform the saint that the *belén* will be joyous, the participants seat themselves on the floor facing the altar, and the first song is sung."[36] What may not necessarily be clear in Price's words is the essential role of music during the event. The "night of the party," according to Losonczy, is "animated by music and dance around the altar, adorned with flowers and candles."[37] The music—comprising genres such as *juga* and *bunde*—is primarily sung by female *cantadoras* (or *cantaoras*), who play bamboo shakers (*guasás*) as they sing. Men accompany the singers on two types of membrane drums: *bombos* and *cununos*. Finally, at an arrullo one might also find a marimba, which is a type of xylophone that is not only treated by local practitioners as a sign of Africa's legacy in the region but also probably comes from a central African technology (see the depiction of a marimba in plate 5 in the color insert).[38] Although the marimba may not necessarily be among the most historically used instruments at arrullos, it nonetheless carries strong imagined ties to the religious tradition.[39] Papá Roncón, for instance, who is undoubtedly among the most well-known marimba players in Ecuador, remembers the marimba fondly as essential to sacred dancing, singing, and—in a way that recalls the Venezuelan celebrations discussed earlier—the recitation of *décimas*.[40]

The texts performed at arrullos are sung or declaimed and can vary from the explicitly sacred to the seemingly profane. Ethnomusicologist Michael Birenbaum, for instance, explains that lyrics often humanize the saints by depicting "them in mundane, human contexts," while Losonczy claims that "no song evokes religious themes."[41] Independent of the content itself, this singing is, it seems to me, always at least implicitly sacred, given its constituent role in arrullos.

In addition to singing, "worshippers dance toward the altar . . . to declaim religious poems called *loas* to the saint."[42] If indeed the *loa* is, as Norman Whitten claims, a "sacred *décima*," the arrullo seems strongly to resemble the alternation between drumming and *décimas* that characterizes the Venezuelan velorio.[43]

The music, together with the gaiety of the participants and the alcohol shared at the event, is especially vital to the creation of the appropriate "heat" (*calor*) for the saint's festival, a fact that is comparatively important, given the importance of "hotness" in moving caboclos to appear at Bahian rezas.[44] Indeed, when the atmosphere at the arrullo is hot enough, the saint is often said to be present at the altar, in the "voices" of the singers or in the hands of the drummers.[45] The heat has an important cosmological foundation since, as Birenbaum explains, "the generating of heat at an arrullo pleases the saint because it counteracts the cold of heaven (divine world), reminding him of his abdicated humanity, and bringing him temporarily to the human world to help those who offer him this human heat."[46] In some cases the saint is said to temporarily enter participants' bodies, causing the drumming to become more vigorous and the singing louder. And although the possessed person may smile or stare at the altar, the possession is not designed to lead one to dance.[47] In this way it is distinct from the Bahian context. Such distinctions are of course expected, given the contrasting histories of Colombia and Brazil. In fact, the demographic data of enslavement and disembarkation alone is stark, let alone all of the broader imperial, social, and economic dissimilarities.

Although figures are less clear for the Pacific coast, we do have illuminating numbers for the most prominent Colombian port of disembarkation, Cartagena. David Wheat explains that "Angola and Upper Guinea provided roughly equal shares of captives to the city [of Cartagena] between 1573 and 1640," which was also the period during which the Spanish colonies (as a whole) imported the overwhelming majority of their slaves.[48] As such, we can surmise that the central African influence may have been far more diffuse in Colombia than, for instance, in Brazil. This does not mean, however, that central Africans were somehow insignificant players in the Colombian context, for Cartagena still received "more slave ships from Angola than from any other single region, even when voyages from the Cape Verde Islands and Upper Guinea are combined."[49]

Dominican Republic and the Velación

In the Dominican Republic, people also hold private saint festivals. These are known locally as *velaciones*, *veladas*, *noches de vela*, *velas*, or *velorios de santo*.[50] In a way that seems to parallel the Brazilian reza, the Dominican *velación*, which can be sponsored by confraternities, families, or individuals, is most typically an inherited obligation.[51] As is the case with all such domestic traditions, *velaciones* demonstrate considerable variety from one home or region to another. Still, the musical structure and content of the rituals appear to overlap in interesting ways with the Venezuelan, Colombian, and Brazilian traditions seen earlier. According to ethnomusicologist Martha Ellen Davis, *velaciones* play out in the following way: "Each of three sections of the rosary (*tercios*)—prayed at 6:00 p.m., midnight, and just before dawn—is followed by three musical settings of the Salve Regina. Each of these is followed by three sacred drum pieces in drumming regions. Then the rest of the event is unstructured with regard to either liturgical or nonliturgical Salves and/or palos for social dance until the next tercio."[52] The back-and-forth nature of the orations, singing, and drumming clearly recall the *velorios de santo* that Brandt observed in Venezuela. But that's not all; the general movement from "structured" to "unstructured" appears to mirror Colombian arrullos and Brazilian rezas.

What's more, the singing style of the velorio is, in broad terms, basically identical to that of the reza. According to Davis, the unaccompanied singing of the first (structured) part of the *velación* is tense-voiced, in a style that is melismatic (i.e., multiple pitches per syllable), antiphonal (i.e., choirs in alternation), unmetered (i.e., no strict beat), and uses modal scales with what is known as a "neutral" third.[53] Precisely the same description characterizes the liturgical hymns sung at Brazilian rezas. The second part of the *velación* shifts radically to include what Davis characterizes as "genres of African heritage," and indeed, although there is much variation in these nonliturgical *salves*, they are generally performed in a call-and-response style to the accompaniment of hand claps, guitars, or various types of drums (often long drums known as *palos*) and include hours of dancing.[54] Furthermore, these African-derived nonliturgical salves, according to Dominican scholar Bernarda Jorge, who labels them as "salves de regocijo" (joyful salves), have a "regular rhythmic pattern," which she describes as being a binary rhythm in a two-four meter with lots of "syncopated" note values.[55] Suffice it say that such a description could characterize Bahia's devotional samba, even if the rhythms themselves are not exactly the same.

The reason for these broad similarities might very well be a common central African ancestrality. After all, Davis claims that "the most overt African customs and enclaves [in the Dominican Republic] . . . stem from contributions by Bantu-speaking peoples from the Congo geocultural region in Central

Africa."[56] This may seem striking, given that Hispaniola's slave arrivals disembarked on the island in large part before the seventeenth century, when the captives were still being taken primarily from Upper Guinea, with limited numbers coming from central Africa.[57] However, it is worth considering that central Africans on the island might have exerted a disproportionate influence, at least in some social spheres. For example, Jane Landers notes that in Hispaniola, despite the fact that the majority of the enslaved had come from the Senegambia region, "one of the most feared of the maroon leaders of the 1540s was Lemba," whose "name has various cultural associations in Kongo," even if his ethnic origin was never specified in the Spanish documents.[58] At the very least, such a case suggests the profound social impact that certain central Africans (and even central African social hierarchies) may have commanded even when not demographically dominant.

With all that has thus far been said, let's take a step back and review: the terminologies, musical instruments, rhythms and rhythmic combinations, cosmologies, timbres, and so on of the domestic patron saint rituals I have heretofore introduced not only overlap with one another in fascinating and at times unexpected ways but also tend to point back to Bantu-speaking central Africa. Furthermore, much like the central African sangamento (see our discussion in the introduction to this volume), the liturgical structures of the patron saint festivities examined in Venezuela, Colombia, parts of Ecuador, Brazil, and the Dominican Republic comprise a complex overlaying of musicoreligious expressivities and logics that point somewhat explicitly to either Europe or central Africa at specific moments or in specific ways. And while solemn prayers followed by festive dances are surely reminiscent of medieval Iberian Christianity and can even be observed in some West African–derived Afro-Atlantic religions, more immediately relevant seems to be the central African connection in each of the four discrete contexts.[59] So why would central African cosmological and aesthetic forms figure so prominently in these Catholic saint festivities? The answer seems indeed to lie in central Africa's Christian history and the region's role in feeding the transatlantic slave trade.

CATHOLICISM MIGHT BE AFRICAN, TOO

To reiterate, I am insisting that residential patron saint celebrations are, not unlike Candomblé and Regla-de-Ocha, part of the African religious legacy in the Americas. But pointing to Catholicism as a locus of "African religion" in the Western Hemisphere seems to fly in the face of the aspects most treasured in the constitution of religions that have been called "African," "Afro-Atlantic," "African-derived," "black Atlantic," "black," and so on. After all, while there is no sole trait that has come to serve as indicative of Afro-Atlantic religions, some markers have come to be especially prominent. One powerful index of Africanity in the Americas—perhaps the single most expressive—is the phenomenon of spirit possession, in which a person becomes the vessel for a deity (usually an African god) who ceremonially enters (or "mounts") the devotee's body to dance, give counsel, or otherwise interact with earthlings. In fact, anthropologist Paul C. Johnson reminds us that possession "has been long applied as the defining and even constitutive feature of Afro-Atlantic religions."[60] Indeed, over a century ago pioneering Brazilian ethnographer Raymundo Nina Rodrigues called possession "the essence of all the religious practices of Negroes," a notion echoed decades later by his compatriot Edison Carneiro, who wrote that "possession by the divinity . . . makes unmistakable cults of African origin [in Brazil]."[61]

What's more, possession is such a powerful marker of Africanity in American religions that even scholars dealing with possessionless religions are drawn to the trope of possession. Ethnomusicologist Lorna McDaniel, for instance, in her study of the Big Drum ceremony on the island of Carriacou, suggests that "while religious trance is rarely a part of the Big Drum drama . . . Big Drum texts are in some ways akin to the language of possession."[62] The implication is that possession is somehow always a part of Afro-diasporic religions, even when the phenomenon itself is not actually present. But why does possession suggest Africanity? In large part, it is simply a result of the historical tendency in the study of Afro-diasporic religions to treat West Africa as the default frame for identifying and understanding the African religious legacy in the Americas. And possession trance dancing undeniably holds a central place in many of the West African religious traditions brought to the Americas. It is therefore within this West Africa–centric frame that possession has been reimagined as an index of Africa.

Already by the beginning of the twentieth century, certain imagined aspects of West African religions (and specifically of the coastal tropical forest region called Lower Guinea) had become synecdochical of a more general "African religion." This was the case not only with possession, which Herskovits called the "outstanding manifestation of West African religion," but also with specific rituals, mythologies, languages, musical styles, musical instruments, and social patterns.[63] I will not here delve into the murky geneal- ogy of this West Africa–centrism except to say that it is primarily a result of the geopolitical circumstances within which the concept of an "African-derived religion" (in the Americas) was crafted in the first place—beginning with Nina Rodrigues in Brazil and followed by Fernando Ortiz in Cuba—compounded by the ubiquity of the erroneous belief that, as Herkovits put it, "New World Negroes are descended mainly from West African stocks."[64]

Certain essentialized West African "traits"—Yoruba and Fon terminology, elaborate mythologies involving West African deities, animal sacrifice, and, of course, possession trance dancing—also fed into a more complex othering process that has taken place for centuries. As Stephan Palmié elaborates, "Biblical imagery, elements of classical and early Renaissance anthropogeography, reports of travelers and traders, stereotypes of the 'character' of various African 'nations,' and concrete New World experiences of interaction with enslaved Africans and their descendants defined a shifting and historically mutable matrix within which changing social constructions of the 'otherness' of *black people* in the New World became representable *as African* (whatever this adjective meant in each particular instance)."[65] Thus, the more clearly *other* a particular American religiocultural form was (and is), the more African it appeared to be. Of course, it cannot be ignored that such otherness has in fact been embraced by many African descendants in the Americas to assert an antiracist and anticolonial position such that difference (and Africanity in particular) is recast as empowerment rather than subjugation.[66] Still, it should not, for this reason, be unproblematic that only a small set of essentialized African religious traditions—those of a specific area of Lower Guinea—might be imagined to represent a continental "African religion." Within this frame, then, it seems quite clear why Catholicism—a religion of (ostensibly) European derivation with no African mythologies or pantheon of gods, no fundamental reliance on West African drum types, and no requisite possession rituals—would escape the interest of scholars in search of Africa in the Americas.[67]

But wait, the reader might protest, *has not Catholicism been present all along*? This is what syncretism in the Atlantic world was supposed to be all about, wasn't it? Was it not our field's forefather, Raymundo Nina Rodrigues, who devoted an entire chapter of his foundational nineteenth-century study, *O animismo fetichista dos negros baianos*, to what he called the "equivalence . . . between Catholic saints and Yoruba *orisás*"? Was it not this medic-turned-ethnographer who, by recognizing in Candomblé what he called the "illusions of catechism in Brazil," paradoxically placed Catholic saints at the center of his study? In fact, the vexing question of syncretism, the supposed fusion of

African gods with saints, an issue that Roger Bastide derided as a "pseudo-problem," continues to plague the literature on Afro-Atlantic religions, all but forcing every scholar of such religions to at least acknowledge the Catholic saints in one way or another.[68]

In this way, the question of Afro-Catholic syncretism seems to be as much a part of the Afro-Atlantic world as are spirit possession and African gods, whether the syncretism is viewed as an evolutionary step in human progress (in the case of Nina Rodrigues), as a sign of "acculturation" (as Herskovits and his followers would have it), or as a strategic form of resistance (salient in Bastide's famous interpretation).[69] For me, however, more important than the ongoing syncretism debate, is recognizing that discussions about Afro-Catholic syncretism have always been much more interested in the "Afro" side of the relationship, whether in cognitive, practical, or social terms.[70] Indeed, in every interpretive scenario of Afro-Catholic syncretism the saints are only part of the African diaspora inasmuch as they are linked to African gods (orishas, *lwas*, *voduns*, etc.), always being somehow *other* than African. But if we reimagine Catholic saints as being much more than merely post–Middle Passage aggregates of African religions then we can begin to see how these Christian figures might, in many cases, be understood as symbols—even agents—of the "African religions" themselves. More specifically, if we remember central Africa's quincentennial tradition of Catholicism, then we are forced to confront how synonymous "Afro" and "Catholic" might actually be.

WHO, IN THE END, HEARS WHICH AFRICAS?

My argument is that domestic patron saint celebrations in Venezuela, Colombia, parts of Ecuador, Brazil, and the Dominican Republic might very well be the contemporary fruits of a type of Catholicism whose roots lie in central Africa. I am not suggesting that these practices *are* central African, just as it would be misguided to intimate that Candomblé or Regla-de-Ocha *are* West African. After all, since the late 1990s, scholars have become increasingly convincing in their insistence that these "classic" diasporic religions are far more Atlantic and American than truly African.[71] Rather, I am maintaining that just as the specific pantheons of deities and ritual practices of Candomblé and Regla-de-Ocha are broadly traceable to Yoruba- and Gbe-speaking regions of West Africa, many of the cosmological and liturgical elements of certain Catholic celebrations in the Americas quite likely have their origins in Bantu-speaking central Africa.

In more general terms, I wish to emphasize that the Catholicism taken to the Americas was never solely European. And while European-Iberian and central African Catholicisms are no doubt just branches of a larger history of global Christianity, they existed and developed relatively independently of each other already by the sixteenth and seventeenth centuries, a time during which America-bound African captives were still overwhelmingly central African. But, of course, my narrative here (admittedly) overlooks differences in the historical particularities in each of the four sites. To take just a minor example, if in fact the triplet rhythmic patterns common today in Brazilian samba are musical evidence of negotiations between central and west Africans in Brazil, as I have elsewhere suggested, in what way might musical negotiations among Africans and their descendants have played out in other parts of the Americas?[72] In Venezuela, as I have already mentioned, similar such negotiations seem to have resulted in drum ensembles that employ a mix of instruments whose prototypes come from disparate parts of Africa. Or, to speak of local clerical contexts, might not the influence of particular mendicant orders have created some of the more striking differences that distinguish the rituals observed here?

But this chapter is decidedly not about differences. After all, differences continue to be the reigning a priori position in the study of so-called popular Catholicism.[73] Rather, this chapter is an attempt to see broader lines of continuity in these distinctive contexts. More precisely, I am seeking to recognize that certain patterns of central African Catholicism may be quite visible in domestic patron saint ceremonies today. At the same time, I am emphatically *not* suggesting that central Africans only brought Catholicism with them to the Western Hemisphere. Inquisition records from Brazil, for instance, clearly document the central African–derived musicodevotional *calundu*, which was practiced all over Portuguese America from the seventeenth to the late eighteenth century.[74] Likewise, seventeenth- and eighteenth-century travelers to various parts of the Spanish- and French-speaking Americas noted the presence of the so-called *calenda* (appearing also as *kalenda, calinda,* or *caringa*).[75] And although the earliest colonial accounts—such as that of Dominican friar Jean-Baptiste Labat—claimed that the *calenda* was of West African origin (from the Guinea Coast), much of the musical and choreographic evidence suggests important links to central Africa.[76]

It seems quite clear, therefore, that central Africans brought with them to the Americas a whole array of beliefs and practices that no one, either then or now, would recognize as Catholic. And while some rituals may have been quite separate from sangamentos and Catholic feast days, others may instead have been innovatively bound up in them, such that Catholic rituals would have interacted and overlapped with *calundus* and *calendas* (and any number of other practices). In at least one documented case from eighteenth-century Brazil, for example, Catholic saints and masses were an integral part of a *calundu* curing ritual.[77] Moreover, it is perhaps anything but coincidental that, as Martha Ellen Davis explains, "the *calenda* is very similar to the long-drum dance, or *baile de palos*, . . . [which] is the Dominican sacred dance, 'a dance of respect,' associated in particular with Afro-Dominican death rites and the patron saints' festivals of religious brotherhoods."[78] Ritual practices and beliefs, in other words, may have circulated quite freely among those central Africans (and other Africans and African descendants) who were enslaved in the Americas.

Still, it would be foolish not to recognize that the sort of origin tracing I have done in this chapter can easily belie itself. After all, how do we even know what we are looking for? Isn't the identification of "hints" of central African "Africanity" in Afro-diasporic Catholicism by way of terminology, musical rhythms, and cosmologies not simply the same class of error as using spirit possession by African gods as an index of a *continental* "African religion"? In other words, am I not circularly conjuring boundaries of Africanity that act less as *proof* of something than merely as a means of reinforcing my own presumptions and projections? And, thinking more ethnographically, how might those devotees who today perform for their Catholic saints in Venezuela, Colombia, the Dominican Republic, and Brazil feel about my deductions, which easily become impositions and thus possibly epistemic violence? Who am I to conjure a (central) African heritage for *their* practices?

In the end, then, the question is really about how we (whoever *we* might be) identify what is or is not of African derivation in a hemisphere (even a global system!) whose economies, political systems, cultures, and institutions largely owe their existence to the forced labor of enslaved Africans. After all, could we not reasonably say that everything on earth (given how interconnected the world has been since the fifteenth century) is African derived in one way or another? While this is too complex a question for me to tackle here, it nonetheless gets to the heart of what I have tried to do in this chapter, which is, quite simply, to recognize the agency of those who were fundamental to creating the Americas we know today. At the base level I hope to have shown the continued impact of central Africans and their descendants on structures typically regarded as European. Yet I also hope to have demonstrated the conceptual (and humanistic) benefits gained from expanding what we might think of as "African religion" not only in the Americas but also beyond. The whole point, in other words, has been to call attention to the forgotten, ignored, and marginalized contributions of central Africans and their descendants. And it seems to me that attempting to return agency to the silenced voices of the oppressed is never a project in vain, even if it is riddled with problematic assumptions about the voice (and face and body) of Africanity.

This has, therefore, been a strategic project, as is every game of origin tracing. To declare something to be African derived, African influenced, or African inspired reveals itself to be more a political position than an objective observation; it is never "innocent."[79] In fact, my goal in this chapter has primarily been to essentialize the religious history of central Africans (as if it could ever be treated as singular!) in an effort to de-essentialize the West Africa–centric discourse that has, for generations, served to homogenize the multiplicity and plurality of the African religious legacy in the Americas, invisibly forcing us to keep silencing the silenced. But the echoes of a great many Africas resound throughout the Americas, and recognizing those sounds is really a matter of having ears attentive enough to do so. The lesson, it seems to me, is that our ability—or, conversely, our inability—to hear "Africa" depends less on what we actually hear than on what we imagine Africa can sound like in the first place.

NOTES

This chapter has been a long time in the making, and the narrative it puts forth has benefited from all of the different contexts in which I have shared aspects of it. I am thankful for the enlightening conversations I have had with Martha Ellen Davis, Johanna Monagreda, Michael Birenbaum Quintero, Fabrício Prado, and Richard Turits. The chapter itself has also been read in its entirety by a number of people to whom I am indebted. Ryan Bazinet provided enriching comments and edits on an earlier version, as did Max Katz and the students in his undergraduate research seminar at William and Mary. I am grateful, moreover, to Cécile Fromont not only for inviting me to contribute to this important collection but also for providing substantive suggestions on the penultimate draft. Finally, an anonymous reviewer (and Cécile, yet again!) offered important critiques that helped me rethink the chapter in the context of the collection as a whole.

1. Roger Sansi, "Sorcery and Fetishism in the Modern Atlantic," in *Sorcery in the Black Atlantic*, ed. Luis Nicolau Parés and Roger Sansi (Chicago: University of Chicago Press, 2011). Discussing the *mandinga* pouch (a type of charm) in Brazil, for instance, Sansi makes a statement that seems to present an all-too-common "given": that which is African and that which is Catholic are mutually exclusive. "The actual material components of these pouches and the spells and rituals prayed upon it were not necessarily African. On the contrary, they were often Catholic" (24).

2. David M. Guss, "The Selling of San Juan: The Performance of History in an

Afro-Venezuelan Community," *American Ethnologist* 20, no. 3 (1993), 452; Maria Matilde Suárez and Carmen Bethencourt, "En Venezuela, San Juan Bautista es el Rey del Sangueo," *Revista Bigott* 30 (1994): 5. Suárez and Bethencourt tell us that Saint John the Baptist is celebrated in the following communities: Barlovento, Borburata, Patanemo, Puerto Cabello, Farriar, Agua Negra, San Rafael de Orituco, the central coast (from Carayaca to Todasana), the villages of Ocumare de la Costa, El Playón, Cata, Cuyagua, Choroní, Turiamo, and Chuao.

3. Angelina Pollak-Eltz, *Cultos afroamericanos* (Caracas: Universidad Catolica Andres Bello, 1972), 193.

4. Max H. Brandt, "Venezuela," in *Garland Encyclopedia of World Music*, vol. 2, *South America, Mexico, Central America, and the Caribbean*, ed. Dale Olsen and Daniel Sheehy (London: Routledge, 1998), 536; see also Juan Liscano, *La fiesta de San Juan el Bautista* (Caracas: Monte Avila, 1973), 54.

5. John K. Thornton, *The Kongolese Saint Anthony: Dona Beatriz Kimpa Vita and the Antonian Movement, 1684–1706* (Cambridge: Cambridge University Press, 1998), 114.

6. Brandt, "Venezuela," in Olsen and Sheehy, *Garland Encyclopedia*, 529; Guss, "Selling of San Juan," 454.

7. Jesús García, *Venezuela: Afro-Venezuelan Music*, vols. 1–2, UNES 08318 (Washington, D.C.: Smithsonian Folkways Recordings, 2013), compact disc liner notes, 15.

8. John K. Thornton and Linda M. Heywood, *Central Africans, Atlantic Creoles, and the Foundation of the Americas, 1585–1660* (Cambridge: Cambridge University Press, 2007), 106; Cécile Fromont, *The Art of Conversion: Christian Visual Culture in the Kingdom of Kongo* (Chapel Hill: University of North Carolina Press, 2014), 23.

9. Jesús García, *Africa en Venezuela: Pieza de Indias* (Caracas: Lagoven, 1990), 86.

10. Luis Felipe Ramón y Rivera, *La música afrovenezolana* (Caracas: Imprenta Universitaria, 1971), 59, 147–48, 165. This song is a good representative of the genre's metrical and rhythmic characteristics. I am uncertain about the etymology of the term *sanguéo*, but it seems

at least worth noting its striking resemblance to the term *sangamento*. J. García, *Venezuela*, disc 2, track 12.

11. Gerard Béhague, "Improvisation in Latin American Music," *Music Educators Journal* 66, no. 5 (1980): 120; Peter Manuel, "From Contradanza to Son: New Perspectives on the Prehistory of Cuban Popular Music," *Latin American Music Review* 30, no. 2 (2009): 193; Katharina Döring, "Samba da Bahia: Tradição pouco conhecida," *Ictus* 5 (2004): 78; Carlos Sandroni, *Feitiço decente: Transformações do samba no Rio de Janeiro (1917–1933)* (Rio de Janeiro: Zahar, 2001), 28.

12. Gerhard Kubik, *Angolan Traits in Black Music, Games, and Dances of Brazil: A Study of African Cultural Extensions Overseas* (Lisbon: Junta de Investigações Científicas do Ultramar, 1979), 16–17; Kazadi wa Mukuna, *Contribuição bantu na música popular brasileira: Perspectivas etnomusicológicas* (São Paulo: Terceira Margem, 2000), 27–29.

13. Julian Gerstin, "Comparisons of African and Diaspora Rhythm: The Ewe, Cuba, and Martinique," *Analytical Approaches to World Music* 5, no. 2 (2017): 13–14.

14. Max H. Brandt, *Estudio etnomusicológico de tres conjuntos de tambores afro-venezolanos de Barlovento* (Caracas: Centro para las Culturas Populares y Tradicionales, 1987), 55.

15. Liscano, *Fiesta de San Juan*, 55; see also Josefa Guerra Velásquez, "La religiosidad popular como practica cohesiva," in *XXVI Congreso de la Asociación Latinoamericana de Sociología: Conference Proceedings from the Asociación Latinoamericana de Sociología* (Guadalajara: Asociación Latinoamericana de Sociología, 2007), accessed October 1, 2018, http://cdsa.aacademica.org/000-066/996.pdf.

16. Guss, "Selling of San Juan," 454.

17. Alex Borucki, "Trans-imperial History in the Making of the Slave Trade to Venezuela, 1526–1811," *Itinerario* 36, no. 2 (2012): 32; Alex Borucki, David Eltis, and David Wheat, "Atlantic History and the Slave Trade to Spanish America," *American Historical Review* 120, no. 2 (2015): 446; Borucki, "Trans-imperial History," 34.

18. Brandt, "Venezuela," in Olsen and Sheehy, *Garland Encyclopedia*, 529.

19. Borucki, "Trans-imperial History," 34; James Sweet, *Recreating Africa: Culture, Kinship, and Religion in the African-Portuguese World, 1441–1770* (Chapel Hill: North Carolina University Press, 2003), 29.

20. Armando Castro, *Irmãs de fé: Tradição e turismo no Recôncavo Baiano* (Rio de Janeiro: E-Papers, 2006), 69–81; Francisca Marques, "Festa da Boa Morte e Glória: Ritual, música, e performance" (PhD diss., Universidade de São Paulo, 2008), 116–72.

21. Michael Iyanaga, "New World Songs for Catholic Saints: Domestic Performances of Devotion and History in Bahia, Brazil" (PhD diss., UCLA, 2013), 91–100.

22. Michael Iyanaga, "O samba de caruru da Bahia: Tradição pouco conhecida," *Ictus* 11, no. 2 (2010): 130.

23. Michael Iyanaga, "On Flogging the Dead Horse, Again: Historicity, Genealogy, and Objectivity in Richard Waterman's Approach to Music," *Ethnomusicology* 59, no. 2 (2015): 188–91.

24. Iyanaga, "New World Songs," 274–77.

25. Edison Carneiro, *Samba de umbigada* (Rio de Janeiro: Ministério da Educação e Cultura/Campanha de Defesa do Folclore Brasileiro, 1961), 6–7; Souza Carneiro, *Os mitos africanos no Brasil* (São Paulo: Companhia Editora Nacional, 1937), 436; Yeda Pessoa de Castro, *Falares africanos na Bahia (um vocabulário afro-brasileiro)*, 2nd ed. (Rio de Janeiro: Topbooks, 2005), 333; Gerhard Kubik, *Extensions of African Cultures in Brazil* (New York: Diasporic Africa Press, 2013), 31; Sandroni, *Feitiço decente*, 84–85; Marília T. Barboza da Silva and Arthur L. de Oliveira Filho, *Cartola: Os tempos idos* (Rio de Janeiro: Fundação Nacional de Artes, 1983), 44. Although for many years *samba* was believed by scholars to be a corruption of *semba*, others have insisted that *samba* is primarily related to Bantu-language-group devotional practices. Most convincingly, Kubik has shown that "the root word, *samba*, where it exists in most Bantu languages, refers to a procedure of motion." *Extensions of African Cultures in Brazil*, 31.

26. Michael Iyanaga, "Why Saints Love Samba: A Historical Perspective on Black Agency and the Rearticulation of Catholicism in Bahia, Brazil," *Black Music Research Journal* 35, no. 1 (2015): 122–23, 136.

27. Iyanaga, "New World Songs," 307.

28. Ibid., 325–26.

29. Michael Iyanaga and Lia Lordelo, "Spiritual Melodies of Living: Praying in the Recôncavo of Bahia," *The Method of Imagination: Multidisciplinary Explorations*, ed. Luca Tateo (Charlotte, N.C.: Information Age, forthcoming); Kairn A. Klieman, "*The Pygmies Were Our Compass*": Bantu and Batwa in the History of West Central Africa, Early Time to c. 1900 C.E.* (Portsmouth, N.H.: Heinemann, 2003), 74.

30. Iyanaga, "New World Songs," 340–41; John M. Janzen, *Ngoma: Discourses of Healing in Central and Southern Africa* (Berkeley: University of California Press, 1992), 87; Victor Turner, *Revelation and Divination in Ndembu Ritual* (Ithaca: Cornell University Press, 1975), 37.

31. Iyanaga, "Why Saints Love Samba," 120.

32. Anne-Marie Losonczy, *La trama interétnica: Ritual, sociedad, y figuras del intercambio entre los grupos negros y Emberá del Chocó* (Bogotá: Instituto Colombiano de Antropología e Historia, 2006), 214–16; Thomas James Price Jr., "Saints and Spirits: A Study of Differential Acculturation in Colombian Negro Communities" (PhD diss., Northwestern University, 1955), 189–203; Michael Birenbaum Quintero, "The Musical Making of Race and Place in Colombia's Black Pacific" (PhD diss., New York University, 2009), 59–65; Norman E. Whitten Jr., *Black Frontiersmen: Afro-Hispanic Culture of Ecuador and Colombia* (Prospect Heights, IL: Waveland, 1974), 135–38.

33. Price, "Saints and Spirits," 189.

34. Losonczy, *Trama interétnica*, 214.

35. Juan Sebastián Ochoa, Leonor Convers, and Oscar Hernández, *Arrullos y currulaos: Material para abordar el estudio de la música tradicional del Pacífico sur Colombiano*, 2 vols. (Bogotá: Editorial Pontificia Universidad Javeriana, 2015), 1:55.

36. Price, "Saints and Spirits," 195.

37. Losonczy, *Trama interétnica*, 215.

38. Robert Garfias, "The Marimba of Mexico and Central America," *Latin American Music Review* 4, no. 2 (1983): 205–7; Kubik, *Angolan*

Traits, 36; Carlos Miñana Blasco, "Afinación de las marimbas en la costa pacífica colombiana: ¿Un ejemplo de la memoria interválica africana en Colombia?," in Músicas y prácticas sonoras en el Pacífico afrocolombiano, ed. Juan Sebastián Ochoa Escobar, Carolina Santamaría Delgado, and Manuel Sevilla Peñuela (Bogotá: Editorial Pontificia Universidad Javeriana, 2010), 327–33; Ochoa, Convers, and Hernández, Arrullos y currulaos, 1:57–58. Garfias's study concerns Central America, turning decidedly away from the Pacific coast of Colombia and Ecuador. Nevertheless, his observations about different styles of African xylophones is entirely relevant. The marimbas found along the Pacific coast of South America are xylophones with wooden keys suspended over bamboo resonators, whose name (or in a variation form, malimba) is, as Kubik reminds us, "found in several Bantu languages in East, Southeast and Central Africa, meaning: xylophone and/or lamellophone" and whose construction, despite some interesting debate, probably comes from Africa. Miñana, in particular, is convincing is his argument for the African origins of the Colombian and Ecuadorian marimba.

39. Ochoa, Convers, and Hernández, Arrullos y currulaos, 1:55; Birenbaum Quintero, "Musical Making," 63; Norman Whitten, Afro-Hispanic Music from Western Colombia and Ecuador, FW04376 (New York: Folkways, 1967), compact disc liner notes, 2.

40. Juan García Salazar, ed., Papá Roncón: Historia de vida, 2nd ed. (Quito, Ecuador: Universidad Andina Simón Bolívar; Ediciones Abya-Yala, 2011), 136.

41. Birenbaum Quintero, "Musical Making," 64; Losonczy, Trama interétnica, 215.

42. Birenbaum Quintero, "Musical Making," 63.

43. Whitten, Black Frontiersmen, 137–38. Whitten explains that the loas he heard recited were textually "quite simple; they include parts of rosaries, phrases of praise to San Antonio, God, [and] Jesus, and terminate in a request for good fishing for the ensuing year" (ibid.). Though I know little about the etymology of the word loa, it does not seem to me a coincidence that the term is also used to refer to the songs sung in the Afro-Brazilian context of maracatu crowning processions.

44. Losonczy, Trama interétnica, 216; Birenbaum Quintero, "Musical Making," 64.

45. Losonczy, Trama interétnica, 215.

46. Michael Birenbaum Quintero, "Las poéticas sonoras del Pacífico Sur," in Ochoa Escobar, Santamaría Delgado, and Sevilla Peñuela, Músicas y prácticas sonoras, 230.

47. Price, "Saints and Spirits," 198.

48. David Wheat, "The First Great Waves: African Provenance Zones for the Transatlantic Slave Trade to Cartagena de Indias, 1570–1640," Journal of African History 52, no. 1 (2011): 12; Borucki, Eltis, and Wheat, "Atlantic History," 437; see also David Eltis, Stephen D. Behrendt, David Richardson, and Herbert S. Klein, eds., Voyages: Trans-Atlantic Slave Trade Database, accessed September 15, 2018, www.slavevoyages.org/assessment/estimates/.

49. Wheat, "First Great Waves," 15.

50. Martha Ellen Davis, "Diasporal Dimensions of Dominican Folk Religion and Music," Black Music Research Journal 32, no. 1 (2012): 165; Bernarda Jorge, El canto de tradición oral de República Dominicana (Santo Domingo: Colección Banreservas, 1996), 44.

51. Jorge, Canto de tradición oral, 45.

52. Davis, "Diasporal Dimensions," 169.

53. Martha Ellen Davis, "Oral Musical Traditions of the Dominican Republic," in Music in Latin America and the Caribbean, an Encyclopedic History: Performing the Caribbean Experience, ed. Malena Kuss, 4 vols. (Austin: University of Texas Press, 2007), 2:201; Martha Ellen Davis, Voces del purgatorio: Estudio de la salve dominicana (Santo Domingo: Taller, 1981), 30. The "neutral" third refers to the third note of a diatonic scale, which would indicate whether the scale is a major or minor. A neutral third thus suggests that there is no clear major or minor distinction in the scale.

54. Davis, "Diasporal Dimensions," 169.

55. Davis, "Oral Musical Traditions," in Kuss, Music in Latin America, 2:202–3; Jorge, Canto de tradición oral, 103, 102.

56. Davis, "Oral Musical Traditions," in Kuss, Music in Latin America, 2:193.

57. Borucki, Eltis, and Wheat, "Atlantic History," 437, 446; Borucki, "Trans-imperial History," 32; Jane G. Landers, "The Central

African Presence in Spanish Maroon Communities," in *Central Africans and Cultural Transformations in the American Diaspora*, ed. Linda M. Heywood (Cambridge: Cambridge University Press, 2002), 235.

58. Landers, "Central African Presence," in Heywood, *Central Africans and Cultural Transformations*, 234–35.

59. William A. Christian Jr., *Local Religion in Sixteenth-Century Spain* (Princeton: Princeton University Press, 1989), 57–59; Ryan Bazinet, "The Sonic Structure of Shango Feasts," *Ethnomusicology Review* 20 (2015), http:// ethnomusicologyreview.ucla.edu/journal /volume/20/piece/877#_ftnref4/.

60. Paul Christopher Johnson, "Introduction: Spirits and Things in the Making of the Afro-Atlantic World," in *Spirited Things: The World of "Possession" in Afro-Atlantic Religions*, ed. Paul Christopher Johnson (Chicago: University of Chicago Press, 2014), 4.

61. Raymundo Nina Rodrigues, *Os africanos no Brasil*, 2nd ed. (São Paulo: Companhia Editora Nacional, 1935), 351; Edison Carneiro, *Candomblés da Bahia*, 6th ed. (Rio de Janeiro: Civilização Brasileira, 1978), 25.

62. Lorna McDaniel, *The Big Drum Ritual of Carriacou: Praisesongs in Rememory of Flight* (Gainesville: University Press of Florida, 1998), 15.

63. Melville J. Herskovits, *The Myth of the Negro Past* (New York: Harper, 1941), 215.

64. Stephan Palmié, *The Cooking of History: How Not to Study Afro-Cuban Religion* (Chicago: University of Chicago Press, 2013), 49–50; Melville J. Herskovits, "The Significance of West Africa for Negro Research," *Journal of Negro History* 21, no. 1 (1936): 28.

65. Stephan Palmié, "Introduction: On Predications of Africanity," in *Africas of the Americas: Beyond the Search for Origins in the Study of Afro-Atlantic Religions*, ed. Stephan Palmié (Leiden: Brill, 2008), 8–9.

66. Kevin A. Yelvington, "The Invention of Africa in Latin America and the Caribbean: Political Discourse and Anthropological Praxis, 1920–1940," in *Afro-Atlantic Dialogues: Anthropology in the Diaspora*, ed. Kevin A. Yelvington (Santa Fe: School for Advanced Research Press, 2006), 36.

67. Gerhard Kubik, "Intra-African Streams of Influence," in *The Garland Handbook of African Music*, vol. 1, ed. Ruth Stone (New York: Garland, 2000), 316. I am referring here specifically to what Kubik calls the "cord-and-peg tension" drum commonly seen in Afro-Atlantic religions. Kubik explains that "outside West Africa, the only area to which cord-and-peg tension traveled was the New World. In fact, wherever across the Atlantic this trait appears, its appearance is a likely sign of an Ewe, Fō, Akan, or (more rarely) Yoruba cultural heritage. . . . Cord-and-peg tension turns up among the 'Bush Negroes' of Surinam, in drums used in *candomblé* cults in Bahia (Brazil), in Haiti, and in Cuba" (ibid.).

68. Raymundo Nina Rodrigues, *O animismo fetichista dos negros baianos*, facsimile ed. (Rio de Janeiro: Fundação Biblioteca Nacional/ Editora da Universidade Federal do Rio de Janeiro, 2006), 110, 107; Sérgio Figueiredo Ferretti, *Repensando o sincretismo: Estudo sobre a Casa das Minas* (São Paulo: Editora da Universidade de São Paulo; São Luís: Fundação de Amparo à Pesquisa e ao Desenvolvimento Científico e Tecnológico do Maranhão, 1995), 41–43; Roger Bastide, *The African Religions of Brazil: Toward a Sociology of the Interpenetration of Civilizations* (Baltimore: Johns Hopkins University Press, 1978), 272.

69. Melville J. Herskovits, "African Gods and Catholic Saints in New World Negro Belief," *American Anthropologist* 39, no. 4 (1937): 635–36; Arthur Ramos, "Acculturation Among the Brazilian Negroes," *Journal of Negro History* 26, no. 2 (1941): 248–49; Andrew Apter, "Herskovits's Heritage: Rethinking Syncretism in the African Diaspora," *Diaspora* 1, no. 3 (1991): 253; Bastide, *African Religions*, 162; Pollak-Eltz, *Cultos afroamericanos*, 191–95.

70. Palmié, *Cooking of History*, 119–30.

71. Stefania Capone, "African American Religions," in *Oxford Bibliographies: Atlantic History*, ed. Trevor Burnard, online database (Oxford: Oxford University Press, 2011), www .oxfordbibliographies.com/view/document /obo-9780199730414/obo-9780199730414 -0080.xml; Palmié, "Introduction," in Palmié, *Africas of the Americas*, 4–5.

72. Iyanaga, "Why Saints Love Samba," 133.

73. William A. Christian Jr., "Catholicisms," in *Local Religion in Colonial Mexico*, ed. Martin Austin Nesvig (Albuquerque: University of New Mexico Press, 2006), 259.

74. Luis Nicolau Parés, *A formação do candomblé: História e ritual da nação jeje na Bahia*, 2nd ed. (Campinas, Brazil: Editora da Unicamp, 2007), 112–17; Sweet, *Recreating Africa*, 144.

75. Thomas J. Desch-Obi, "'Koup Tet': A Machete Wielding View of the Haitian Revolution," in *Activating the Past: History and Memory in the Black Atlantic World*, ed. Andrew Apter and Lauren Derby (Newcastle upon Tyne: Cambridge Scholars, 2010), 252; Dena J. Epstein, "African Music in British and French America," *Musical Quarterly* 59, no. 1 (1973): 69–72; Peter Fryer, *Rhythms of Resistance: African Musical Heritage in Brazil* (Middletown: Wesleyan University Press; Hanover: University Press of New England, 2000), 114–15; Julian Gerstin, "Tangled Roots: Kalenda and Other Neo-African Dances in the Circum-Caribbean," *New West Indian Guide* 78, nos. 1–2 (2004): 7–9; Jean-Baptiste Labat, *Nouveau Voyage aux Isles de l'Amerique*, 8 vols. (Paris: Pierre-François Giffart, 1722), 4:154–56; Antoine Pernety, *History of a Voyage to the Malouine (or Falkland) Islands* (London: Jefferys, 1771), 120–21; Médéric Moreau de Saint-Méry, *Description topographique, physique, civile, politique, et historique de la partie française de l'Isle Saint-Domingue*, 2 vols. (Paris: Dupont, 1797), 1:45.

76. Thomas J. Desch-Obi, *Fighting for Honor: The History of African Martial Art Traditions in the Atlantic World* (Columbia: University of South Carolina Press, 2008), 141; Jeroen Dewulf, "From the *Calendas* to the *Calenda*: On the Afro-Iberian Substratum in Black Performance Culture in the Americas," *Journal of American Folklore* 131, no. 519 (2018): 16–19; Gerstin, "Tangled Roots," 25–26. There are certainly interesting parallels between descriptions of Kalendas/Calendas and the types of dancing witnessed in southern Brazil as well as in central Africa during the colonial period. As Dewulf has argued, the *calenda* (a term of probable Latin origin) may have referred less to a specific dance than to dancing more generally. This means that the *calenda* may have taken on any number of aesthetic forms depending on the performers. But this does not change the fact that, independent of being labeled as "calenda" or not, at least some of the musical moments described by colonial travelers appear to have employed dances and musical instruments traceable to central Africa.

77. Iyanaga, "Why Saints Love Samba," 131–32.

78. Davis, "Oral Musical Traditions," in Kuss, *Music in Latin America*, 2:194

79. Palmié, The Cooking of History, 248..

FURTHER READING (AND LISTENING)

Primary Sources

Davis, Martha Ellen, Roberto Rodríguez, and Verna Gillis. *Yo vine a amanecer: Panorama de la música tradicional dominicana*. Santo Domingo: Archivo General de la Nación República Dominicana; Washington, D.C.: Smithsonian Folkways Recordings, 2015, compact disc.

García, Jesús. *Venezuela: Afro-Venezuelan Music*, vols. 1–2. UNES 08318. Washington, D.C.: Smithsonian Folkways Recordings, 2013, compact disc.

Naidy, Grupo. *¡Arriba suena marimba! Currulao marimba music from Colombia*. SFW CD 40514. Washington, D.C.: Smithsonian Folkways Recordings, 2005, compact disc.

Secondary Sources

Brandt, Max H. *Estudio etnomusicológico de tres conjuntos de tambores afro-venezolanos de Barlovento*. Caracas: Centro para las Culturas Populares y Tradicionales, 1987.

Davis, Martha Ellen. *Voces del purgatorio: Estudio de la salve dominicana*. Santo Domingo: Taller, 1981.

Döring, Katharina. *Cantador de chula: O samba antigo do Recôncavo Baiano*. Salvador, Brazil: Pinaúna, 2016.

García, David F. *Listening for Africa: Freedom, Modernity, and the Logic of Black Music's African Origins*. Durham: Duke University Press, 2017.

García, Jesús. *Africa en Venezuela: Pieza de Indias*. Caracas: Lagoven, 1990.

Losonczy, Anne-Marie. *La trama interétnica: Ritual, sociedad, y figuras del intercambio entre los grupos negros y Emberá del Chocó*. Bogotá: Instituto Colombiano de Antropología e Historia, 2006.

Ochoa, Juan Sebastián, Leonor Convers, and Oscar Hernández. *Arrullos y currulaos: Material para abordar el estudio de la música tradicional del Pacífico sur Colombiano*, vol. 1. Bogotá: Editorial Pontificia Universidad Javeriana, 2015.

Palmié, Stephan. *The Cooking of History: How Not to Study Afro-Cuban Religion*. Chicago: University of Chicago Press, 2013.

Thornton, John K., and Linda M. Heywood. *Central Africans, Atlantic Creoles, and the Foundation of the Americas, 1585–1660*. Cambridge: Cambridge University Press, 2007.

Contributors

KEVIN DAWSON is an associate professor of history at the University of California, Merced. His scholarship is situated at the intersection of the African diaspora and Atlantic history and primarily considers how captives recreated and reimagined Atlantic African maritime traditions in the Americas, where their cultural heritage provided their lives with a sense of meaning and worth, while generating significant capital for slaveholders. He has written *Undercurrents of Power: Aquatic Culture in the African Diaspora* (2018), as well as several articles, including "Enslaved Ship Pilots in the Age of Revolutions: Challenging Perceptions of Race and Slavery Between the Boundaries of Maritime and Terrestrial Bondage," *Journal of Social History* (2013), and "Enslaved Swimmers and Divers in the Atlantic World," *Journal of American History* (2006).

JEROEN DEWULF studied at the University of Ghent (BA), the University of Porto (MA), and the University of Bern (PhD), and is currently an associate professor in the Department of German and Dutch Studies at the University of California, Berkeley, where he is also the director of the Institute of European Studies. He has been a visiting professor at the University of São Paulo and the Federal University of Ceará, in Brazil. His most recent book publications are *Shifting the Compass: Pluricontinental Connections in Dutch Colonial and Postcolonial Literature* (2013), *The Pinkster King and the King of Kongo: The Forgotten History of America's Dutch-Owned Slaves* (2017), and *From the Kingdom of Kongo to Kongo Square: Kongo Dances and the Origins of the Mardi Gras Indians* (2017).

CÉCILE FROMONT is an associate professor in the History of Art Department at Yale University. Her writing and teaching focus on the visual, material, and religious culture of Africa and Latin America with a special emphases on the early modern period (ca. 1500–1800) and the Portuguese-speaking Atlantic world. She is the author of *The Art of Conversion: Christian Visual Culture in the Kingdom of Kongo* (2014). It was named the American Academy of Religion's

2015 Best First Book in the History of Religions and received the 2015 Albert J. Raboteau Prize for the Best Book in Africana Religions, the 2017 Arnold Rubin Outstanding Publication Award from the Arts Council of the African Studies Association, and an honorable mention for the 2015 Melville J. Herskovits Award of the African Studies Association. Her articles on African and Latin American art have appeared in the *Colonial Latin American Review, African Arts, RES: Anthropology and Aesthetics,* and *Art History,* as well as various edited volumes and exhibition catalogs.

JUNIA FERREIRA FURTADO is a full professor of early modern history at the Universidade Federal de Minas Gerais in Brazil. She holds a master's degree and doctorate in social history from the Universidade de São Paulo. She has been a visiting scholar at Princeton University, the École des Hautes Etudes en Sciences Sociales in Paris, the John Carter Brown Library, the Instituto de Ciências Sociais at the Universidade de Lisboa, and Stanford University. She has written extensively on slavery and on the history of cartography in Brazil. Her books and articles include *Chica da Silva: A Brazilian Slave of the Eighteenth Century* (2009), *Oráculos da geografia iluminista: Dom Luís da Cunha e Jean Baptiste Bourguignon d'Anville na construção da cartografia do Brasil* (2012), and *The Map That Invented Brazil* (2013), which won the 2014 Jabuti Award for best book in human science from the Brazilian Chamber of Books.

MICHAEL IYANAGA (PhD in ethnomusicology, UCLA) is an assistant professor of music and Latin American studies at William and Mary. Prior to his current teaching post, Iyanaga taught at the Universidade Federal do Recôncavo da Bahia, the Universidade Federal da Paraíba, and UCLA. His scholarship focuses on Afro-Catholic musical practices in Brazil and the wider Atlantic world, as well as on broader issues of method, theory, and intellectual history in ethnomusicology and anthropology, and his work has appeared in journals and books in both the United States and Brazil. His award-winning publications include "Why Saints Love Samba: A Historical Perspective on Black Agency and the Rearticulation of Catholicism in Bahia, Brazil," which received the 2016 Jaap Kunst Prize from the Society for Ethnomusicology and the 2016 Irving Lowens Article Award from the Society for American Music.

DIANNE M. STEWART is an associate professor of religion and African American studies at Emory University. Her research and teaching interests cover a wide range of topics under the umbrella of Africana religions, namely, religious cultures of the African diaspora with particular emphases on African heritage religions in the Americas and the Caribbean; women and religion in Africa and the African diaspora; African religions; black, womanist, and Caribbean liberation theologies; theory and method in Africana religious studies; and interreligious dialogue among communities in the African diaspora. Dr. Stewart is the author of *Three Eyes for the Journey: African Dimensions of the Jamaican Religious Experience* (2005). Her second co-authored book, *Obeah and Orisa Religious Identity in Trinidad: Between and Beyond Colonial Imaginations*, is forthcoming. Dr. Stewart's current book project, "Local and Transnational Legacies of African Christianity in West-Central Africa and the Black Atlantic World," was inspired by a year and a half of archival and field research as a Fulbright Scholar in the Democratic Republic of Congo, where she focused on the history of religions in Central Africa during the slave period and prophetic religious movements in Congo today.

MIGUEL A. VALERIO is an assistant professor of Spanish at Washington University in Saint Louis. His research and teaching focus on the African diaspora in the literatures and cultures of the Iberian world from the late medieval period to the present. His article "The Queen of Sheba's Manifold Body: Creole Afro-Mexican Women Performing Sexuality, Cultural Identity, and Power in Seventeenth-Century Mexico City" appeared in *Afro-Hispanic Review* in 2016. His work has also appeared in *Confraternitas*. Valerio is currently working on his first book, *The Black Kings and Queens of Mexico City: Identity, Performance, and Power, 1539–1640*.

LISA VOIGT is a professor in the Department of Spanish and Portuguese at Ohio State University, where she focuses on the literatures and cultures of colonial Latin America, the Spanish and Portuguese empires, and the early modern Atlantic world. She is the author of *Writing Captivity in the Early Modern Atlantic: Circulations of Knowledge and Authority in the Iberian and English Imperial Worlds* (2009), which won the Modern Language Association's Katherine Singer Kovacs Prize for an outstanding book published in the field of Latin American and Spanish literatures and cultures; and *Spectacular Wealth: The Festivals of Colonial South American Mining Towns* (2016).

Index

waters, cultural importance of, 49–50
Wheat, David, 175
Whitten, Norman, 175
Widmer, Ted, 27
Williams, Jerry, 60
Wood, Marcus, 132

Xavier, Francis, Saint, 31
xylophones, 18n31, 174, 186n38

Yanga, Gaspar, 63
Yoruba-Orisa religion in Trinidad
    Catholic elements in, 140, 141
    custodians of, 142
    deities, 140, 141, 147, 148
    discussion of "syncretism" of, 161n36
    new interpretation of, 15
    public rituals, 143
    ritual architecture, 143, 147, 153
    ritual vocabulary, 144
    roots of, 141
    sacred text of, 160n33
    Ṣàngó warship, 148–49, 161n35

scholarly debates on, 141
Yoruba people
    identity of, 160–61n33
    religion of, 141
Yoruba Trinidadian diaspora
    adoption of Euro-colonial norms by, 144,
        152
    commemorative rituals of, 150
    coronation ceremony in, 145
    cultural exchanges of, 150, 151
    emancipation-celebration rituals, 144–46,
        150–51
    formation of, 144, 150
    historical accounts about, 144–46
    involvement with Catholicism, 151
    liberation of, 143, 144, 156n3
    palais structure of, 144
    religion of, 142
    scholarship on, 144, 152–53
    Shango ritual system of, 143, 144, 149
    songs and chants of, 143, 149, 150, 154–55
Young, Jason, 44